The imperative to read the times where an unp[...] have been displaced around the globe, along w[ith] Scripture and the witness of Jesus Christ, is ur[gent]. journey, Dr. Barnabé Anzuruni Msabah lays the groundwork to grasp the breadth and depth of the global and African challenge of migration and refugees to move the body of Christ to action. Practical paths for engagement are provided for people of faith and faith-communities to embody the good news. This book issues a call to use our collective power of Ubuntu towards hope and transformation, while recognizing the God-given image and resource of the stranger in our midst.

Selena D. Headley
Community Development, Sociology & Theology Lecturer,
Cornerstone Institute
Formation Coordinator,
Institute for Urban Ministry, Cape Town, South Africa

Dr. Barnabé Anzuruni Msabah has provided the scholarly community and the church a rare opportunity in which to engage with the prophetic and righteous work of siding with and supporting those on the margins. In Matthew 25:31–46, Jesus is recorded as saying that what we do for "the least of these" we are doing for Christ's very self. Dr. Anzuruni's book outlines the means by which the church can respond to the critical needs of refugees. In doing so, this work makes a defiant claim for the radical nature of God's identification with those on the margins. This book is a must read!

Anthony Reddie
Professor Extraordinarious, University of South Africa
Director, Oxford Centre for Religion and Culture, University of Oxford, UK

Forced displacement is a defining issue of the twenty-first century. It is concerning this issue that Dr. Msabah speaks to the church at large. His life has been profoundly shaped by repeated forced displacement. He was born a refugee and later experienced the challenges of "returning" to a "homeland" that he had never seen. He was later internally displaced by war, separated from family, and uprooted across borders to once again become a refugee. He has reflected deeply concerning the experience of forced displacement and the mission of the church. He offers a clarion and passionate voice calling the church to holistic mission – to advocate for the dignity of all human beings and to serve as a catalyst for the integration of refugees into their host society.

Thomas Albinson
Ambassador for Refugees, Displaced and Stateless People,
World Evangelical Alliance
Founder and President, International Association for Refugees, USA

The Wayfarer

HIPPOBOOKS

The Wayfarer

*Perspectives on Forced Migration and
Transformational Community Development*

Barnabé Anzuruni Msabah

HIPPOBOOKS

© 2021 Barnabé Anzuruni Msabah

Published 2021 by HippoBooks, an imprint of ACTS and Langham Publishing.
Africa Christian Textbooks (ACTS), TCNN, PMB 2020, Bukuru 930008, Plateau State, Nigeria
www.actsnigeria.org

Langham Publishing, PO Box 296, Carlisle, Cumbria, CA3 9WZ, UK
www.langhampublishing.org

ISBNs:
978-1-83973-225-6 Print
978-1-83973-555-4 ePub
978-1-83973-556-1 Mobi
978-1-83973-557-8 PDF

Barnabé Anzuruni Msabah has asserted his right under the Copyright, Designs and Patents Act, 1988 to be identified as the Author of this work.

All rights reserved. No part of this publication may be reproduced, stored in a retrieval system or transmitted, in any form or by any means, electronic, mechanical, photocopying, recording or otherwise, without the prior written permission of the publisher or the Copyright Licensing Agency.

Requests to reuse content from Langham Publishing are processed through PLSclear. Please visit www.plsclear.com to complete your request.

Unless otherwise stated, Scripture quotations are from the New Revised Standard Version Bible, copyright © 1989 National Council of the Churches of Christ in the United States of America. Used by permission. All rights reserved.

Scripture quotations marked (NIV) are taken from the Holy Bible, New International Version®, NIV®. Copyright © 1973, 1978, 1984, 2011 by Biblica, Inc.™ Used by permission of Zondervan.

Scripture quotations marked (NKJV) are taken from the New King James Version (NKJV). Copyright © 1982 by Thomas Nelson, Inc. Used by permission. All rights reserved.

British Library Cataloguing-in-Publication Data
A catalogue record for this book is available from the British Library

ISBN: 978-1-83973-225-6

Cover & Book Design: projectluz.com

The publishers of this book actively support theological dialogue and an author's right to publish but do not necessarily endorse the views and opinions set forth here or in works referenced within this publication, nor guarantee technical and grammatical correctness. The publishers do not accept any responsibility or liability to persons or property as a consequence of the reading, use or interpretation of its published content.

To
Rev. Dr. Hyung Kyu Kim
A spiritual father, close friend, and prayer partner who
ignited in me the love of Christian spirituality.

Contents

Foreword xi
Acknowledgements xiii
The Immigrants' Creed xv
1 Introduction 1
2 Forced Migration: Facts and Figures 13
3 Two Contexts, Four Constants 53
4 Transformational Community Development as Ubuntu in Action .. 73
5 Transformational Community Development as Hope in Action 99
6 Narratives of Hope 123
7 Principles of Transformational Community Development 151
8 Conclusion 177
  Bibliography 195

Foreword

I heard Dr. Barnabé Anzuruni Msabah's story for the first time when I asked him to teach a class for me on migrants in an undergraduate theology and development class at the University of Stellenbosch. It is a story filled with challenges, hope, and resilience which begins this book. His story, and those of other refugees on the continent, are compellingly woven throughout and draw readers into the realities and pain of this journey in such a way that we cannot look away.

These stories together with a solid sociological description of the intersecting challenges of refugees paint a stark picture of the cross-cutting issues of armed conflict, gender-based violence, economic hardship, continuing dictatorships and corruption, climatic factors, and exploitation by the Global North of the mineral wealth of Africa. These are stories and challenges which we as Africans cannot look away from, and in terms of African integral mission discourse, we must continue to emphasize the intersectional and complex nature of poverty and marginalization on our continent in order to begin to seek to engage it.

This book is at its best in its rich theological engagement which seeks to deeply challenge the church to not only relieve the suffering of "those on the Jericho road" and welcome the strangers in their midst, but also to be a bearer of *shalom* – of hope, restoration, justice, and healing. I am particularly struck by the following quote from the book:

> That is what this book is all about, assisting the local church in fixing the road and making it safer for all so that whoever walks on it in their life's journey – including refugees – will not be mugged and left half dead on the roadside but will finish their journey and reach their intended destination unharmed.

This is the call of the book, and in challenging the church, Dr. Msabah puts forward several theological perspectives which are integral to our understanding of mission, but he re-inscribes them creatively. Perhaps most fittingly for a book written by an African scholar for Africans, Ubuntu is highlighted as a precious gift offered by Africans. Dr. Msabah calls on us as Africans to live out this gift and offer Ubuntu as a gift to each other and the world. This call to be contextual and intercultural is also distributed throughout the book. On our continent where tribalism and racism remain constant, *The Wayfarer* engages the church to make the kind of shifts which will not only accommodate refugees or advocate for their rights, but will indeed assist them in assuring livelihood sustainability and full integration into the community.

The Wayfarer contributes to the field of transformational development, and indeed to African practical theology, and creates new boundaries in doing so. Not only is the church positioned as an agent of change in addressing the refugee phenomenon, the book importantly positions migrants as having agency and recognizes them as putting hope into action. During the Apartheid years in South Africa, and indeed throughout the world, there has been a call for those on the margins to shape their own discourse with the rallying cry: "Nothing about us without us." It remains troubling that so much written about marginalized groups comes from the centres of power – those who are removed from the realities of the topic they are engaging. I remember very well at an international conference on migrants that Dr. Msabah and I attended together that he was very clear that migrants' voices must be centred, and in this book, he does exactly that.

I was personally challenged by this book, and I have no doubt that you will be, too. May this book assist us to see the issues related to refugees more clearly, evaluate the situation with theological discernment, and act boldly with compassion and justice based on the biblical call.

Nadine Bowers Du Toit
Professor of Theology and Development
University of Stellenbosch, Cape Town, South Africa

Acknowledgements

I would like to express my sincere gratitude to all those who made meaningful contributions to this book directly or indirectly. I acknowledge that my expression of gratitude does not measure up to the support and encouragement they offered. Particular gratitude to my wife, Dr. Susan Anzuruni, for her prayerful support, encouragement, and reassurance during this laborious process. I would like to also thank Rev. Dr. Hyung Kyu Kim as well as my parents, By'elongo Sangara and Justine Mlebinge, who constantly fall to their knees whispering my case to God. Glory, honour and thanksgiving to the only wise God who has made this possible!

Barnabé Anzuruni Msabah

The Immigrants' Creed

I believe in Almighty God,
who guided the people in exile and in exodus,
the God of Joseph in Egypt and Daniel in Babylon,
the God of foreigners and immigrants.

I believe in Jesus Christ,
a displaced Galilean,
who was born away from his people and his home,
who fled his country with his parents when his life was in danger,
and returning to his own country suffered the oppression
of the tyrant Pontius Pilate, the servant of a foreign power,
who then was persecuted, beaten, and finally tortured,
accused and condemned to death unjustly.
But on the third day, this scorned Jesus rose from the dead,
not as a foreigner but to offer us citizenship in heaven.

I believe in the Holy Spirit,
the eternal immigrant from God's kingdom among us,
who speaks all languages, lives in all countries,
and reunites all races.

I believe that the church is the secure home
for the foreigner and for all believers who constitute it,
who speak the same language and have the same purpose.
I believe that the communion of the saints begins
when we accept the diversity of the saints.

I believe in the forgiveness of sin, which makes us all equal,
and in reconciliation, which identifies us more
than does race, language, or nationality.

I believe that in the resurrection
God will unite us as one people
in which all are distinct
and all are alike at the same time.

Beyond this world, I believe in life eternal
in which no one will be an immigrant
but all will be citizens of God's kingdom,
which will never end.

Amen.[1]

---

1. "The Immigrants' Creed," Rev José Luis Casal, *The Book of Common Worship: 2018 Edition* (Nashville: Westminster John Knox, 2018).

1

Introduction

I grew up enjoying the melodic sound and lyrical depth of *Vieux pèlerin qui vagabonde* – a French hymn that my dear mother taught us when we were still very young. The hymn was first recorded by the Vaughan's Texas Quartet in 1930 but later popularized in 1958 by Bill Monroe. The first stanza of Monroe's version goes like this:

> *I'm just a poor wayfarin' stranger,*
> *While travellin' through this world below.*
> *Yet there's no sickness, no toil, nor danger,*
> *In that bright land to which I go.*[1]

This song has never stopped ringing in my ears since I learned it as a first-grade pupil in lower primary school. I loved the song (and I still love it) not only for its eschatological profundity, but also for its irrefutable assertion that we are all strangers here on earth. The song convincingly communicates the eternal truth that although we are strangers here, someday we never will be, and our tired body will eventually find rest in the bosom of God's celestial solace. The truth about this song's lyrics rekindled my hope for a better future every time I sang it; in particular, because I have literally lived as a "wayfaring stranger" for most of my life.

In the 1970s the sociopolitical context in the Democratic Republic of Congo (DRC) forced my parents to seek asylum in Burundi. As a result, I was born in Burundi. Life in Burundi was very difficult, but we survived through God's providential care. So it was in Burundi that I learned at a young age that life is not easy, and the meaning of another famous French children's song always vibrated in my ears with renewed meaning: "*La vie est tellement*

---

1. Bill Monroe and the Blue Grass Boys, "Wayfaring Stranger," http://www.songlyrics.com/bill-monroe-and-the-bluegrass-boys/wayfaring-stranger-lyrics/.

difficile, travaillons pour gagner notre vie" (life is very difficult, let us work hard [if we are] to make it in life). This was one of the songs many children used to sing in primary school but which conveyed a special message to me personally seeing the conditions of life we lived in as refugees. The song taught me the importance of hard work and the value of diligence when executing assigned duties.

Because I was born in a country where my parents were asylum seekers, I, too, was born an *asylum seeker*. On 21 October 1993, war broke out in Burundi following the assassination of Melchior Ndadaye, the first democratically elected president of the country. We then left Burundi in April the following year, 1994, and went to Uvira in the DRC. In Uvira, we lived at the mercy of humanitarian assistance from some charitable international organizations because we were *returnees*. We were going through a "reverse culture shock," so we needed humanitarian assistance from the United Nations High Commissioner for Refugees (UNHCR) and other organizations to allow us settle in our new setting that was literally our "home away from home." However, before we could fully settle, another war broke out in 1996, barely two years later. We left the city of Uvira and fled to Swima, a village situated a few dozen kilometres away. In Swima, we were *internally displaced persons* (IDPs) because we were uprooted from our original abode and displaced elsewhere without crossing any of our national borders. However, this "label" was short-lived because two months later, on 9 December 1996, leaving the other family members behind, my brother and I decided to cross Lake Tanganyika aboard a little wooden boat.

Our trip to Tanzania was a journey of hope because of the desperation that had encroached on our lives. We tried to leave Swima on 9 December, but that night when the Mayi-Mayi fighters – armed militias – learned that our boat was leaving and that the destination was Tanzania, they went down to Lake Tanganyika and attacked us. They shot in the air and threatened to shoot us if we left because they did not want people to leave the country. They said fleeing was not patriotic, which is why they urged people to stay and fight for their country. We managed to escape through the *lùbenga* – a large plantation of mango, avocado and palm trees – where we hid before returning home. The next evening, 10 December, we tried again, and this time we were successful. We did not go directly from Swima to Tanzania as we made several stops in different villages along the Ubwari peninsula, picking up passengers along the way.

Our wooden boat was powered by a Mariner 45 engine, but had some mechanical issues. At one point the engine malfunctioned and our little boat nearly capsized because it was overloaded with both people and their luggage.

During our 6-day journey as boat people, many, especially children, suffered from dehydration and intense hunger. When we finally arrived in Kigoma, we did not go straight to the harbour as the police would have arrested us since we did not have the proper documents to enter Tanzania. We were boat people and undocumented migrants. We sailed to Kigali, a rural area on the outskirts of Kigoma near Kalalangabo along the shore of Lake Tanganyika. It was around 9:00 a.m. when we arrived. From Kigali, we walked to the city of Kigoma. From there, we were taken to the Nyarugusu Refugees' Camp. The camp was literally "in the middle of nowhere," as we used to say in those days, considering its location in the jungle. The Tanzanian immigration authorities referred to us as *those boat people.*

The Nyarugusu camp is located in the province of Kigoma, Tanzania, approximately one hundred and sixty kilometres from the city of Kigoma, east of Lake Tanganyika. Nyarugusu is one of the largest and best-known refugee camps of the twenty-first century, with more than one hundred and fifty thousand refugees as of 2018.[2] When we arrived there, the camp was just one month old and housed approximately eighty thousand people – all from DRC. The camp was later expanded as some other refugees from different camps such as Lugufu, Mutabila, etc. were brought to Nyarugusu. Because the camp was located at a place that had never been inhabited before the arrival of refugees, our frequent visitors were initially wild animals. It was quite common to come across, for example, big snakes, antelopes, and monkeys, at any given time. At night it was common to hear sounds of wild animals such as hyena and, geographically, being in a forest, Nyarugusu was very wet and cold in those early days. Life was unbearably difficult. While in the camp, I did part of my schooling. Initially, our classrooms were under trees and we sat on cut pieces of trees or rocks. We had no blackboards or any school materials such as books or pens. Many stopped going to school considering the conditions. A few of us endured the conditions and soldiered on.

The world is experiencing the largest refugee crisis in history. Without a doubt, forced migration worldwide is at record numbers. According to a UNHCR report, by the end of 2019 about 79.5 million people had been forcibly displaced around the world "as a result of persecution, conflict, violence, human rights violations or events seriously disturbing public order."[3] This

---

2. See the ReliefWeb, "North West Tanzania: Nyarugusu Refugee Camp Profile," UNHRC (2018), https://reliefweb.int/sites/reliefweb.int/files/resources/65654.pdf.

3. UNHCR, "Global Trends: Forced Displacements in 2019," Copenhagen: Statistics and Demographics Section (2020), https://www.unhcr.org/5ee200e37.pdf.

basically means that on average, one person around the world is displaced from their homes every two seconds. These figures correspond to three main groups: refugees, internally displaced persons (IDPs), and asylum seekers. Beside these three main groups are millions of other populations of concern such as stateless people who have been denied citizenship and access to basic rights like education, healthcare, employment, and freedom of movement. About twenty-six million people are refugees, forty-six million are internally displaced, and four million are asylum seekers. Many have dangerously crossed borders at the risk of their lives in search of security and protection. As a result, many die or go missing during the course of their emigration.

This situation is one of the explanations for the current "boom" in theological reflection vis-à-vis contemporary trends in human mobility. The factors that give rise to this increased attention are multiple and sometimes subject to prejudiced reasons such as the passionate interest and personal experience of some theologians, which is partly the reason this book has been written. It addresses the current debates on the relationship between forced migration and transformational development by exploring ways in which refugees contribute to the development of their host country. It also highlights the relevance of their contribution to the socioeconomic welfare of the local community. In the context of this interdisciplinary approach, the question of refugees is presented in a way that befits the acumen of theologians and benefits development practitioners in reflection and action. The question of refugees and asylum seekers in this twenty-first century commands common interest and presents an opportunity for and the means to research other ends. The current situation is proof that both theological researchers and church leaders need a cutting-edge perspective and a more critical sense due to the complexity of this discipline. So this book provides pointers on how we can take the challenges related to the refugee phenomenon and turn them into opportunities for ministry as the church.

The faith articulation and spirituality of refugees are evidently among the areas of interest to practical theologians. This interest could be informed by the fact that forced migration leads to deeper theological reformulation. The faith of refugees reveals new faces of God, and in the phenomenon of forced migration, various religious perceptions and spiritualities converge in the same social context.[4] For many refugees, faith constitutes a support system during

---

4. Anthony H. Richmond, *Global Apartheid. Refugees, Racism, and the New World Order* (Oxford: Oxford University Press, 1994), 3.

their migratory journey. For example, they would perform some religious rites before their departure and would thank God as soon as they cross the border among other things. Hence, in most cases, their migration experience represents a test of their faith in God. As it were, forced migration is ever present in the Bible, and aspects of a God who is ever on the move are found throughout the pages of this sacred writ. Basically, forced migration is a central feature of the biblical narrative, although too often it has not been considered as such in Christian thought. Therefore this book promotes a theology that calls us the church to champion the protection and integration of refugees into our immediate communities.

When one observes the ministry of Jesus Christ during his time here on earth, one realizes that he was the defender of the oppressed, the marginalized, and those excluded by the evil human systems. From the beginning of his ministry, Jesus explained his mission: he came to bring good news to the poor, to proclaim deliverance to prisoners, to announce recovery of sight to the blind, and to set the oppressed free (cf. Luke 4:18–19). This mission is quite integral and provides evidence of the depth of Christ's love and his care for humanity. The mission of Jesus further provides pointers to the fact that God does not tolerate any of us being subjected to systemic poverty or suffering oppression and socioeconomic exclusion. Through his love, Jesus calls us to follow in his footsteps by helping the needy, the heartbroken, the wounded, the forgotten, and the captives among us. Because of this call, we have the responsibility to renew hope. It is our duty to advocate for the dignity of all human beings – especially those who are unable to get by on their own – in a constant attempt to create a *shalom* community.

In his Sermon on the Mount, Jesus taught deeper truths concerning the lives of wayfarers here on earth when he told the disciples about the effect of salt and the influence of light. As salt brings out the flavour of any food and preserves, cleans, and helps to heal infections, so should we wayfarers. For us to be "salt" in this world, we must keep our distinct properties and salty flavour. When we assimilate the ways of thinking and acting of the world through which we are only passing, we lose our salty taste. Our engagement in matters of social concern is meant to add flavour and change the taste of this current system. In the same way, as light expels darkness, the presence of wayfarers in this world is *de facto* to brighten all surrounding places. However, a light hidden under a table cannot lighten up anything. When we hide inside our places of worship and refuse to bring that light into the community, we are spiritually ineffectual. When we speak, we shed light on social problems with the truth of God's word and allow its light to shine through. When we learn that people are plagued by poverty, we must apply the truth of God to our lives and do all we can to help. When injustice reigns, we must speak for the oppressed as the Lord Jesus did. In short, we should be socially active as the church. God expects us to be salt and light in our immediate communities, flavouring, stimulating, and lighting up every corner as much as we can.

Certainly the history of humanity is marked by migratory movements, and we are wayfaring strangers travelling through this world. This is true spiritually just as it is physically because we are a generation on the move. The motivations for migration have been and still are varied. To wonder about the causes and the effects of the migratory flows we are currently facing implies considering the meaning of the present global evolution. In the context of globalization organized on political bases, it is important to define the peculiarity of today's migratory movements, identify their many causes, and derive results for reflection and action. For this reason, I make use of the SEA (See, Evaluate, Act) approach – a contextual method for interpreting Scripture socio-scientifically. This approach is here employed through the lenses of forced migration and transformational development.

Following the SEA approach, the process of biblical interpretation starts with a reflective study of the original context, that is, "see." Then follows an analysis of the text to allow it to speak of the context, that is, "evaluate." Finally, the interpreter moves to action by applying the meaning of the text to a current situation as a response, that is, "act." The SEA approach allows the interpreter to make sense of contemporary realities out of a Bible narrative, event, or scene. Thus the rereading of the biblical text makes it possible to assess whether our reality is as God wants it; and whether our plan of action allows us to work with God in bringing about holistic transformation and sustainable change. This interpretation process is continuous and therefore "praxical" as each action leads to further reflection, further analysis, and even more action. This is the cycle of praxis encouraged in this book.

With such a praxical approach to socio-scientific hermeneutics, we are here challenged to speak on human acceptance and equal opportunity so that people will come to realize that we ought to be excited about living together as one human race and as members of one human community in tolerance, coexistence, and mutual respect. Both the refugee community and the host community are therefore reminded of their roles in society by championing the ethos of communal living and social cohesion as in a *shalom* community, which is a community characterized by peace, harmony, and just relationships. So this book presents a paradigm shift in the theology of development as it uses practical methods to theologize about those millions of refugees around the world for whom poverty is systemic, hunger is daily, opportunity is restricted, and hope is in short supply.[5]

A collective effort is necessary to avoid further forced migrations, and as a church we can play a role by not being absent when people suffer. The suffering and misery of our people should be a great concern to us. The idea of a collective effort in response to forced human migrations should cause us to "say in unity: enough is enough" with Thabo Mbeki because "we have seen too many dead bodies littering the African landscape; we have seen too many displaced Africans . . . crossing national borders, driven by fear of death at the hands of fellow Africans; we have seen enough of death and destruction."[6] By urging Africans "to say in unity: enough is enough" because of "too many dead bodies . . . [and] too many displaced [people]," we affirm our conviction that all is not lost. Africa can still rise again above armed conflicts, rebel movements, and sociopolitical problems. This is our firm conviction, and our hope against hope.

This book is written with a strong conviction that despite the complexities of the problems in our various African countries, this continent shall once again be at peace. However improbable this may sound, one day Africa shall flourish. This is why the book reflects on the images of God in the lived experiences of refugees, asylum seekers and all those in refugee-like situations by highlighting the mission of a God who does not stay on the other side of the border but crosses over in an attempt to accomplish his redemptive plan. It focuses on the mission of the migrant Christ who traverses the divine-human frontier so as to break the boundaries that separate us from ourselves, and us from God. The book also draws attention to the work of the ever-moving Holy Spirit who always roams around inspiring us to shared humanity in solidarity, unity, and mutuality. This book is born from the synthetic identity of those who have been excluded or pushed away to the periphery such as refugees. For them, the book reveals a sense of double belonging and expresses a process for redefining their identity in an attempt to reclaim the centre.

At a time when theology is shunned by other academic disciplines, it is claiming its place within them because it deals more and more with themes

---

5. See W. S. Mooneyham, *What Do You Say to a Hungry World?* (Waco, TX: Word Books, 1975), 31–32.

6. Thabo Mbeki, "Africa – War and Peace," public lecture, Tshwane University of Technology, 16 September 2010 (Pretoria: Tshwane University of Technology, 2010), https://www.polity.org.za/article/sa-mbeki-public-lecture-by-the-former-president-of-south-africa-on-africa-war-and-peace-pretoria-16092010-2010-09-16.

associated with human and social sciences. Many of these themes were once the domain of theology and were removed from them in favour of emerging disciplines. This book sends a nod to the humanities and social sciences to kindly welcome theology within their academic boundaries. Theology is at a crossroads. It is in the process of being redefined outside the institutional shackles to which until recently it has been subject. To rediscover its place of nobility within the humanities and social sciences, theology must be transdisciplinary. It must be connected with the reality of the world in which it is built so as to link faith and doctrines with the realities of the world.

Throughout the pages of the Bible, foreignness plays a critical role. In Luke 10:25–37 for example, we read one of the most famous parables of Jesus: the good Samaritan. We are told that a man was going from Jerusalem down to Jericho. He was attacked, beaten, robbed, and left in a state of vulnerability – half dead. First, we see a priest pass by, but he does nothing to help the dying man. Although the priest was a symbol of hope, he passed to the other side of the road, deliberately keeping a safe distance between himself and the vulnerable man who was fighting for his life and needed urgent help. In so doing, the priest only amplified the hopelessness of this vulnerable man. Second, we see a Levite pass by. The Levites were a highly respected group for many reasons including the fact that they taught the law, served in the temple, and were the tribe of the priests. Nevertheless, the Levite also walked away and wanted nothing to do with the vulnerable, dying man. He also amplified the hopelessness of the vulnerable man.

As the story continues, we see a foreign migrant from Samaria come and help this dying man; and Jesus openly refers to this foreigner as "good." Jesus then tells the legal specialist to "Go and do likewise" (Luke 10:37). Here Jesus uses a foreigner as a moral yardstick and an example to follow if one wants to be "good." The implication of this truth is of critical relevance for us today. Indeed, the goodness of this foreigner from Samaria was a temporary solution to the problem as it was achieved by an individual. What was really needed was a collective effort to make the road from Jerusalem to Jericho a bit safer so people would never again be beaten and left half dead. It is important to note the role of this foreigner from Samaria and his contribution to the socioeconomic welfare of the local citizenry as he came to help this dying Jew on the road to Jericho. Jesus told that legal mind of Jewish descent to go and do as this foreigner from Samaria did if he wanted to be truly "good" and therefore deemed "a neighbour." It was this despised foreigner who felt compassion for the dying man and approached him in order to help, unlike the priest and the Levite who had decided to walk on the other side of the road.

The despised foreigner from Samaria even dressed and bandaged the wounds of this wounded Jew who had been left half dead.

Despite his foreignness, the Samaritan was compassionate enough to be willing to help a Jew who was in urgent need of humanitarian assistance. This means the Samaritan ignored racism, xenophobia, and all kinds of preconceived attitudes toward him as a foreign migrant and acted justly and with mercy. Although he was a foreigner, he had enough money to pay for all the expenses. He probably managed the little he had so well that despite being on a presumably tight budget, he had enough for unforeseen expenses. This ability shows that not all foreign migrants are a burden or parasites – living at the expense of local citizens or humanitarian charities. Given a chance, most refugees can put their potential to good use and serve those in need using their own resources. The fact that the innkeeper trusted the Samaritan might show that he was well-known or even famous for his integrity in the area despite being a foreigner. If we want to be good neighbours, we must be more like this foreign migrant from Samaria whom Christ qualified as "good." The implied message of the story is that the church needs to be financially strong so we have the means to act on our good intentions and plans for society.[7] Jesus concludes with this warning: "Go and do likewise."[8] Our challenge is that people are always attacked as they go "on the road to Jericho" in an attempt to grow financially and flourish. We need to do more than the Samaritan and make the road safer, which is an act of integral mission.

The parable of the good Samaritan lays bare the hypocrisy of meeting the needs of the other according to religious or ethnic expectations, which often shows the cracks in the human character, yet provides us with the definitional context of a neighbour: every human being in need. Continuing the Old Testament tradition of God's preferential treatment of the poor, the scene of the last judgment in Matthew identifies God with the foreigner, the thirsty, the hungry, the sick, the prisoner (Matt 25:31–46). Welcoming the other is therefore at the heart of human reality for Christians. We are called to embrace otherness and welcome the other. Caring for others is a Christian requirement and is accompanied by a moral imperative of resisting the exclusion of foreigners including refugees.

---

7. Joe Plemon, "The Parable of the Good Samaritan: 5 Lessons Learned," Crosswalk.com (6 January 2019), https://www.crosswalk.com/family/career/the-parable-of-the-good-samaritan-5-lessons-learned.html.

8. See Plemon "Parable of the Good Samaritan."

Integral mission explains the mission of Christ or the *missio Christi* as found in Luke 4:18–19 and results from the integration of word and deed. In integral mission, evangelism and social action are integrated in order to do away with conceptions of church mission that distinguish evangelism from social responsibility. The word "integral" therefore refers to the idea of holism, which is going beyond the dichotomous parallel between the gospel and social action. Holism is putting forward the evangelism dimension of social action and the social dimension of evangelism. In other words, the social consequences of the gospel must be integrated into the practice of *missio ecclesiae* so that personal transformation can be accompanied by a transformation of the structures of society because the spiritual and the material go hand in hand. In essence, this is the theological meaning of integral mission.

The *missio Christi* can be expressed by three important terms – revelation, restoration, salvation. It is a revelatory mission because Jesus came to declare the love of the Father's heart. The Father entrusted to the Son the manifestation of his love. So the Father's love for a guilty and dying world is the substance of Christ's message. The *missio Christi* is a restorative mission because Jesus was sent to unveil the righteousness and love of the Father, and he sends faithful followers to carry out the plan which he exemplified. Lastly, the *missio Christi* is a salvific mission because it is sacrificial and redemptive. This means that Jesus came to do what no human or angel could do, that is, to expose what is eternally present in the heart of the Father and to carry the expression of perfect holiness and unlimited mercy to their paroxysmal peak. His mission therefore ensures that complete reconciliation, repentance, submission to the Father will inaugurate the beginning of a new and eternal life. Now we are sent to take part in the ministry of our Lord. Our service is to represent him on earth by continuing his restoration ministry. In other words, our work is inextricably linked with that of Christ, the Redeemer. We are brought into a partnership with one who "came not to be served but to serve, and to give his life as a ransom for many" (Mark 10:45; see Matt 20:20–28; Mark 10:35–45). It is a mission of salvation because Christ came into the world to express God's absolute hatred for sin and to root it out from the heart of human beings, taking upon himself all his curse and his shame until the end.

When the church engages in transformational development and integral mission, we enable a *shalom* community to emerge and thrive. We are challenged to do more because "to whom much has been given, much will be required" (Luke 12:48 NRSV). Since we have been given much as the church – for example, we are led by the word of God, empowered by the Holy Spirit, and enabled by Jesus who is eternally present – it befits us to go beyond the good act of the Samaritan, who did not have these gifts, and be more than just a neighbour. We should ensure that the road is fixed and made safe for everyone so that all people from all backgrounds can flourish and experience life in its fullness. That is what this book is all about, assisting the local church in fixing the road and making it safer for all so that whoever walks on it in their life's journey – including refugees – will not be mugged and left half dead on the roadside but will finish their journey and reach their intended destination unharmed. Such a process is transformational. Those of us who proclaim the gospel of Jesus Christ on the African continent must be concerned with the crucial questions of transformation within the broader context of development practice. This is why this book lays a strong foundation for a theology of transformational development based on the word and actions of Jesus toward the poor and marginalized, among whom are refugees. In other words, the book is based on a rich theological tradition that places forced migration at the centre of the biblical message.

It has become urgent today to promote a different perspective on migration and to build a new framework for migration policies. For my part, I have tried to understand the intersection of African migration and the dynamics of transformational development resulting from mobility within sub-Saharan Africa. On the migratory routes, development areas are opening up and diversifying. My remarks are particularly aimed at the phenomenon of sub-Saharan migrants in their social and cultural diversity. Their experience that echoes certain biblical figures will constitute the framework of this contribution which will be structured around eight chapters. The next chapter discusses about facts and figures of the refugee phenomenon in Africa so that our interventions will be informed by existential experiences of forced migration that reflect the realities on the ground.

Discussion Questions

1. What did we learn in this chapter, and how does it affect our relationships with refugees in our communities?
2. How important is the SEA approach in interpreting and applying the Bible in context?
3. Read Luke 4:18–19.
    - What does Jesus say about himself and the nature of his mission?
    - What is "the year of the Lord's favor" that Jesus came to proclaim (v. 19)?

- Read Leviticus 25:8–13. Thinking about the year of Jubilee, what do you think is good news, and what does it mean to bring this good news to refugees?

4. Read Luke 10:25–37. The Samaritan asked the innkeeper to look after the vulnerable man while he went about his other business, paid the innkeeper, and promised to cover any additional expenses the innkeeper might incur.
    - What does this parable tell us about the contribution of refugees to the socioeconomic transformation of their host communities if given equal opportunities?
    - What does this passage tell us about mutual support to meet the needs of vulnerable people?
    - Jesus told the rich young ruler to "go and do likewise"; but why are we challenged to do more than the Good Samaritan if we are to holistically transform our communities?

5. Read Jeremiah 38:7–13. Ebed-melech was an official in the royal palace of Judea during the time of the prophet Jeremiah. He was an African foreigner from Ethiopia.
    - How was Ebed-melech a blessing for Jeremiah?
    - What does this account tell us about the integration of refugees into the local community?

2

Forced Migration: Facts and Figures

Ben is a Congolese man. He fled both the 1993 war in Burundi and the 1996 war in the Democratic Republic of Congo (DRC) when he was still a teenager. Like me, he first escaped bullets in Bujumbura, and did the same two years later in the DRC, the country of his nationality. Ben narrates his experiences with a mixture of anger and courage. For quite some time, the entire population of Uvira, DRC, was overwhelmed with panic due to contradictory information transmitted by word of mouth. During those days, only a select few among the elite owned phones, and the social networks that we currently enjoy were inexistent. Therefore it was difficult to tell exactly what was really going on in the plain of Ruzizi, a few kilometres from the city of Uvira. The only certainty was that the Stalin Organ – this formidable weapon from Kinshasa which would drop bombs every day toward the mountains to attack the rebels – had been removed from the city of Uvira by the Navy and taken to Kalemie, another coastal city on Lake Tanganyika hundreds of kilometres away southwards. Even the military officers did not know much about what was going on.

It was a Friday, 25 October 1996. Like every morning, Ben recalls how most people rushed down the main streets to listen to the latest "*Bihuha*," the unverified information widely disseminated by word of mouth. Uvira had become an over-militarized city because of the presence of several divisions of the armed forces. So on this day, 25 October, tens of thousands of people fled the heavy fighting on the Ruzizi plain and passed through Uvira going to a destination they did not know themselves. Some families stayed in the city of Uvira; others continued all the way to the territory of Fizi. Nobody took them seriously even when they said that places like Luvungi, Luberizi, Sange, and Kiliba had already fallen into the hands of the rebels. At around nine in the morning, a wave of people came into the city of Uvira, and panic went a notch higher. Ben remembers seeing a guy coming and informing them that he had just seen, with his own eyes, the Rwandan soldiers at the Kavimvira roundabout, approximately ten kilometres away. However, no one believed him. The man was even booed, and narrowly escaped mob justice.

At around 10:30 am, some crackling of bullets sounded from afar. The time had come for Ben and his family to follow the movement of people that they had watched until then. They locked their house and took some blankets with them, but hoped to return at night to sleep. This was the beginning of a long, five-day march that would take them to the territory of Fizi, before the rebels found them in Swima and asked them to return to Uvira, which they did. Those who decided to go further to Mboko found themselves caught up in a fierce battle. On one side were elements of the *Front pour la Défense de la Démocratie* (FDD), the armed wing of the *Conseil National pour la Défense de la Démocratie* (CNDD), the Burundian rebel group that operated in the eastern DRC and supported the Zairian armed forces, and the *Interahamwe*, a Rwandan rebel group that also operated in the DRC and supported the Zairean armed forces. On the other side were the *Inkotanyi*, the *Armée Patriotique Rwandaise* (APR), the Rwandan armed forces. Their conflict resulted in several deaths, while tens of thousands walked toward this destination. Many abandoned their cars along the way because the roads were packed with thousands upon thousands of people, so it was impossible for those driving to get through.

While returning to Uvira with his family, Ben saw human bodies lying down for the first time in his life. At a checkpoint established at the Kalundu Harbour by the rebels, men were being separated from women for a thorough search. All the men were ordered to completely undress so that a systematic search for any form of scarification could be carried out. People with scarification were suspected of being members of the Mayi-Mayi fighters. Only those who had no *machanjo*, form of scarification on their bodies, were allowed to go beyond Kalundu and enter the city of Uvira. The fate of those thousands of people who were found with *machanjo* or scarification on their bodies remains unknown – only God knows what happened to them.

Upon entering the city of Uvira, Ben and his family discovered this strange inscription in Kinyarwanda on most of the good-looking houses: *irafashwe*, meaning "it has been taken" or "confiscated." They also realized that most homes had been systematically looted. As soon as they reached home, Ben realized the phrase *irafashwe* had also been inscribed on their house. The young man did not know how to hold back his tears, but his dad, who was a church bishop, told him with a firm sense of hope that God would provide. A week later, Laurent-Désiré Kabila arrived in Uvira from Bujumbura, escorted by a big contingent of soldiers. He held his first popular meeting at the Catholic Cathedral of Uvira where he introduced for the first time the AFDL (*Alliance des Forces Démocratiques pour la Libération du Congo*), a conglomerate of four political parties of Congolese revolutionaries who had the same will and resolve to overthrow Mobutu's dictatorial regime.[1]

Forced migration has always been part of life for many people, particularly those of us from the Great Lakes region of Africa. Personally, forced migration influenced my being, my belonging, and my becoming. All of the challenges associated with the refugee life including the pain of being an unaccompanied child and the experience of unfair treatment by some host communities are all part of my life story. However, these challenges are actually familiar to the entire forcibly displaced population, as seen in the story of Ben whose lived experiences are common to thousands of people from the Great Lakes region of Africa. Such events have placed this region in a fragile and complex situation, and most countries are yet to recover. The region is constantly in need of aid as millions of refugees are scattered around the world. The causes of forced migration are multiple but can be grouped under three distinct dynamics: sociopolitical, economic, and "other" dynamics.[2]

Sociopolitical Dynamics of Forced Migration

Many factors contribute to the phenomenon of refugees in sub-Saharan Africa, including those of social and political origin. Political factors include lack of participatory democracy, exclusion of certain people from running public affairs, exclusion from being a beneficiary of service delivery, lack of political will to empower local governments, persecution, lack of specialized institutions to combat intolerance, and all other forms of prejudice. There are also social factors. For example, in sub-Saharan Africa, one of the main reasons for emigration is extreme poverty; although poverty can also be classified to some extent as an economic factor, it is often triggered by social and political factors

---

1. Benjamin Babunga Watuna, "*Et Si Nous Parlions d'Histoire?*" Facebook (26 October 2019). The original text of this testimony is in French, which I translated. https://www.facebook.com/groups/528706633982349/?multi_permalinks=1265851536934518&notif_id=1572090676267850&notif_t=group_activity&ref=notif&__m_async_page__=1&_rdc=1&_rdr. Used by permission.

2. See E. G. Ferris, *Beyond Borders: Refugees, Migrants and Human Rights in the Post-Cold War Era* (Geneva: World Council of Churches, 1993).

in most African countries. This situation explains why most of the refugees from sub-Saharan Africa have chosen to settle in well-off countries including South Africa. It should be noted, however, that mobility has characterized humanity since time immemorial. Today, in a world marked by globalization, human migrations have become even faster mainly due to progress in transport and communication. In other words, generally speaking, mobility is a factual part of human life.

Although most migrants of yesteryear faced challenges similar to those of modern migrants, the contexts are different, and the conditions of their displacement raise different expectations. In the past, people had the choice to migrate where it seemed preferable to survive, but today the movement of people is regulated by competent bodies. This situation explains why forced migration is a big challenge to manage. Forced migrants are limited in many ways because they have to follow certain rules and regulations in the host country, unlike in the past when human migration was more a form of free movement. Forced migration is moving from one place to settle in another for reasons beyond one's control. It is also changing location periodically by moving from one region to another due to the lack of safe settlements. Therefore, forced migration is sometimes voluntary depending on the circumstances that occasion the move. In my lived experiences, it has become clear that all forms of forced migration are beyond the control of refugees, whether voluntary or involuntary. Some refugees are forced to make the decision to migrate due to sociopolitical or economic challenges they face at home. Indeed, their migration is voluntary because it is premeditated, but at the same time it is forced because the decision was taken because they felt persecuted by the socioeconomic and political systems of their country. Thus, forced migration can be voluntary or involuntary depending on how refugees left and the circumstances that led to their decision to leave. Forced migration can also be internal – within the borders of the refugees' own country – or external, which is a border-crossing experience.

The quest of refugees for freedom and safety is understandable considering that most are forced to leave their countries for various reasons including conflicts and wars. Many displaced people undertake dangerous journeys to reach the borders of a host country. However, in the face of this wave of crisis, several African countries have resolved to strengthen their immigration policies to prevent non-citizens from residing within the borders of their territorial space and thereby limit the refugee influx. Nevertheless, people look for protection beyond the geographical borders of their countries because they have been forced to leave their homes. Their decision to emigrate is often guided by many reasons including sociopolitical situations that keep threatening their lives, wars and conflicts, and other forms of violence or human rights violations. Hence, most people prefer to live their lives peacefully as refugees rather than living in their home country in situations that endanger their dear lives. But in many host countries, refugees are often treated as insignificant people. At times they are even confined to below average living standards and subjected to xenophobic attitudes or attacks.

The existence of refugees in any given country indicates that something is wrong somewhere, and somehow someone's peace and freedom are threatened. The trauma of abandoning one's home and belongings, and the experience of finding oneself in unfamiliar territory with unfamiliar people who sometimes speak unfamiliar languages and often eat unfamiliar foods make refugees vulnerable in multiple ways. In some African countries, refugees are regarded as a serious problem to the local community. They are also often considered a threat to the wealth and health of the host country.[3] Nonetheless, refugees use their skills to prove their tenacity to survive against all odds in the host country, which explains their readiness, determination, and willingness to do any job, regardless of their education or social status. However, in most African countries, refugees compete with local citizens for already scarce jobs, often leading to conflict between the two communities.[4]

In some countries, despite the wretched conditions in which refugees often live, common attitudes and convictions are that they are taking vacant posts that locals could have filled and that they are responsible for much of the crime and other illegal activities in the host country. This thinking often leads to ill-feelings; then ill-feelings lead to resentment; and resentment eventually erupts in violent attacks and deaths. A case in hand is what has been happening in South Africa. However, new trends in forced human migration require global attention and new strategies. Some of these trends that are pushing millions of people from place to place to seek asylum include population growth, urbanization, food insecurity, and climate change. Protecting and assisting refugees has become a very complicated matter in most African countries as these trends are increasing and thus forcing people to seek asylum.

---

3. L. B. Landau, *The Humanitarian Hangover: Displacement, Aid and Transformation in Western Tanzania* (Johannesburg: Wits University Press, 2008).

4. J. Stemmett, "A Biblical Theology of Ministry to Refugees for Baptist Churches in South Africa" (Master of Theology Thesis, University of Fort Hare, 2008), 14.

Overview of the sociopolitical dynamics of forced migration in Burundi and Rwanda

Burundi is a small country in the Great Lakes region of Africa whose postcolonial history is known by interethnic massacres and a long civil war complicated by a bitter power struggle between the main ethnic groups. In 1972, a Hutu insurrection broke out against the Tutsi minority, who initially held sociopolitical power and influence. The repression quickly turned into systematic massacres of members of the Hutu ethnic group, killing an estimated three hundred thousand people. In 1976, a coup d'état brought Jean-Baptiste Bagaza to power, and in 1987, he was overthrown, and Pierre Buyoya, also Tutsi and cousin of his predecessor, became head of state. In 1988, new massacres bloodied the country in the two territories of Ntega and Marangara, leaving fifty thousand dead.

In June 1993, the first democratic elections were held in Burundi and were won by *Sahwanya* FRODEBU (*Front pour la Démocratie au Burundi*), an opposition party led by Melchior Ndadaye – a Hutu. Unfortunately, he was assassinated on 21 October of the same year during a rebellion organized by soldiers from his own predominantly Tutsi army, and a situation of civil war returned to Burundi between the army and the Hutu rebels. Civilians, Hutus, and Tutsis, alternately actors or hostages in the tragedy, were the main victims. Ndadaye's successor, Cyprien Ntaryamira, a Hutu, was also killed in April 1994, along with Rwandan President Juvénal Habyarimana, whose plane was shot down in Kigali.

In July 1996, a coup d'état against another Hutu president, Sylvestre Ntibandunganya, brought back to power Pierre Buyoya, a Tutsi, who began negotiations with the political and armed opposition. A peace agreement was signed in 2000 in Arusha, Tanzania, and at the end of 2003, the main rebel group, the *Conseil National pour la Défense de la Démocratie – Forces pour la Défense de la Démocratie* (CNDD-FDD), laid down their arms. In 2006, the government signed a ceasefire with another rebel movement, the *Forces pour la Libération Nationale* (FNL). This civil war in Burundi from 1993 to 2006 left nearly three hundred thousand dead, mostly civilians, and displaced hundreds of thousands of Burundians around the world.

As for the situation in Rwanda, from 6 April to 4 July 1994, about eight hundred thousand Rwandans, mostly Tutsis, were massacred by other Rwandans, mostly Hutus. Perpetrated in about one hundred days, the Rwandan genocide holds the sad record for the fastest genocide in history. To understand the reasons for this massacre, we have to go back to the time of the colonization of the country. Under German domination from the beginning of the twentieth century, Rwanda suffered the throes of an already strong ethnological ideology, which designated the Tutsi tribe as being superior to the Hutu and the Twa tribes. The colonizers then affirmed that the Tutsis constituted a smarter ethnic group that was closer to the European peoples. At the end of the First World War, Belgium took up the torch of colonization, and they found nothing to fault with this situation which seemed to be well established. The Tutsis had access to education and occupied positions of responsibility in the administration. The Hutus cultivated the land and remained confined to the lower socioeconomic classes.

Racial discrimination went further when in 1931, the Belgian colonizers decided to put in place a registration system designating the ethnic groups in both Rwanda and Burundi. From then on, the inhabitants started to be characterized by their Tutsi, Hutu, or Twa ethnic groups. However at independence, the historical situation was reversed in Rwanda, and many Tutsis were forced into exile in the late 1950s and early 1960s. Animosity between Tutsis and Hutus continued to grow. The exiles tried on several occasions to return to the country, but the repression was bloody. In 1990, a civil war broke out between the rebel movement Rwandan Patriotic Front (RPF) and the Rwandan government. The civil war fueled this propaganda of hatred and fear, according to which the minority Tutsis were presented as a threat to the survival of the majority Hutus. This propaganda facilitated the recruitment of militias, the *Interahamwe*, who were the armed wing of the genocide. On 6 April at 8:50 pm, the presidential plane was shot down as it was preparing to land in Kigali. This attack was the spark that caused the explosion. The genocide of the Tutsis began, and hundreds of thousands of Rwandans, mostly Hutus, fled the country to seek refuge in neighbouring countries, mainly the Democratic Republic of Congo.

Overview of the sociopolitical dynamics of forced migration in the DRC

The Great Lakes region of Africa is characterized by complex realities that illustrate the fragility of most countries in the region. The crisis in the DRC which started in 1996 was preceded by the crises in Burundi and Rwanda as explained in the previous section. The crises that have marked the history of Burundi and Rwanda for years particularly illustrate the political dimension of ethnic conflicts. Melchior Ndadaye – a Hutu – was assassinated on 21 October 1993. The following year in Rwanda, the killing of Juvénal Habyarimana, then president of Rwanda, and Cyprien Ntaryamira, then president of Burundi, sank Rwanda into an unprecedented crisis that resulted in a terrible genocide.

These two major conflicts in Burundi and Rwanda were, to a certain extent, the precursors of the wars in the DRC. We could go back very far to understand the conflict in the Democratic Republic of Congo, but it suffices here to underline the effects of the Rwandan genocide of 1994.

After the genocide which killed more than eight hundred thousand people, thousands of refugees crossed the border from Rwanda to the DRC, in particular to the regions of North Kivu and South Kivu, in and around the cities of Goma, Bukavu, and Uvira. Among these Rwandan refugees it was suspected were several leaders who had orchestrated the genocide in Rwanda and mercilessly killed their Rwandan compatriots, mostly Tutsis and moderate Hutus. In the DRC, it is believed that these suspected genocidaires quickly took control of the refugee camps from which they planned to reconquer Rwanda. The new Rwandan government saw the presence of the Hutu refugees in the DRC, most of whom are suspected genocidaires, as a significant threat to their country. A Rwandan military intervention resolved the problem quickly in 1996, but the troops remained in the DRC.

Confident of their success, the Rwandan attackers opted for another objective: to overthrow the regime of DRC President Mobutu. When their candidate, Laurent-Désiré Kabila, seized the capital Kinshasa in 1997 and replaced Mobutu, events accelerated. Kabila sought to get rid of his Rwandan allies who had put him in power. A struggle for power ensued and quickly fell into violence. Kabila's "breakup" against his former allies who had helped him take power triggered another war. Rwanda, Uganda, and Burundi armed the anti-Kabila Congolese rebels. Kabila was saved by the rapid intervention of African states including Angola, Namibia, and Zimbabwe which were particularly active, as well as Chad, Libya, and Sudan which were also involved but in a limited and short-term manner. In this context, the war in the DRC took on a whole different form. Trafficking, economic predation, and looting of all kinds of mineral resources became the privileged means of financing the war. As a result, the war in DRC became particularly cruel to civilian populations and by its nature difficult to stop. The Congolese conflict is therefore considered the deadliest, and it is believed to have killed more than five million people.[5]

Thus, the war in the DRC reached the highest level of complexity to the point that it was renamed the "African World War," having involved at least eight African nations and more than twenty armed groups. Minerals such as gold, tin, tungsten, and tantalum, which is mined in the form of coltan,

---

5. Armin Rosen, "The Origins of War in the DRC," *The Atlantic* (26 June 2013), https://www.theatlantic.com/international/archive/2013/06/the-origins-of-war-in-the-drc/277131/.

play an essential role in the financing of these armed groups and therefore in prolonging the conflict. The country is indeed rich in resources, but also rich in conflicts, violence, and all sorts of human rights abuses. The DRC is currently experiencing one of the greatest crises of forced migration on the African continent. As a consequence, many Congolese have not experienced lasting peace since 1996.

The DRC continues to face governance, public service delivery, and poverty reduction challenges because of the long-lasting armed conflicts that have had serious and long-term impacts on the functioning of the state. At the moment, the DRC is experiencing the world's most complex humanitarian crises but, seemingly, the most ignored and most forgotten as a 2019 Mercy Corps report indicates.[6] The rise of the Ebola virus has always worsened the situation in the DRC due to its endemic nature. Until recently, the DRC was battling its tenth Ebola outbreak, which killed thousands of people. The epidemic is said to have been the worst in the history of the DRC.[7]

It should be noted that the size of the DRC is equal to that of Western Europe, making it the second largest country in Africa after Algeria – with an area size of 2,345,804 km^2 and an estimated population of 105,044,646 people.[8] In eastern DRC, most people have fled and sought asylum in neighbouring countries due to the violence ravaging their home areas. They then seek safety and security, as well as new opportunities that will help them earn an income so they can survive. They do this as the conflict has forced them to abandon their land, their loved ones, and their belongings.[9] In the eastern DRC, many women and girls have been victims of sexual violence. According to a 2019 Mercy Corps report, women usually "leave their homes with very little." They only take "their children and the clothes that they are wearing" at that time. As for the men, some of them leave the country because they are afraid "of being killed or of being forcibly recruited into armed groups."[10] In this part of the DRC, the massacres have never stopped completely since October 1996. In Beni and its surroundings such as Butembo as well as in other corners of this part of the country such as Mulongwe in Uvira and Makobola in Fizi,

---

6. Mercy Corps, "The Facts: The Humanitarian Crisis in the Democratic Republic of Congo," Mercy Corps (17 July 2019), https://www.mercycorps.org/blog/drc-humanitarian-crisis.
7. Mercy Corps, "The Facts."
8. World Fact Book, "Congo, Democratic Republic of the" (9 March 2021), https://www.cia.gov/the-world-factbook/countries/congo-democratic-republic-of-the/.
9. Mercy Corps, "The Facts."
10. Mercy Corps, "The Facts."

South Kivu province, heinous massacres have been committed, while both the international community and the media remained indifferently silent.

The DRC contains large quantities of natural resources including gold, diamonds, coltan, tin, zinc, uranium, and oil to name but a few. The country is the largest copper producer in Africa and the world's leading source of cobalt – a metal whose value has tripled in the last few years due to the surge in demand for electric cars.[11] DRC is also home to immense biodiversity and the second largest tropical forest in the world, which is a significant carbon sink storing greenhouse gases.[12] In addition, DRC's rivers have a hydroelectric potential that could eventually supply half of sub-Saharan Africa with electricity. Equipped with eighty million hectares of arable land and climatic conditions of great diversity, the DRC has agricultural potential that could feed a large part of the African continent. In addition, the volcanoes, gorillas, and exceptional landscapes of this country present enormous opportunities for the tourism sector.[13]

Yet despite all this wealth of natural resources, DRC is ranked as one of the poorest countries in the world. Thus the country is richly blessed with a copious supply of all kinds of mineral resources, but its population is among the poorest in the world due to inadequate use of resources, the lack of adequate infrastructure, food insecurity, malnourishment, the impacts of colonialism, corruption, diseases, and many years of conflicts.[14] Widespread abuses perpetrated by armed groups as well as members of the Congolese security forces have hindered the country's development for years. These abuses are reinforced by widespread impunity and struggles for control of the country's considerable resources. As a result, millions of Congolese nationals are in urgent need of humanitarian assistance including food, sanitation, running water, shelter, and education.[15] In addition, factors like lack of adequate healthcare services and social marginalization deprive people

---

11. Mercy Corps, "The Facts."

12. Rhett A. Butler, "The Congo Rainforest," Mongabay (1 August 2020), https://rainforests.mongabay.com/congo/.

13. Ida Sawyer, "Présentation sur la crise politique en RD Congo et ses répercussions en matière humanitaire, de droits humains et de sécurité," *Human Rights Watch* (9 April 2018). See also L. Xu, S. S. Saatchi, A. Shapiro, et al., "Spatial Distribution of Carbon Stored in Forests of the Democratic Republic of Congo," *Scientific Reports* 7, no. 15030 (8 November 2017), https://www.nature.com/articles/s41598-017-15050-z.pdf.

14. Kara Roberts, "Understanding the Causes of Poverty in the DRC," *Borgen Magazine* (6 September 2018), https://www.borgenmagazine.com/poverty-in-the-drc/.

15. Sawyer, "Présentation sur la crise politique en RD Congo."

of their rights for survival just as they rob them of their freedom and their dignity. A number of African leaders conduct themselves dictatorially despite espousing democracy and multiparty politics in their respective countries, and they seem unaware that democratic leaders are accountable to the people they govern. The combination of all these social challenges and political crises often results in forced migration.

It needs to be emphasized that people are the backbone of democracy and should be the beneficiaries of the material and cultural benefits that flow from it. Sharing these benefits is a requirement for any democratic government. However the refusal to alternate political powers, the refusal to admit electoral defeat, the lack of dialogue, and in many cases the demonization of political opponents all work to validate the popular claim in Africa that "democracy is not an African thing." This assertion is ascertained in most African countries because many leaders do not defend democratic values as they are expected to due to their unconstitutional and autocratic leadership styles. Such behaviour ends up producing tension, endless conflicts, and other types of violence which often lead to forced migration. Due to these interminable sociopolitical crises, the presence of refugees from sub-Saharan Africa in various other African countries, including South Africa, is so evident. South-South forced migration is indeed a reality that cannot be ignored or pushed into the annals of oblivion.

Economic Dynamics of Forced Migration

Various economic factors lead to forced migration. The main factors among others are low economic growth, unequal distribution of wealth, and overpopulation linked to high demographic growth, as well as high unemployment rates. All these factors are linked to the country of origin. The natural disposition of people to migrate to resource-rich areas has been traditionally regarded as an inextinguishable phenomenon. Recognized in the world economy as a factor of economic development, the mobility of populations has increased sharply in recent decades. Today, migrations are generally ordered by the existence of economic and political but also social factors. In a knowledge-based economy, economic issues are crucial for African countries whose advantages of globalization and technology are reinforced by the attractiveness of skilled workers.

In Africa, economic migration is due to the fact that, despite economic progress in all regions of the world, most people in sub-Sahara Africa remain below the poverty line.[16] Migrating for work has become a common practice for many due to the globalized system we now live in because it constitutes a way of securing sufficient income for the survival of the immigrant. The effects of this type of forced migration are more perceptible in the country of origin because emigrants take their knowledge with them.[17] Migration in general is made up of emigration and immigration. To emigrate means to leave one's country to go and settle in another. It is therefore in relation to the country of departure or origin that we speak of emigration. Conversely, immigrating means entering a foreign country in order to settle there. It is therefore in relation to the country of arrival or host country that we speak of immigration. So, emigration is *out*-migration while immigration is *in*-migration. The loss of labourers from the country of origin can be profitable for the host country because it brings in skilled labourers. At the same time, a country of origin that experiences a "brain drain" balances the loss of human resources with the influx of other skilled labourers from other countries. However in general, this situation confirms the deduction that emigration without immigration impacts any country's economy negatively because the workforce decreases when emigration is significantly high.[18]

As refugees stay longer in a country, the host government risks serious economic effects. However, upon their return to their country of origin, refugees are likely to boost the economy with skills acquired in their country of asylum. This means that most returnees increase their domestic productivity, especially if they were in a country known to be better off. Ironically, many African countries exist in a paradox of wealth in terms of mineral resources and an extremely poor population – and an example in hand is the DRC. Understanding this paradox is a big challenge for many African countries, which is why many people prefer to seek asylum elsewhere in search of better opportunities. Others seek asylum for economic reasons because they think their chances of survival are higher elsewhere than in their own country. In

---

16. Albert G. Zeufack, Cesar Calderon, Gerard Kambou, Megumi Kubota, Catalina Cantu Canales, Vijdan Korman, "Africa's Pulse, No. 22" (October 2020). Washington, DC: World Bank, https://openknowledge.worldbank.org/bitstream/handle/10986/34587/9781464816482.pdf.

17. C. Harzig, D. Hoerder, and D. Gabaccia, *What Is Migration History?* (Cambridge: Polity, 2009), 11.

18. Benjamin Elsner, "Does Emigration Increase the Wages of Non-Emigrants in Sending Countries?" (n.d.), https://wol.iza.org/articles/does-emigration-increase-wages-of-non-emigrants-in-sending-countries/long.

some cases, people send a few members of the family away to a foreign country so that they can support the rest of the family through remittances.[19]

Many people in Africa are forced to migrate due to economic crises in their own country, and others seek asylum because they are attracted by economic opportunities in host countries. There are many questions about whether this second reason really qualifies someone as a refugee or simply as an economic migrant. However, trade and industry have an impact and influence on markets, and these impacts could lead people to seek asylum for new opportunities. For instance, an increase in food production in a neighbouring country could be a factor behind forced migration for economic reasons. Among those who migrate for money reasons are often those who have been seriously affected by unemployment or poverty in their country of origin. Their displacement is therefore the result of their desire to work in another country because they are dissatisfied, unemployed, hopeless, or helpless in the circumstances prevailing in their own country.

Lack of basic needs

In most African countries, the lack of basic needs is caused by unemployment, which is one of the many causes of poverty. In other words, the lack of basic needs indicates that most people in African countries live in abject poverty. Therefore, those who have relatives or friends in another country, or those who simply hear about opportunities elsewhere, are forced by the circumstances of their home country to migrate to that country so they can also improve the prospects of their well-being. This migration is both forced and economic mainly because of a "pull factor," what they hear from this rich country or the concrete proof they see in the remittances that their friends or relatives send, and a "push factor," the economic hardships they are facing in their own country. The presence of friends or relatives in a better-off country can trigger forced migration on account of economic factors, especially if the soon-to-be emigrant lives in poverty or is unemployed. These pull and push forces explain why Africa is one of the continents with the highest number of transnational forced migrants and why the demands for development are increasing compared to other continents in the world.

---

19. Bimal Ghosh, "Migrants' Remittances and Development: Myths, Rhetoric, and Realities," IOM-International Organization for Migration (2006), https://publications.iom.int/system/files/pdf/migrants_remittances.pdf.

The UNHRC Convention and Protocol Relating to the Status of Refugees, which includes the 1951 Convention Relating to the Status of Refugees and its 1967 Protocol, is the key legal document that defines who are refugees, their rights, and the legal obligations of states to them. This document defines someone to be a refugee based only on that person's "well-founded fear of being persecuted" and with the prerequisite that he or she has crossed a national border.[20] This means that without crossing a national border, someone is technically not a refugee per se but an internally displaced person (IDP), despite the fact that IDPs also live in situations similar to refugees but in their own country. So considering a refugee on the sole basis of having "a well-founded fear of being persecuted for reasons of race, religion, nationality, membership of a particular social group, or political opinion"[21] has a certain level of ambiguity that creates challenges when determining one's refugee status. This "persecution clause," as it is referred to, suggests that victims of other problems, such as economic difficulties in home country and various other social or environmental problems, should not be considered refugees upon arrival in a host country because their flight was not caused by a so-called "fear of persecution."

The ambiguity of this persecution clause gave rise to debates in the attempt to clarify what it really means to be a refugee. It was in this context that the 1969 "Organization of African Unity (OAU) Convention Governing the Specific Aspects of Refugee Problems in Africa" redefined the term "refugee" by expanding its meaning in Africa to "every person who, owing to external aggression, occupation, foreign domination or events seriously disturbing public order in either part or the whole of his country of origin or nationality, is compelled to leave his place of habitual residence in order to seek refuge in another place outside his country of origin or nationality."[22] This statement means that the internationally accepted refugee definition has proven inadequate to address the challenges posed by millions of forced migrants in various parts of the world. As a result, regional definitions, such as that presented by the 1969 OAU Convention, have been put forward. They

---

20. UNHRC, "Convention and Protocol Relating to the Status of Refugees," including the "1951 Convention Relating to the Status of Refugees" and "1967 Protocol Relating to the Status of Refugees," Geneva: UNHRC (2010), http://www.unhcr.org/3b66c2aa10.html.

21. UNHRC, "Convention and Protocol Relating to the Status of Refugees," 3, 14.

22. UNHRC, "OAU Convention Governing the Specific Aspects of Refugee Problems in Africa," UNHRC, Addis-Ababa (10 September 1969), https://www.unhcr.org/about-us/background/45dc1a682/oau-convention-governing-specific-aspects-refugee-problems-africa-adopted.html.

represent a concrete attempt to adapt international refugee laws to existing refugee problems at regional levels. For this reason, the 1969 OAU Convention prohibits *refoulement*, unlike the 1951 Convention and its 1967 Protocol, and it is the first international instrument to codify the principles of free and voluntary repatriation. The 1969 OAU Convention thus broadened the definition of a refugee's identity according to the 1951 UN Convention and its 1967 Protocol by including accidental situations such as flight from socioenvironmental disasters like famine, drought, and anything that disturbs public order even if it is not caused by the political circumstances of the country. The depth and breadth of this definition provides African leaders with guidelines of relevance to African contextual issues. In other words, the description of a refugee by the 1969 OAU protocol includes those who are forced to leave their home countries for a myriad of reasons regardless of whether they are physically threatened or personally in danger of persecution.

Besides to a great extent the term "persecution" could refer to whatever threatens one's life or freedom. In this regard, a denial of or menace to one's basic rights – economic, cultural, social, religious, etc. – is therefore considered to be persecution. One does not need to be physically harmed or emotionally deprived to be deemed persecuted. Thus, the lack or deprivation of basic human rights is also a form of persecution. In the same way, since a human being has the rights to work, to earn a living, to education, to worship, to own land, etc., any denial or threat to such basic rights is also within the persecution clause. So, the breadth of the term "persecution" makes the meaning of the term "refugee" even more extensive for people who leave their country of origin to seek asylum. Therefore, people who are forced to leave their country due to economic factors including poverty and unemployment are genuinely refugees and not merely "economic migrants" because they are economically persecuted and their freedom is severely threatened.

Deprivation of capabilities

Amartya Sen finds that development is a process of expanding the real freedoms that people enjoy which can only be done by removing the major sources of unfreedom such as poverty, tyranny, and systemic deprivation.[23] Sen's theory of development demonstrates that quality of life should be measured by human freedom, not by opulence. According to the theory, one can be considered persecuted even when, for example, public facilities such as toilets are neglected

---

23. Amartya Sen, *Development as Freedom* (Oxford: Oxford University Press, 1999), 3.

by local authorities or when schools are closed for no apparent reason by the local chief. When these things happen, freedom is at stake, and people might be forced to migrate as a result of these specific forms of persecution. Hence, the attempt to draw a line between a genuine refugee and an economic one only leads to false analogies, as Maluwa argues.[24]

In this regard, Sen considers poverty to be a "deprivation of basic capabilities," and not just a fact of lacking or earning less money.[25] Such deprivation causes early mortality, malnutrition, disease, illiteracy, and many other failures. This deprivation of basic capabilities is further reflected in unjust distribution of wealth, which often forces many to seek asylum. Poverty is ill-being. This is why Swanepoel and de Beer associate it with factors such as poor housing, a lack of safe water and sanitation services, poor educational facilities, and little opportunity for employment.[26] To transform the lives of those living in poverty, they must be given a chance to look after their own well-being through programmes of self-reliance.[27] It cannot be overemphasized that most refugees are in a similar situation as they are deprived of basic human needs and find little opportunity for employment in both their home country and their host country. Most of them pursue livelihoods themselves and contribute to their own process of transformation by involving themselves in various socioeconomic activities. Refugees are not ashamed to even vend some small items on the streets, which raises the level of competition in the microeconomic sector.

The economic activities of refugees seem to be a threat to the host population in many countries. In South Africa, for example, the rate of unemployment and poverty is quite high. As a result, tensions over economic concerns and different expressions of national interest are common between the host population and the migrant population in the country. Such a "sentiment of nativism," as Daniel Carroll calls it, usually leads to waves of violent attacks.[28] Here nativism could be a policy to promote natives as opposed to immigrants. Thus nativists oppose immigration, and this sentiment is based on the fear that immigrants distort the existing order or spoil cultural

---

24. T. Maluwa, "The Refugee Problem and the Quest for Peace and Security in Southern Africa," *International Refugee Law Journal*, University of Cape Town (1995): 64.

25. Sen, *Development as Freedom*, 20.

26. H. Swanepoel and F. de Beer, *Community Development: Breaking the Cycle of Poverty*, 4th ed. (Lansdowne, South Africa: Juta, 2006), 8.

27. Swanepoel and de Beer, *Community Development*, 9.

28. M. Daniel Carroll, *Christians at the Border: Immigration, the Church, and the Bible* (Grand Rapids: Baker Academic, 2008), 30.

values. In situations where immigrants outnumber the original inhabitants, nativists prevent cultural change. When an individual is animated by the spirit of nativism, they tend to have a feeling of fear and / or hatred toward a foreign minority which, according to them, constitutes a danger or a threat to their heritage or their national culture. Likewise, a development process that benefits only a small minority of the population and maintains or even increases the disparities between the different layers of the population is not transformational development. It is more of an exploitation and explains the need for a new development strategy which will contribute to the eradication of poverty, promote a self-reliant process of transformation, and intervene sustainably in terms of ecology because indeed transformational development, like mission, should be integral.

In most African countries, members of the host communities tend to believe that the majority of foreign migrants commit crimes in order to survive, and those who do not commit crimes for survival will take their jobs. This situation explains why terms like "illegal immigrants," "economic migrants," etc. are used interchangeably with the term "refugee" or even, like in South Africa, alongside derogatory terms such as *amaKwerekwere* when describing refugees. The term "*kwerekwere*" is an onomatopoeic neologism[29] used pejoratively to refer to foreigners. The term supposedly suggests those who speak unintelligibly, so their unfamiliar language sounds like someone saying *kwere, kwere, kwere*, which has since been xenophobically used as an insult directed at foreigners. Such name-calling and assumptions that refugees take jobs belonging to the local population only reinforce speculation that refugees, and various other African migrants, are either criminals or a socioeconomic burden that adds to poverty and unemployment already experienced in the host country. Thus, the very presence of refugees displeases many in the host country. Inequality and unemployment are among the main factors that make the host population feel threatened by refugees. Unemployment, for example, is so severe in sub-Saharan Africa that most public and even private institutions do not know whether skilled refugees are eligible for even managerial positions in a company or whether they are eligible for grants or scholarships like their local counterparts. As a result, refugees often live in a situation of limbo – not knowing where they stand legally or socially.

The involvement of refugees in the microeconomic sector of many African countries points to the fact that their small businesses contribute to the transformational development of their country of asylum. It is evident that most

---

29. Meaning a new word formed from a sound associated with what is named.

refugees are susceptible to discrimination, intolerance, and xenophobia because refugees are considered to be the source of most of the problems affecting the national economy of the host country.[30] Indeed, the unemployment rate of the local population of the host country is often high. This is the case in South Africa and the cause of the many cases of xenophobic violence in the country.

The presence of abject poverty

It is difficult to know the main reason for someone's decision to leave. However, most causes of migration are linked. For example poverty results from conflicts, and conflicts are always linked to political and social crises. In sub-Saharan Africa, one of the determining reasons for leaving is extreme poverty, which explains the settling of migrants in a relatively richer country. Some leave in search of better socioeconomic prospects as they face extreme poverty in their home country. They flee wars, ethnic and religious conflicts, human rights abuses, and the like. Some are immediately recognized as refugees while others become asylum seekers and wait for their cases to be determined by the relevant authorities in the host country. They are not always allowed to work, but many get to work illegally. All of these factors are linked in one way or another to the question of poverty.

Poverty is both a challenge and a problem with life-threatening implications. In Africa, poverty is widespread, and its prevalence is evidence of the ever-widening gap between the rich and the poor. This situation amplifies the magnitude of people's vulnerability. For several decades, eastern DRC has not ceased to be at the mercy of an infernal cycle of armed conflicts which are the direct consequences of the colonial history of the Great Lakes region of Africa and of the geopolitical situation built on globalized capitalism. At the heart of the Great Lakes region, the eastern part of the DRC is a migration hub. Since the 1990s, especially in the wake of the Rwandan genocide, the situation has continued to deteriorate, increasing the number of armed groups which continue to perpetrate fights, massacres of innocent civilians, looting, and rape. Thus to flee the atrocities experienced by the populations of this part of the country, as well as the socioeconomic crisis created by so many hardships that persisted among us, many Congolese have been forced to seek asylum in neighbouring countries. It was in this context that I found myself a refugee in

---

30. P. Mususa and F. Nyamnjoh, "Migration and Xenophobia in Southern Africa," in *Building Peace in Southern Africa*, ed. D. Hanar and C. Saunders (Cape Town: Centre for Conflict Resolution, 2010), 36.

various countries. Through my life story, I can say that being a constant witness to the suffering of others constantly confronts me with my own vulnerability.

This situation also explains why humanitarian organizations lead a twofold battle: helping to reduce the effects of forced migration by assisting refugees with basic needed services and trying to alleviate the plight of poverty by partnering with the government on programmes that sustainably ensure transformational development. In view of these efforts, there is a need to understand the positive role that migration in general plays in reducing poverty so that we can explore the possibilities of mobilizing ourselves in fighting this societal scourge. Attempts to manage both poverty and the refugee phenomenon require new strategies that focus on the whole person and aim at restoring dignity. Partnerships between the private and the public sectors are therefore *sine qua non* if we are to manage the causes of poverty and reduce its many effects that lead to forced migration. According to Dryden-Peterson and Gilles, this situation also shows the coherent link between poverty and the refugee phenomenon in the global economics of wealth. They argue that poverty exacerbates conditions of forced migration and exile no matter the economic class, ethnic group, or gender involved.[31]

The link between poverty and migration should not always be viewed negatively because there are cases where poverty forces people to migrate and that migration helps them out of poverty, which should be considered a positive outcome.[32] The main challenge for sub-Saharan Africa is that a great number of people find themselves in situations of abject poverty due to the lack of basic needs and/or the absence of modern tools for economic activities such as agriculture and fishery, among other activities for sustenance and economic growth. Unfortunately, the maladministration and accumulation of funds by the local elite increases the level of "underdevelopment" in many African countries. That is to say, the elite exploit the needy – and this behaviour reinforces poverty as those in need become dependent on those who have something to offer. Situations like this often cause people to look for an alternative country to live in. The refugee phenomenon thus presents a dual challenge for African countries since many also have their own socioeconomic problems to deal with. So many countries seek to address the root causes

---

31. S. Dryden-Petersen and W. Gilles, "Introduction: Higher Education for Refugees," *Refuge: Canada's Periodical on Refugees* 27, no. 2 (2010): 5.

32. R. M. Collyer Black, R. Skeldon, and C. Waddington, "Routes to Illegal Residence: A Case Study of Immigration Detainees in the United Kingdom," Geoforum 37, no. 4 (2006): 552–64.

of poverty in a holistic way, mostly through transformational community development processes and humanitarian interventions or activism. Focusing on transformational community development ultimately improves the holistic well-being of people through both word and acts of service. Transformational community development in the context of the refugee phenomenon can be church-led process through which refugees identify and overcome the obstacles that prevent them from living life in all its fullness.

It is for these reasons that as the church, we need to stand in the gap and be the voice of reason to give the voiceless refugees a sense of belonging and self-worth. We have a responsibility to ensure that transformation is sustainable by empowering the refugee community to sustainably contribute to the process of development in their host country. It is part of our Christian responsibility to join the civil society groups in their attempts to raise awareness on how to treat refugees with human dignity. So, what is the role of the church in all this? One approach to conceptualizing the reduction of poverty from an ecclesial perspective is to understand the role of the church, which requires us to examine the benefits that the poor can derive from religious or faith-based organizations. In addition to material and financial support, church association with these organizations can create a diverse set of resources for refugees ranging from individual empowerment and well-being to social network development and social mobilization, and finally to civic engagement.

This approach harmonizes well with Sen's conceptualization of the multidimensionality of poverty in his book *Development as Freedom* which widens the description of poverty centred mainly on income to a notion that encompasses autonomy, empowerment, and dignity, thus moving from the set of individual actions to collective action.[33] As migrant populations are often denied the right to claim social benefits due to restrictions on their stay, poor migrants are desperate for help in any form. Church contributions in kind such as food vouchers, which may seem like little to most ordinary families, could offer migrants quick and essential assistance. Migrants also establish social networks by joining religious groups; they find emotional support in religion and help their children build their human capital. All of these factors contribute to the reduction of poverty.

---

33. Sen, *Development as Freedom*.

Other Dynamics of Forced Migration

It is difficult if not impossible to draft an exhaustive and precise list of the causes of forced migration. This is why, apart from the sociopolitical and economic dynamics, it is safer to classify the rest of the dynamics in the "other" category. Many of these factors are either pull factors or push factors. Push factors are those that drive people away from their home country, while pull factors are those that attract them toward another country. Push factors include but are not limited to natural disasters, demographic changes, climate change, environmental pollution, fear of persecution, the various forms of "unfreedom," and poverty and unemployment. Pull factors include but are not limited to the various forms of freedom, jobs or money-making opportunities, better living conditions, and strong democracy, as well as peace and security. So push and pull factors are what drive people to move away from a location and to move to a new location. Push and pull factors work together when people migrate, pushing them away from one country and dragging them to a new country. These factors create either new avenues for holistic transformation or barriers to social progress if they threaten people's emotional stability and well-being. As a result of these factors, people change their original abode in the quest for that which they need most or which they lack in their home country.

Climate change and other environmental challenges

In the Nyarugusu refugee camp, life was hard. Those of us who arrived there in 1996 when it had just opened for human habitation used the available resources for our survival. We used to cut trees to construct our tented houses and to use as firewood for cooking. Indeed, we were causing environmental degradation by cutting down trees with reckless abandon, but using firewood for cooking was a fundamental need for all the refugees since the camp was located in the jungle. It should also be noted that cutting trees is a very common practice on the African continent, despite the impact it causes on the environment, because sun-dried pieces of trees are used for firewood and for making charcoal. In addition, some houses are built using branches of trees. So without cutting trees down, our life equation would have been even more complex in this camp environment. Therefore it could be said that from an ecological point of view, our cutting of trees in Nyarugusu caused environmental deterioration, but from the point of view of our living experiences as refugees in a camp of concentration, it was a survival strategy. This contrast of perspectives is important because it shows that in Africa, climate change must be addressed within the context of poverty and deprivation so as to give the matter contextual relevance in the region.[34]

Environmental disasters linked to climate change are fast becoming a major cause of forced migration. It is estimated that by 2050, about two hundred million people will have been forced to relocate because of environmental disasters, which is more than the current number of immigrants in the world.[35] However, the approach to the phenomenon remains complex: in addition to the uncertainty of climate change and the ignorance of current internal migratory flows is the questioning of the appropriate concepts to describe these forced displacements. The authors of a study carried out at the United Nations University in Bonn suggest three categories: "environmentally motivated migrants," "environmentally forced migrants," and "environmental refugees."[36] Environmentally motivated migrants are those who decide to leave a degraded environment to avoid the worst; this movement can be temporary or permanent. Environmentally forced migrants must leave to avoid the worst; this movement is permanent. As for environmental refugees, they are people fleeing an ongoing disaster such as flooding; this movement can be temporary or permanent.

It is of course obvious that the Bible does not say anything explicit about climate change due to human activity; however, there is no reason to believe that the Bible has nothing relevant to say on the subject. In our technological world are many topics the Bible does not speak directly about, yet biblical principles have frequently been used to shed light on such topics. For example, the Bible does not directly address the issues of abortion or euthanasia, but few Christians would say it has nothing relevant to say about these areas. Biblical doctrines which affirm that human life is sacred and that its value depends not on physical or mental capacity but on the creative act of God are put to good use to develop ethical reflection on these subjects. For instance, many Christians consider it fundamental to engage with politics and develop a commitment to it. Christians have also used the Bible on other contemporary issues including apartheid, AIDS, and nuclear power. So claiming that one can

---

34. D. Simon, "The Climate Change Challenges for Regional Integration in Southern Africa," paper presented at Research and Policy Seminar on Building Peace in Southern Africa (Cape Town, South Africa, 2010), 34–35.

35. E. Piguet, "Climate Change and Forced Migration," Research Paper 153 (Geneva: UNHCR, 2008), 4.

36. F. Renaud, J. J. Bogardi, O. Dun, and K. Warner, "Control, Adapt or Flee: How to Face Environmental Migration?" Bonn: United Nations University – Institute for Environment and Human Security (2007): 29–30.

discuss climate change without first looking at the Bible is to deny the authority and scope of the word of God.

Climate change poses innumerable challenges to both the host country and refugee-producing countries. For example in sub-Saharan Africa, the effects of climate change are causing natural forests to slowly disappear, and local people are being forced to relocate. There is a need to find new strategies that protect both the environment and the refugee community as climate change poses a threat to vulnerable communities. Policies which empower vulnerable communities to become agents of their own transformation must be encouraged if we are to provide holistic and sustainable solutions to the challenges facing the continent. Climate change is thus a complex, transboundary challenge on the continent and particularly in sub-Saharan Africa which calls for new and more contextual approaches to its management and mitigation. Ferris affirms this complexity when she argues that historically, people have always tried to move when they were unable to survive.[37] Although it is not easy to say the exact reasons for the first migrations, it is well-known that one of the reasons for this mobility was climate change that led to food insecurity or food shortages. When people moved from one place to another, they crossed geographical areas and cultural groups to hunt and reunite their families.[38]

It should be noted, however, that all the countries contribute to the increase in greenhouse gas emissions, even though China, the United States, India, Russia, and Japan are the top emitters.[39] In Africa, South Africa is the main emitter of greenhouse gases which explains why South Africa is also very vulnerable to the threat of global warming and the various effects of climate change. Changes in rainfall patterns and droughts and floods affect the agricultural sector, water resources, and the whole ecosystem. Adapting to these changes is imperative and should be included in various social assistance programmes and socioeconomic development plans. Extreme weather patterns put communities at risk as natural disasters become more of a threat.

Disasters undermine the ability to cultivate land, which is the main socioeconomic activity of many in the rural areas. Pushed to the margins,

---

37. Ferris, *Beyond Borders*, 68.
38. Harzig, Hoerder, and Gabaccia, *What Is Migration History?*, 10.
39. Andriy Blokhin, "The 5 Countries that Produce the Most Carbon Dioxide (CO2)," *Investopedia* (27 October 2020), https://www.investopedia.com/articles/investing/092915/5-countries-produce-most-carbon-dioxide-co2.asp.

poor communities are often not protected and are unable to protect themselves. This is a double tragedy for them because it makes them more vulnerable to the effects of climate change. Their situation also provides evidence that the earth's climate is constantly and rapidly changing. The magnitude of these changes is widespread and results in wide-scale forced migration. In view of this situation, climate change increases the possibility of rivalry between refugees and the host community as they all compete for available resources such as water and food. While not all natural disasters happen as a result of climate change, most cases of climate change cause natural disasters, which force people out of their original homes.

The presence of refugees increases the population of the host community. Population and climate change are inextricably linked because humans also generate greenhouse gases in the atmosphere. So each additional person increases carbon emissions; for example, we all breathe out, produce vast quantities of waste, and need energy. In this case, the refugee community increases the population of the host country, which affects the temperature or weather conditions as the carbon is emitted even more and then increases the level of greenhouse gases. All of these dynamics are coherently linked to demographic factors and have a significant impact on climate change. They also have consequences for agricultural productivity and other economic factors. When these impacts happen, the entire population is exposed to ecological vulnerability, and its holistic well-being is threatened. This situation contributes to conflicts between the host community and the refugee community, the latter being considered as a total nuisance and an economic burden to the country.

The more refugees continue to pose a threat to the host community and to put additional pressure on the local government and inhabitants, the more local authorities get frustrated, and the more they create and reinforce laws and regulations that infringe on the freedoms and entitlements of refugees. This is not the first time in human history that people have had to migrate because of environmental problems. There are cases in Africa and elsewhere where people have been evacuated due to volcanic eruptions, for example. Yet climate refugees present evidence of the climatic changes we are facing. The 1951 Geneva Convention and its 1967 Protocol were signed in the post-war years in a migratory context very different from that prevailing today. People were fleeing their countries because of easily identifiable persecution, mainly emanating from state authority. In recent decades, migratory flows have diversified under the influence of the changing international context, and new causes of exile have gradually appeared. However, the convention does not contain any reference to victims of natural hazards.[40]

The question of ecosystem should therefore be used to mend the ills in the management of environmental resources and to foster perceptions of mutuality and solidarity in relation to the refugee phenomenon.[41] Brown notes in his report prepared for the International Organization for Migration (IOM) that the world will be much hotter in the future than it is today.[42] The patterns of rainfall are also expected to change, and the rain is more likely to fall in floods which will "wash away the soil" as Brown puts it.[43] Therefore, the frequency and severity of extreme weather conditions such as droughts, storms, and floods will increase in the future. This basically means that sub-Saharan Africa will be more affected by these weather conditions because crop growth is generally rain fed. Many African countries will face serious problems as weather conditions linked to rainfall affect food security.

Global warming and destruction of biodiversity are accelerating and are already having consequences on the social and political stability of vast areas of the planet. We must therefore accelerate awareness and concrete decisions. However with the intensification of climatic disturbances and the decrease in biodiversity, it is becoming increasingly difficult not to recognize these elements as factors aggravating the risks of conflicts related to water, land, and other finite resources in a world with a growing population. The link is not systematic, and the intensity of the effects of global warming and the extent of the destruction of biodiversity differ from region to region of the world. Rather, these issues play the role of catalysts, exacerbating factors of preexisting political, social, or economic imbalances. Several cases of conflicts and migratory phenomena have been amplified by the degradation of the climate and biodiversity. The killings between farming and herding populations have claimed lives in several African countries for years. As a result of soil degradation, pastoralists are often forced to leave their land and go elsewhere to find water and food for their herds, leading to conflicts over access to resources. These conflicts often lead to forced migration to another country.

---

40. S. Castles, "Environmental Change and Forced Migration: Making Sense of the Debate," Working Paper 70 (Geneva: UNHCR, 2002), 4–5.

41. See Brown, *Migration and Climate Change*; Simon, "Climate Change Challenges."

42. Brown, *Migration and Climate Change*.

43. Brown, 16.

To develop effective responses to the refugee phenomenon, it is not enough to understand the root causes of climate change; we must also understand how it influences the country's biodiversity. Land distribution is one of the contentious issues affecting many people in Africa. The privileged elites use land for development projects or some commercial activities such as agriculture or construction. This land use has resulted in people being forcibly displaced from their homes to the periphery, and sometimes these peripheral areas are barely sufficient for subsistence activities. People moving to the margins may also impact the area's environment. An illustration can be found in the eastern DRC. Coltan, a mineral used in the manufacture of electronic device components such as mobile phones and computers, is being exploited by various rebel groups. As a result, local residents are forced to move out as they may not live on a site where mining activity is happening on a daily basis. They become landless, and the whole ecosystem and even the local climate is impacted by the mining operation.

It cannot be overemphasized that climatic factors often cause forced migration regardless of the nature and severity of global climate change. In Africa, drought has made large tracts of land arid and unproductive, forcing people to migrate to cities where jobs are scarce and food is more expensive. Migration is then the only viable solution. This phenomenon shows how climate change issues have sparked international migration. Admittedly, there is a correlation between the level of desertification and the number of forcibly displaced migrants. However, a multitude of other causes come into play in these migrations including political instability, security threats, and population growth. So, we can say that any migration linked to drought or any other climatic factor is also economic migration. Therefore, it should be noted that rural populations are displaced to the cities during the dry season and often settle in the city because climatic challenges have so impacted agricultural production that they can no longer live in agricultural areas.

As guardians of God's creation, it is our duty to promote sustainable livelihoods that meet the needs of today's generation and the generations to come. God created the world for his purposes, which is why he eagerly awaits the restoration of our relationship with the entire creation, and we have a responsibility to partner with him as coworkers in achieving the divine plan by taking care of the creation (cf. 1 Cor 3:9; Gen 2:15; Num 35:33). The "restoration of all things," to use Peter's phrase in Acts 3:21 (NKJV), will not be fully accomplished until Christ returns. However, our desire to be faithful stewards should motivate us to interact with this fallen world because of what it will someday be, which is part of our work as bearers of the image of God.

In fact as Genesis 1–2 reveals, the earth was not designed to function properly outside of human care. God created the earth to be under the stewardship of humanity. The Old Testament considers that God, human beings, and the rest of creation are closely related, so our sins affect not only our relationship with God, but also our relationship with the entire created order. The sin of Adam and Eve not only led to their separation from God, the earth began to produce thorns, and agriculture became more difficult (cf. Gen 3:17–19). Thus biblically, human behaviour affects how the earth actually functions, which includes the climate.

So the question of climate change is not just a scientific and political issue. It is above all a moral question. Unfortunately, the sense of good and evil in our moral conscience was mainly developed for small-scale personal interactions rather than long-term global challenges like climate change. We are to ask ourselves unprecedented and unfamiliar questions of justice which should lead us to understand how to make lifestyle and political choices that allow us to flourish. These questions should also help us understand what it means to say "Jesus Christ is Lord" in times of climate change. The Bible was written before the impact of humanity on the climate was global; therefore, we need to find out how we can make such an ancient text relevant to such a modern question. In other words, as the church we need to find answers to the following question: What can the Bible tell us about our place in nature and our responsibilities to the planet?

The church is a good place to raise awareness, mobilize, and make a relevant Christian contribution to debates on the environment and climate. We must give a place to creation in teaching, preaching, and Bible studies, and develop recognition of the wonders of creation including the unique place God has given to humans: the ability and the mandate to understand and act. We must also integrate into the life of the church actions for creation such as reflecting on global warming, climate change, environmental degradation, and ecological stewardship. Apart from such seemingly complex topics, we can for example encourage a Sunday when members come to worship without driving their own personal cars as a way of raising awareness on ecological stewardship.

From the Psalms it is also clear that the earth is not for us to use and abuse with reckless abandon. "The earth is the LORD's and all that is in it," proclaims the psalmist (Ps 24:1). Regarding how we should treat the earth and its resources, the implications of this passage are profound. Although the Bible never uses the language of management to describe how we are to care for creation, management is nonetheless a fitting picture when properly understood. God is the owner of all creation, and our role can never be greater than that of custodians who carefully manage the property of the owner. The moral implications of a biblical theology of creation must include both wonder and restraint at the same time. It is right that we be moved to wonder at the beauty, breadth, complexity, and delicacy of nature, and that we see the character of God in creation. We now live in a very impoverished world; we are surrounded by deforested landscapes and oceans filled with plastic, and we breathe air that contains more pollutants than any generation before us. We must therefore recognize before God how we have responded to him and how we have exercised our responsibility. As we know the damage we have caused and are causing to God's creation, we should be made to repent and lament that there is very little left today of what God said was "very good." We need to be more restrained in how we use the resources of the earth, ensuring that they are taken to meet needs and not simply to feed our greed.

Climate change is an issue that should concern us all because it affects the life of the entire planet. The earth with all of its ecosystems is a precious gift that we have received from God. In the face of world crises – economic, ecological, or of any other nature – we are called to live in ways that manifest our faith and our hope, our love for God, and our respect for all of God's creation. We must promote lifestyles that prevent the misuse of God's gifts in creation and encourages good stewardship of all that God has given us. With all of this in mind, we must reduce our dependence on energy consumption. Industrialized countries must take the lead in these efforts particularly because of their responsibility for the accumulation of greenhouse gases in the earth's atmosphere for decades. The cumulative effect of these greenhouse gases is one of the many challenges we face when making political decisions. We also need to change our behaviour in daily life, as communities and as individuals.

In the Bible, the story of Joseph can help us think about our response to climate change. God warned Pharaoh in a dream that a time of scarcity was coming. What did Joseph do? First, he turned to God to interpret the dream and tell them what to do, realizing that this was a problem he could not solve on his own (Gen 41:1–45). Second, Joseph led the Egyptians so that sufficient food supplies were provided (Gen 41:46–57). He stored wheat and limited its consumption when the crops were plentiful, instead of allowing it to be overconsumed or wasted. His principle of storing food (Gen 41:48–49) is important to Africans and all who live in societies dominated by short-term consumption. Finally, when the time of famine arrived, Joseph showed generosity and a spirit of justice to those who lived in countries near and far (Gen 41:56–57). His action was local, but his outlook and compassion crossed borders. Today as more and more climate refugees seek refuge in other countries for their survival, we must welcome them as Joseph did. Indeed, climate change affects us all for several reasons, even though it is largely caused by rich countries and disproportionately affects the poorest. In dealing with the matter, fairness and justice must apply.

The need to belong and the quest for identity

The quest for identity and a place to belong lead to asylum seeking. When refugees arrive in the host country, they feel in limbo because their identity has not always been linked to their status as asylum seekers. In my case, the civil wars and consequences of the sociopolitical crises in my country led to my forced migration. When you have to leave your country for another, you experience a kind of disjunction, a rupture, a leap, or even a confrontation between two places: the place of origin and the new settlement. A feeling of vulnerability always resides in refugee migrants who have to leave their country. First is the fear of the unknown, a kind of anxiety about the new reality to be discovered: new environment, new sociocultural codes, new networks, new language. One becomes like an uprooted tree that must be rooted in a new land. Of course I am aware of my immigration status, but to be reminded of it always causes a pang of heart. Such a reminder is the same as saying, "Hey, you are not at home here; you come from elsewhere." In contact with a new culture and new people, the original identity of refugee migrants undoubtedly undergoes a certain reshuffle and reconfiguration. Also, they carry the heritage of their place of origin as well as that of the host country. It is this multi-affiliation that makes me a global citizen.

This mindset made it easy for me to fit in everywhere – whether in Burundi, Tanzania, Mozambique, South Africa, or Kenya. The awareness of my own identity is a primary factor in my existence and relationship to the world and is the result of a complex process that closely links my relationship to myself, my relationship to others, and my relationship to the world. The question of my deep identity has always been at the centre of my concerns. Having spent most of my life as a foreign migrant, I always felt like I did not know where to stand in terms of my origins, my culture, and my identity. Sometimes I constantly interrogated my parents because I did not know the different members of my family who had remained in the country. Identity is also a dynamic phenomenon that evolves throughout life and is marked by ruptures and crises. Refugees are people who have been forced to leave their country, and therefore developing a feeling of belonging in the host country is essential for them because their identity has been intertwined with homelessness.

In this sense, integration into a new culture constitutes an opportunity to recreate oneself while at the same time being afraid of the possibility of losing oneself. My multiple interactions in various local activities enable me to understand the cultures of my host countries, to forge human bonds, and thus to feel valued in my uniqueness. However, even with this integration, in my ways of being and doing I have found that it is not easy when you are constantly reminded that you are a foreigner. Unfortunately when I visit my country, I still experience a culture shock. Most friends and neighbours whom I had known before are no longer there. The geographical environment is no longer the same, as it has undergone some forms of transformation over time. Thus I have become a stranger even in my own country. This situation has made me a stranger everywhere, even among my own people. I no longer totally belong to either my original culture or the host culture. I rightly understand that my identity is always in motion; it evolves throughout life and at the rate of lived experiences. This understanding reminds me that even the founding event of Israel's identity as a people, namely the exodus, was a migratory movement and a quest to belong.

Indeed, the arrival of refugees in a new setting creates a number of challenges for various parties. It creates socioeconomic challenges for the local community, the producing country, and even to the international community. In general, as the church we need to educate members and communities concerning the refugee phenomenon. However, specifically and practically, the local church needs to provide refugees with a sense of belonging and homely warmth because the church is the truest sanctuary for those pushed to the margins of society by broken human systems. In other words, we should not keep apart those who find themselves in conditions of vulnerability nor push them away since we are called to build bridges between the excluded and the included, the insider and the outsider. The refugee community needs to belong in the church community and in the host community. By providing refugees with a sense of belonging, we live up to our calling to be reconciliatory, redemptive, and transformational.

Constructing the feeling of belonging is not so easy because it is a very subjective concept. Each person can use multiple criteria to feel part of the new host country. In addition, beyond a reorganization of belonging, forced migrants are often faced with questioning their identity, which can happen in different ways. The feeling of belonging and identity are strictly linked to each other because belonging to a specific social group allows everyone to identify as an individual subject but at the same time as a part of the group. Forced migration leads individuals to position themselves between two worlds: their country of origin where they grew up and developed important emotional and social ties, and their host country where they are now. This situation is what creates the challenge of identity and belonging.

Having to be between these two significant worlds generates a certain instability, which in turn causes ruptures; that is to say, interruptions of the normal flow of events. People leave their country of origin for very different reasons, and sometimes because they are forced to do so. Throughout their journey, they take up different identities. For instance, when they leave their country of origin, they are *emigrants*. From the moment they arrive in their new setting, they become *immigrants* and face a variety of challenges in their new environment that are social, economic, cultural, and religious. These challenges occur when migrants interact with individuals, groups, or institutions. In this case, being a migrant translates into the dynamism of rebuilding identity every day. Such an identity is transnational or bicultural in nature, but it also often involves idealizing the country of origin and creating parallel societies so the migrant does not have to enter into cultural or religious relations.

For many refugees, faith is a great support during their journey. Religious rites such as prayer accompany their departure, and they thank God as soon as they cross the border. For most, the migration experience is a test of faith in God: it is a spiritual experience or a new opportunity offered by God to reach God. Their experience begins a process of deepening faith, and migrants feel that God is revealed to them in different ways. In other words, during the refugee's journey, God is a travelling companion. He travels with them and does not stay on the other side of the border. In a way, the formation of Christian communities and expressions such as "refugee church" are very important in the process of identity reconstruction and also explains why refugees go to church to meet their compatriots, speak their own language, and share their faith. As a result, faith acquires a community and cultural dimension. The Christian community becomes a community of people sharing identity, culture, and language. We become the refugee community struggling to find a place in the new society. This Christian community will then offer help to newcomers, especially those who are forced to remain undocumented. In refugee churches, refugees find a network that helps them settle, such as finding a home and a job, learning the language of their new country, and so on.

The history of human migration in Africa predates the era of colonialism and the establishment of today's artificial boundaries. This means that forced migration is neither a new phenomenon nor a recent political concern because it has been happening for ages. Migratory movements have a historical depth in Africa, and the history of humanity is a history of migration.[44] It is difficult to say with absolute certainty the genesis of these migratory movements because the populations of the past moved from one territory to another when and as there was need. These early migrations contributed to the establishment of new communities and identities. They also played a major role in the social progress and economic life of peoples through the fusion of their abilities, their spirituality, and their emotions. For example across southern Africa, there is a long history of population movements for work in what is now South Africa, way before 1910 when the country became self-ruling, and this is the case for many countries on the continent. Mususa and Nyamnjoh claim that none of these workers have ever been offered permanent residence, although they have contributed to the construction of the country for decades.[45] Many of these workers still live in South Africa, and although some now have citizenship, they are vulnerable to xenophobic treatment.

The problems faced by refugees in host countries or those they experienced in their own country of origin are often stereotyped. Potential dangers exist when we concentrate on statistics for budget purposes and forget that behind these numbers are real human beings with real human needs. Most refugee data focus on basic information such as name and surname, age, sex, country of origin, and some simple details to identify unaccompanied children, vulnerable women, and orphans for statistical purposes. This information may be sufficient for organizations wishing to adapt their support to the needs of the population, but is not sufficient for understanding the different challenges and dimensions of the suffering of the population.[46] Behind the statistics are real people who are suffering and hurting inside. This is why in the host country refugees need appropriate documentation to access specific services. The granting of refugee status recognizes a number of rights and obligations, even though seeking asylum is an option for any individual.

Refugees have various rights including the right to employment, education, and freedom of movement, among other rights. This means that the legal status of refugees in the host country should reflect the real rights they must enjoy. Tom Sine suggests that we respond to the emerging refugee

---

44. Harzig, Hoerder, and Gabaccia, *What Is Migration History?*, 8.

45. P. Mususa and F. Nyamnjoh, "Migration and Xenophobia in Southern Africa," in *Building Peace in Southern Africa*, ed. D. Hanar and C. Saunders (Cape Town: Centre for Conflict Resolution, 2010), 36.

46. M. N. Getui and P. Kanyandago, eds., *From Violence to Peace: A Challenge for African Christianity* (Nairobi: Acton, 1999).

movements in the world with humanity because refugee flows are a by-product of political destabilization.[47] We need to analyse politically unstable regions of the world and determine where future refugee flows will come from so that refugee programmes can be developed before new movements begin. Sine's statement also indicates the possibility of preventing migration trends by identifying and addressing issues that contribute to migration. In other words, the first step in improving the governance of forced migration is to identify and analyse the trends that give rise to new migratory movements. This exercise in identifying and analyzing migratory trends is important because migration offers opportunities but also challenges related to vulnerability and discrimination. However, people leave their country for a variety of reasons ranging from abuse to hostilities, so such predictions cannot necessarily counteract migration trends.

The identity of a refugee can no longer be reduced to situations of lack, instability, fragility, insecurity, and suffering. Being a refugee expresses the dynamism of an identity that is being rebuilt every day. It is a transnational identity that bears a human richness – a richness to be welcomed, not to be feared. Indeed, forced migration is part of human experience going back thousands of years, but it is also part of modernism because globalization allows most refugees to find themselves easily and quickly in distant countries, even thousands of kilometres from home. Many refugees bring with them a variety of skills and knowledge that host countries use to their advantage. In my case, for example, although my decisions to migrate were caused by traumatic events in the country of origin – push factors – my migratory movements often ensured the flow of ideas, knowledge, and skills from one country to another. This is the case of most forced migrants, especially if the doors of opportunity are open to them. Forced migration nurtures a dense and vibrant human fabric that links cultures, societies, and economies. This situation explains why the journey of forced migrants is sometimes a paradox in search of identity and belonging, and therefore welcoming migrants means offering them a part of our identity and accepting migration as the quest to belong.

The "gender factor"

With the intensification of certain phenomena such as armed conflicts and climate change, international migration continues to increase. Furthermore, it

---

47. Tom Sine, "Development: Its Secular Past and Its Uncertain Future," in *The Church in Response to Human Need*, ed. V. Samuel and C. Sugden (Grand Rapids: Eerdmans, 1987), 12–13.

is becoming more diversified and feminized. Migration inevitably affects gender relations. In many African societies, the role of the main economic provider of the family rests on men. For this reason, migration is mainly perceived as a male phenomenon: the active actors are considered to be men while women are only passive escorts of their male counterparts. However, today, researchers of the sociology of migration are now paying more attention to the role and place of women in human migration, and a number of assumptions about gender are being debunked. This research reveals the importance of focusing on the challenges that women face during the process of forced migration because although women's migration is not a new phenomenon, women have long been ignored in migration research.

Today, migratory movements have intensified considerably across the world, and the face of this migration is that of a woman, alone or with children. Women constitute the largest number of migratory flows, although they are often not highlighted.[48] The migration of women is a path strewn with pitfalls because they are often confronted with much physical, psychological, and sexual violence. Once they arrive in the host country, women do not necessarily see their situation improve because of the difficulties they often face in finding a job. When they find a job, working conditions are often very difficult for them. Wages are generally too low and insufficient to meet the needs of the family, and the jobs often lack adequate measures for their protection. Indeed, all these challenges are faced by refugees regardless of their gender, but they are much more amplified for women.

Leaving one's country to settle often involves risk, violence, fear, extreme suffering, and sometimes even death, for both men and women. However, women face specific challenges before, during, and after their migratory journey. Because of their status as women, they face discrimination and violence at different points in their journey. In the country of origin, women are sometimes victims of rape that the perpetrators use as a weapon of war; they are often sexually exploited; they have limited access to education and appropriate health care; they are subjected to forced marriages and suffer domestic violence, etc. These gender factors are some of the specific reasons for women to migrate. During their migratory journey, they can be victims of forced prostitution, sexual assault, and abuse by smugglers or customs agents and lack privacy and access to basic health products. In the host country, women feel a great sense of insecurity and can be victims of harassment, discrimination, and sexual assault.

---

48. Susan Forbes-Martin, *Refugee Women* (Maryland: Lexington Books, 2004), 26.

Indeed, women face certain kinds of persecution that require international attention and protection.[49] Some of the challenges they face when seeking and obtaining asylum relate to asylum procedures, recognition of the harm or abuses they have had to endure, and obtaining refugee status on the basis of the type of persecution they have suffered. The mistreatment of women is why migration and poverty have been feminized.[50] Many women and girls experience various forms of victimization including rape, sexual exploitation, or harassment prior to their emigration. When they flee from such situations to a foreign country, they do not expect to be in a state that is going to bring back memories of their horrible past. However, refugee women are often targeted for prostitution by organized crime and experience victimization in work and commercial agriculture. The treatment they receive makes them believe that their past has followed them, their present is a failure, and their future is hopeless.

When we fled from the Burundi ethnic war which started in 1993, our youngest sibling was still breastfeeding. The conditions under which we left the country were such that we could not use any means of transport to the border. My mother carried two of my younger siblings to Gatumba, where there is a border post between Burundi and the DRC, on foot. Two years later in 1996, when we left the DRC after the outbreak of the Congolese war, my mother had to flee with her youngest child who was now four years old, so he still needed her full attention during the flight. It should be noted that my mother walked for about thirty kilometres while carrying a four-year-old child on her back and some of our few belongings on her head. In many instances, women in Africa carry their children on their backs with food or their few possessions on their heads during the flight, just as my mother did, which illustrates how much the refugee phenomenon renders women vulnerable not only in their place of origin or destination, but also during their flight to a place of safety.

In the host country, women struggle to find work for the mere fact that they are women and the workplace is predominantly male. Their abilities and experiences are often not acknowledged, and their competencies reduced to nothingness simply because they are women and worse, refugees. This gender-

---

49. K. Newland, *Seeking Protection: Women in Asylum and Refugee Resettlement Processes*, United Nations Division for the Advancement of Women – Consultative Meeting on "Migration and Mobility and How This Movement Affects Women." 2–4 December 2003 (Malmö, Sweden: United Nations, 2004).

50. J. Crush and V. Williams, *International Migration and Development: Dynamics and Challenges in South and Southern Africa*, United Nations Expert Group Meeting on International Migration and Development (New York: United Nations, 2005).

based discrimination is accompanied by a strong sense of humiliation which suggests that refugee life is embarrassing, leading to loss of dignity. As a result, most refugee women find themselves in unworthy jobs taken for their survival. For example, my mother, despite her level of education, had to engage in both small business and small-scale farming so we could survive in Burundi. She mainly grew beans and corn. She sold sun-dried *dagaa*, a type of sardines, at the Kinama market during the day and at the Kamenge market in the afternoon. During the harvest, she would sell part of the produce and keep some for food at home. This business sustained our family when my father was still unemployed.

Women are an important asset of sustainability. As I have seen in my family, women do more about the survival of children. Indeed, men have an important role to play – and my father was instrumental in our education – but the role of women in the upbringing and survival of children should not be relegated to oblivion especially when it comes to social progress, which is essential for improved well-being. A better understanding of the impact of the refugee phenomenon on women is therefore a more important step toward a fuller understanding of its dynamics. Those conducting research on refugee issues must do so from a gender perspective to deepen their knowledge.

At times women seek asylum because they are survivors of certain abuses such as rape, sexual harassment, or gender discrimination, among other things. Because the 1951 UN Convention Relating to the Status of Refugees and its 1967 Protocol do not refer to such abusive acts as forms of persecution, refugee women find it difficult to report them for the fear of being stigmatized and denied asylum. These key legal documents that govern refugee affairs provide some of the basic principles for dealing with the refugee phenomenon such as the principle of non-refoulement, which asserts that a refugees should not be returned to a country where they are under serious threat of their life or their freedom. However, the UN documents do not protect people against all kinds of harm, even if the harm is serious enough to amount to persecution or create vulnerability.[51] Since the 1951 UN Convention and its 1967 Protocol do not specifically mention gender abuse and sexual harassment as forms of persecution, it is assumed that they do not qualify as reasons for seeking asylum and the assigning of refugee status. Thus, the gender factor is not part of the criteria for seeking asylum under the key legal documents regulating the affairs of refugees, but it is possible for a woman to be recognized as a refugee if she shows well-founded fears of persecution because of her status as a woman. In

---

51. Newland, *Seeking Protection*.

other words, the international laws that regulate the status of refugees do not recognize a woman who seeks asylum on account of gender-based violence, sexual, and domestic abuses as a legitimate refugee because, according to the UN, rape and other sexual abuses do not fall under, nor fit in the grounds of the persecution clause.

Another aspect of the victimization of refugee women is their health. For instance, migration is a key feature of the HIV/AIDS epidemic, and it has played a role in its spread in various African countries.[52] Yet most public administrators and even health professionals in Africa do not always know how to deal with refugees when they seek healthcare services in the host country. This situation is even worse when it comes to dealing with women, which is why refugee women often go through many more health challenges compared to local women.[53] Sexual and reproductive health problems are also experienced specifically by migrant women. In particular, maternal health is an important aspect of women's health. The related problems are the main cause of death and disability for women around the world. Women experience pregnancy complications that result from not having family planning or being unable to access safe procedures though the majority of these complications could be prevented.

Military interventions in most war-torn African countries have been associated with rape and other sexual violence against women, which is very evident in countries such as the DRC and Central African Republic. Because of this sexual violence, refugee women are often at greater risk of contracting sexually transmitted diseases including HIV. Some women migrate without their partners or husbands as it is common for family members to go in different directions as they run for their lives to places of safety. This separation increases the possibility of having their sexual desire satisfied outside established relationships, and at times promiscuously with multiple partners. Women who lose their husbands or partners in violent conflict in their home countries also look for solace in the arms of other men in the host country. Those who have survived sexual or gender-based violence often remain hopeless, helpless, and in desperate need of psychosocial support. Some tend to be involved in sexual activities to make some money to survive, which often leads to many other social ills including human trafficking.

---

52. Black, Skeldon, and Waddington, "Routes to Illegal Residence," 113.

53. A. J. Gagnon, L. Merry, and C. Robinson, "A Systematic Review of Refugee Women's Reproductive Health," *Refuge* 21, no. 1 (2002).

Being a refugee renders women vulnerable to various illnesses and to being victims of varied practices. The excessive stress of adapting to the new conditions in the host country also affects their psychosocial equilibrium. Their situation becomes even more complicated when they are single parents – raising the children alone. The provision of adequate sustenance, safe water, and vaccinations against various illnesses can improve and protect the wellness of refugee women, as can educating them on the various aspects of health consciousness.

One of the ways to protect refugee women is to ensure they have access to effective justice. Most of them are victims of various forms of injustice and need help but are unable to report the offenses they have suffered. Refugee women who are in an irregular situation and who are victims of violence or other abuses are in a particularly difficult situation because they often are reluctant to lodge formal complaint. Special attention needs to be given to women refugees since they may face additional obstacles including cultural barriers that prevent them from reporting violence to the police and receiving appropriate protection.

The challenges facing women before and during forced migration propel us to act with justice, which explains why asylum procedures must be gender sensitive. Women and girls, especially those travelling alone, are at high risk of experiencing some form of violence against them, including sexual violence. During the course of this research, concern has been expressed about the ignorance of local government authorities who do not seem to know about this phenomenon. This ignorance can be explained by the lack of data on some offenses endured by refugee women and the reluctance of victims to talk about their experiences. For instance, in South Africa, there is a detention centre where refugees are meant to be held before they are repatriated back to their homes. The Lindela Centre, as it is called, was originally designed as a reception centre for the registration of newcomers, but it has become a detention centre despite all the risks that it presents for migrant women who stay there. Here, women are detained even when they are pregnant. The detention of refugee women also raises serious concerns because they are often detained with men who are not part of their family.

It should be emphasized that women benefit from the support of the extended family both in the performance of household tasks and in maternal responsibilities in their country of origin. However, they often do not have family support in their new environment. This loss and major change in their usual way of life, especially their community way of life which characterizes their African character, constitutes a real source of stress. The change of scenery also causes women many inconveniences throughout their daily lives and has a negative impact on the educational progress of those who have chosen to return to school. When refugee women become pregnant, they again become prone to being gossiped about, ridiculed, and shown contempt, especially by health professionals who laugh at them for continuing to have babies even when they do not have the financial means to raise these children. In view of this behaviour, getting pregnant and the possible arrival of a new baby bring additional stress and worry to refugee women.

Migration is a phenomenon that has characterized human experience since time immemorial. Today in a world marked by processes of globalization, human migration has become even faster, mainly thanks to advances in transport and communications. In this chapter, we learned about the facts and figures of forced migration and understood that millions of people have been forced to leave their countries of origin and currently live outside of their national borders as refugees. The situation is dire in Africa as the number of refugees and of people in refugee-like situations is increasing. As many leave their country by choice, others have no choice but to leave because of existential unfreedoms which disrupt public order and the usual way of life. Thus, various dynamics are at play in setting various forms of forced migration into motion, including sociopolitical and economic ones. This situation indicates that migratory movements generally occur when a country no longer offers any prospect of life, or even when it has become extremely dangerous to stay there (push factors), but also when another country seems much more attractive or at least more secure (pull factors). Every country feels concerned, be they countries of emigration, transit, or immigration, because migration is emerging as a reality that affects everyone.

The normal mobility of people on earth is a basic human right because the earth is a gracious gift of God's creation. The artificial division of the earth into territories, countries, and continents should not constitute an obstacle to the ability of every human being to go and settle in any place. No one should be discriminated against on the grounds of nationality, origin, or race. This right of asylum seekers and refugees to mobility leads to the fundamental rights to settlement and to a decent living. At the same time, the right of mobility forms the basis of the right to be a foreigner in any part of the world. To best manage forced migration, an educational approach which integrates ethical and spiritual values that promote the worth and socioeconomic contribution of refugees in society is needed. Ultimately, only the values of Christian ethics such as love, charity, solidarity, justice, and above all fairness can be used as the basis of our missional approaches and our advocacy as a church. These approaches will help to influence policymakers in shaping positive migration policies. This discussion is developed further in the next chapter, as the different contexts of integral mission vis-à-vis the refugee phenomenon are highlighted within specific constants of biblical Christianity.

Discussion Questions

1. What have you learned from the facts and figures of forced migration?

2. Why do some people feel driven out of their country and others feel drawn to another? What role should we as a church play in the management of these push and pull factors?

3. Read Matthew 5:13–16.
   - Why does Jesus say that Christians are "the salt of the earth" and "the light of the world"?
   - How can we be "salt" to refugees, and how can we lose our "saltiness" to them?
   - As light, how do we shine on the refugees around us and how can we shine more brightly?

4. Read James 2:14–17.
   - Why does this passage tell us to demonstrate our faith through practical actions?
   - How can we apply this passage when responding to the needs of refugees in our community?

5. Read Exodus 2:1–15; Ruth 1:1–2; 1 Samuel 22:1–2; 1 Kings 17:1–6; Acts 8:1. In each of these biblical passages –
   - Who is fleeing, and what is their reason for fleeing?
   - Which of these reasons for fleeing do refugees have today?

3

Two Contexts, Four Constants

The rumours of imminent war in the Democratic Republic of Congo (DRC) began in July 1996. We had just resumed classes in Uvira but stopped again a few weeks later due to panic. In the DRC, the school calendar starts in September and ends in July, the following year. Instead in September of 1996, we were doing the *rondo*, a practice where all the young men were asked to patrol their neighbourhood at night to ensure that no intruder walked into the area. Anyone who was not from the neighbourhood was considered to be an intruder and suspected of being a spy. Only God knows the fates of such suspects! The actual armed conflict between the rebels and the national army started in the Ruzizi plain, a few kilometres away from the city of Uvira, which became the first main city in the DRC to fall into the hands of rebels. That happened on Friday, 25 October. My parents decided the previous night, 24 October, that we should leave Uvira because everyone else was already vacating the city. Thousands upon thousands were on the road fleeing. We joined the crowd and headed south to an unknown destination, where everyone else was heading. Actually, the road south was the only way out. The geographical location of Uvira is such that everyone had to run southward because the rebels came from the north, on the east is the great Lake Tanganyika, and on the west is the great Mitumba mountain range. Little did we know that this journey would end in a refugee camp in Tanzania.

In reality, being a refugee has a propensity to reduce one's worth to nothingness because in most countries the moment someone knows you are a refugee, their attitude towards you usually changes, and they become indifferent. The experiences I had as a refugee in various African countries are ubiquitous in almost all other countries that allow in refugees. There are a few exceptions, but the attitudes that many demonstrate toward refugees tend to be constantly negative in almost every context. If as the church we are to make a difference in our local communities and transform our attitude in every context in which we find the less privileged, we need to develop biblical constants on God, his word, and his work. A biblical constant is something about which God has made his will and wisdom clear. When we apply or teach such a constant, we are convinced that we have the authority of God for it. In this case, we consider it as something that is immutable and invariable. What is not constant is variable, and therefore something that God has made no clear statement about. The contexts explained in this chapter are variables because they can change according to the circumstances, and the constants are invariables because they remain unchanged under all circumstances. In this chapter we explore four constants of transformational development and two of the contexts within which we may intervene in forced migration. These foundations contribute to our understanding of God, humanity, and the rest of creation, and they emphasize the salvific plan of God for all humanity, which includes forced migrants. Putting these four constants into context explains the need to reflect on how to serve the poor, the wounded, and the excluded. The two contexts in this chapter present a challenge to a sedentary type of church in a community, while the four constants present us with an opportunity to reflect with a broader perspective on a theology that seeks to appreciate God's creation.

Bevans and Schroeder theorize the notion of constants in the many contexts of Christianity.[1] They understand that constants are questions that remain ever present and ever urgent because how they are answered determines how Christians find concrete identity.[2] Groody puts forward the theological foundations for ministry which constitute the basis of the constants discussed in this chapter.[3] As the church, we need to always address these constants in specific contexts because they shape the way we function: they influence the way leaders serve and ministers preach and affect the way members witness in the world. In other words, these constants have a strong effect on the life of the church and our immediate community. They are a theological ground for our engagement in social affairs and our ministry to displaced communities.

The four constants remain unchanged both in theory and in practice. The four constants are (i) *imago Dei*, restoring God's image; (ii) *Verbum*

---

1. S. B. Bevans and R. P. Schroeder, *Constants in Context: A Theology of Mission for Today* (New York: Orbis, 2004).

2. Bevans and Schroeder, *Constants in Context*, 34.

3. D. G. Groody, "Crossing the Divide: Foundations of a Theology of Migration and Refugees," *Theological Studies* 70 (2009): 638–67.

Dei, proclaiming the Word of God; (iii) *missio Dei*, participating in integral mission; and (iv) *visio Dei*, transforming lives through God's vision. The two contexts within which these constants need to be applied are (1) *the church as a sanctuary* and (2) *the church as a reconciler*. The four constants applied within the framework of the two church contexts explain why it is our responsibility as the church to be engaged in transformational community development and all matters of social interest for the common good. As sanctuary, the church functions to provide hope and love to the outsider as well as a place to belong, and as reconciler, the church functions to integrate the outsider and the excluded into the community of the insider and the included in order to promote peace and unity.

Two Contexts			
of the church in ministry to refugees			
Context #1 *Church as Sanctuary*			Context #2 *Church as Reconciler*
Function: Provision Ministries: Hope and Love			Function: Integration Ministries: Peace and Unity
Key references			
Matt 12:21; 1 Cor 13:13; Eph 1:18; 1 Thess 1:3			Micah 6:8; Matt 12:18–20
Four Constants			
of transformational community development			
Constant I *imago Dei*	Constant II *Verbum Dei*	Constant III *missio Dei*	Constant IV *visio Dei*
Function: Restoration	Function: Proclamation	Function: Participation	Function: Transformation
Key references			
Gen 1:26–27	Matt 3:1–2; 4:23–24; 9:35	Luke 4:18–19	Isa 65:17–25

Context #1: The Church as Sanctuary

The term "sanctuary" means a temple or holy place, but it can also mean a protected place that shelters someone from possible attack or acts of vengeance.

According to the medieval European law, a sanctuary was a secure place where a persecuted person could take refuge, and using force to drive a person out of this place of refuge was considered an act of sacrilege. Through Moses, God commanded the Israelites to establish six cities that would serve as places of refuge for those who accidentally killed someone and for refugees and travellers (Num 35:13–15). These cities in Israel were open to all migrants, and throughout the ancient world, sanctuary was offered to the oppressed and the persecuted.

In modern times, the protection of refugees is subject to national policy. As a result, many refugees are labelled as illegal migrants, economic migrants, or aliens, whereas in the biblical cities of refuge, the right of asylum was given to whoever fled for fear of being persecuted, as per the UN definition of a refugee. Anyone threatened with death, either without a trial or without having done something punishable by death, was to be protected in the sanctuary, thus given a chance to live. In the biblical and medieval examples, it is obvious that sanctuaries were a kind of guarantee of renewed hope as the city or church leaders intervened in favour of those being persecuted. In so doing, biblical justice was upheld.

The notion of sanctuary is complex yet central to understanding certain realities of the Christian life and the church. There is certainly a need to explore how the church does and should operate in this global era of challenges and opportunities. Offering sanctuary to a refugee whose life is threatened is restorative and liberating. The church as sanctuary of hope and love gives refugees homely warmth away from home. The constants that we need to emphasize within our context of the church as sanctuary are *imago Dei* and *Verbum Dei*.

Constant I – Imago Dei: Restoring God's image

The theme of *imago Dei* is central to the Christian faith. This doctrine, which has its source in Genesis 1:26–27, is dear to all who have endeavoured to understand the work of redemption. The doctrine has become intricate and supported by many different nuances for ages. It can be summarized as follows: human beings were created in the *imago* (image) and *similitudo* (likeness) of YHWH. These dispositions have been damaged by sin, but by the grace of Christ's redemption, human beings are able to experience God's process of restoration. So, considering that refugees are symbols of the distress and the injustices of our modern world, our response to their calls is also a reaction to the chaos that reigns in our societies and in ourselves. God reveals the most sacred through the most vulnerable, which is why to be with refugees is to bear the pain and risk the complete overthrow of all cultural values and certainties. The refugees among us who are victims of our own society's inability to meet their needs are questioning the meaning of life. If we consider human life as a sacred gift and a reflection of God, then we become aware that refugees are a sacred *imago* and *similitudo* of God.

It should be noted that *imago Dei* has to do with what humans are inherently, which is the *substantive* view of the image of God, because all human beings have a will (Phil 2:13), emotions (Rom 12:15), and other intrinsic values which are characteristically God's (1 John 4:8, 16, 19–21).[4] In other words, this view suggests that the image of God in us relates to specific qualities within us, especially human reason, which means we not only have the ability to choose, but also the responsibility to choose wisely. Also, *imago Dei* is a *relational* concept (Gen 1:26; John 14:16–17; 17:20–23). Like the triune God, humankind was created to coexist; that is, we are meant to be in relationship with God, with each other, with ourselves and with the rest of God's creation. This relational aspect of humanity is consistent with the relationship of the whole Trinitarian council, which explains the image of God in us. That is to say, a human being is the image of God by virtue of his or her relationship with God, the self, the other, and the whole created order. Lastly, the *imago Dei* ought to be understood *functionally* (Gen 1:26–28; 2:15–17; John 1:1, 14). As human beings we are the representatives of God on earth, and as such we have a capacity and privilege to function as rulers, which is an image of what God functionally is. In other words, the functional interpretation of the *imago Dei* is that the image relates to the role of humanity as royal agents of God in the world. Each of these views has a biblical basis and highlights our specialness and value as human beings. We all bear God's image, and each one of us has a particular standing before God and in the world. Therefore when faced with the injustice of the refugee recognition process within our own society, we should consider that offering sanctuary to refugees becomes a moral testimony.

Sanctuary protects a person in danger. When we offer refugees a sanctuary, we make a prophetic gesture of hope, and we show great love and respect for the justice the sanctuary represents. This gesture is not to be done in a spirit of challenge but in the hope of correcting or changing the system or prevailing situation. Our offer of sanctuary should stem from our desire to be with the poor, the dispossessed, the displaced, the outsider, the excluded, and the people without defined status, sharing their insecurities day by day and by engaging

---

4. See Carroll, *Christians at the Border*, 67.

with them in sustainable ways. The church as a sanctuary is also called to cry in the desert until we are heard by those in positions of authority. We are called to exhaust ourselves in making material arrangements and to endure boredom, frustration, and quarrels for days, weeks, or months while waiting for a solution.

God's goal for human beings is that his image in them be completely restored. The passage about God creating human beings in his image (Gen 1:26–27) shows that all human beings bear the *imago Dei* despite the fact that each appears different from the others. The constant of *imago Dei* promotes a clear understanding of humanness and the realization that all forms of discrimination and injustice go against God's goal. In fact, discrimination and injustice undermine the very image of God. To counter this, we as the church need to assume the responsibility of bringing into God's kingdom those who are systematically excluded by human structures or policies. This practical responsibility of the church as a sanctuary attests to the verticality of our relationship with God and exhibits the truth that God's love surpasses by far what human beings can offer. It is due to the constant of *imago Dei* that God sees divine traits and potential in our fallen humanity.

Leviticus 19:33–34 states that a host community should treat refugees in the same way they treat their fellow citizens. Here a refugee is considered a human measurement for one's dimension of love. Hence the church is a sanctuary not just of hope but also of love. That is to say by welcoming a refugee, we pass the test of love toward the other. The more we understand this, the more we will value the *imago Dei*, and the more the "us-and-them" syndrome will be healed. Created in God's *imago* and *similitudo* but wounded by sin, we therefore need this image to be fully restored in us. This is the ultimate goal of the Christian life. The Son of God, who was *in forma Dei* (in the form of God), did not fear renouncing his sacred privileges but humbled himself (Phil 2:6–7), becoming one of us and like us in all but sin (Heb 4:15). In other words, he chose to lose the beauty of his *forma* and be disfigured to the point of no longer being recognized (Isa 53:2). He even experienced death. The Father raised him up and made him sit on his right hand after making him our *Kyrios* (Lord, Phil 2:9). Having been deformed by sin, we must therefore be reformed and gradually transformed so we can be conformed to the *imago Dei* and have the form (*forma*) of the risen Christ.

The constant of *imago Dei* brings the identity of the other into perspective. Traditionally, the concept of "otherness" means that the other is different from the self, which suggests that "other" is foreign. That is, the other is an outsider and therefore from "there," while the self is an insider and therefore from "here." In other words, otherness as a concept is traditionally an exclusionary tendency. The constant of *imago Dei* shows that being from "there" or from "here" is not a qualification for being human; nor does it constitute a motive to include or exclude anyone or set up any foundation for social classification. In fact, foreignness is a construct of human identity if we consider the fact that all of humanity is from "there" and not from "here." Therefore, the word "foreigner" should not be used as a discriminatory description of some, since all are on a wayfaring pilgrimage.

As a church, our understanding of *imago Dei* reveals our belief that people's basic needs must be met so that all can live a meaningful life. In other words, everyone ought to be able to lead a life that is truly human and have what is necessary to survive holistically, which includes enjoying respect from others, having the guarantee to eat something on a daily basis, having the right to education and employment, etc. These enjoyments and entitlements are inclusive of those who have been pushed to the periphery and excluded systematically by the social and governmental structures. The constant of *imago Dei* gives transformational development the cutting-edge it needs for the promotion of human dignity. The *imago Dei* is also a double-edged sword that positively functions as an affirmation of the value and worth of every person while evaluating and challenging any tendencies to dominate or oppress the poor and needy in the society.[5] The *imago Dei* reveals that human discrimination is sinful because it dehumanizes as well as deforms the original *forma* of the *imago Dei*.

Constant II – Verbum Dei: Proclaiming the Word of God

Another constant to observe within the context of the church as sanctuary is the *Verbum Dei*, which simply means the Word of God. It is worth noting that the Old Testament concept of the *imago Dei* is concretized in the New Testament by Christ, the *Verbum Dei*, who crossed the divide between divinity and humanity. On that ground, he alone is able to help human beings cross over back to God. It is Christ who restores God's *imago* through the ministry of reconciliation. This is verified through his kenotic incarnation, which is Christ's movement from divinity to humanity. Christ's incarnational movement is special because he kept both his divine nature and human identity, but it is also similar to how refugees keep the identity of their country of origin even as they belong to and are identified with their host country. By becoming human,

---

5. Groody, "Crossing the Divide," 648.

the *Verbum Dei* never ceased to be divine as he was always God although in bodily *forma*. Likewise by becoming refugees, people do not cease being citizens of their country of origin despite living in a foreign country. John in his Gospel narrative rightly points out that Christ is actually the *Verbum Dei* who "became flesh" and dwelt among us (John 1:14). The purpose of his becoming flesh was to reconcile humanity back to God and restore our Edenic relationships with God and the whole of creation.

This becoming flesh of the *Verbum Dei* is further explained by Paul in his epistle to believers at Philippi. He introduces the subject with a different tone through the kenotic theory (Phil 2:7). The divinity of Christ was not affected in any way by his incarnation and humiliation until death on the cross. Rather, he voluntarily renounced his traits of divine glory. The dispossession of his divine glory was actually a veil when he took up the form of a servant. In other words, his divine nature was not the object of dispossession as it was not affected by the incarnation. Kenosis therefore has a transient status and does not affect the divinity of the *Verbum Dei*. The *kenosis* of Christ denotes the taking of human form by crossing the divide between humanity and God. Thus, Christ's *kenosis* is the greatest migratory movement as it indicates the divine migration or movement of God to humanity in love.[6] As a result of this divine migration, the *Verbum Dei* lived amid the controversies, dynamics, and experiences of human migration on earth. For instance, Matthew 2:13–15 records that Jesus experienced the refugee life as a young child. Not long after his birth, his parents fled with him to Egypt escaping King Herod's planned persecution and execution of infants in Bethlehem.

In 1 John 4:20, the apostle John alludes to the fact that loving the other is a measuring rod for all claims about loving God who is unseen. In this context, we are the embodiment of the *Verbum Dei* because we are the body of Christ. Thus the *Verbum Dei* is the reason for the hope and dignity of refugees. As the church in this secularized, global world, we require a cutting-edge perspective on the *Verbum Dei* if we are to revive authentic Christianity in the life of followers of Christ. To be faithful representatives of God's kingdom, our communities of faith are called to practice a transformational theology of development that meets the current demands of globalization. Using the *Verbum Dei* as an approach of church ministry to those living on the margin of society implies that there is no boundary that cannot be crossed by God in the world he created. Because of the kenotic incarnation of the *Verbum Dei*, the church is a valued catalyst for transformational development.

---

6. Groody, 649.

Understanding the kenotic nature of the *Verbum Dei* is essential for proclaiming the gospel through words and deeds. When the incarnation becomes a reality in the life of individuals, they become committed to the proclamation of the truth imbedded therein because one of the guiding biblical principles of the Christian life is the double commandment of love which is, to some extent, the duplication of a single command. This double command is to love God, the Ultimate Truth, and the other. Our mission as the church is to proclaim the incarnate Word of God and his gospel to the world so as to infuse happiness in both the self and the other. The *Verbum Dei* is in this regard the proclamation of the Word of God for salvific ends with the aim of making the world believe and hope. It is noteworthy and explicit that the "world" in this instance does not exclude the other. Therefore, the proclamation of God's word is not to be restricted to those akin to oneself.

The word of God is perfect and pure; however, it is proclaimed by imperfect human beings. There are therefore two dimensions: one is human and the other is divine. It is a human being who speaks and human beings who listen. In this dimension, one can exclude neither the speaker's mistakes of style or substance nor the listeners' errors of comprehension. In the divine dimension, the Holy Spirit speaks to the heart of hearers and strengthens or arouses faith in them. The imperfect words and sentences spoken by human vessels do not prevent God from bringing the message across with power and causing it to penetrate the inner faculties of the hearers. Thus, proclaiming the word of God as the *Verbum Dei* is to translate the words and deeds of Jesus in ways that reflect his earthly ministry. This proclamation may or may not be conveyed orally because God speaks to human beings even through *diakonia*, deeds or social actions. The *Verbum Dei* as the proclamation of God's word is a demonstration that God intervenes in all human circumstances and that a human being is always fully human irrespective of age, gender, race, tribe, origin, or religious affiliation. In this regard, the *Verbum Dei* as the proclamation of God's word promotes human dignity to refugees.

Context #2: The Church as Reconciler

The theme of reconciliation is rich and diversified. Paul uses reconciliation as a figure of salvation. In ecclesiology, reconciliation is presented as a sacrament, and various approaches to reconciliation have been developed in countries long divided by conflicts. Sin is by extension the inability to be reconciled with ourselves, with others, with nature or the environment, and with God. Sin is therefore always a breach of the love that comes to us from God or of the love for our neighbour and for ourselves. This lack of love is conscientious and voluntary, and this rupture hurts its authors, their entourage, and their relation to God. The sacrament of reconciliation, therefore, is a process of returning to the Father from whom we have strayed. It is the recognition of a personal process that allows us to receive forgiveness from God. This sacrament guarantees sinners the love of a God to whom they are reconciled and because of whom they are reconciled with themselves, others, and the rest of creation.

In any case, reconciliation is a fruitful theological activity. Considering the multiple meanings of the concept, it is important to clarify the perspective used here. First, the angle is not the sacramental dimension which emphasizes the individual as a character to be reconciled because reconciliation not only affects individuals but most often concerns the whole of society, or even the whole of humanity. The horizon of reconciliation here is not based on a situation of sin in the sense of an act involving personal or collective accountability. Here reconciliation with God – that is, faith – requires the reconciliation of human beings – that is, justice. Faith and justice must be inseparably together if reconciliation is to take place.

This notion of reconciliation provides the framework for an original reinterpretation of the biblical, historical, spiritual, and existential foundations of our mission as the church against the backdrop of the tensions of the modern world. In the end, a new theology of mission vis-à-vis refugees which assigns a differentiated value to the agents of reconciliation is required because a detailed use of reconciliation to describe our mission as the church highlights both its flexibility and fruitfulness. The conception of the church as reconciler is not only based on circumstantial experiences but on a broader horizon because reconciliation is also understood as the renewal of broken relationships between God and people, as well as between people and the rest of the creation. God initiates this process, and humans respond to his initiative through faith. The result is the reconstitution of the human community as a new creation. Therefore, for Christians, the hope of reconciliation is strictly linked to faith in the redemptive action of Christ.

In the context of the refugee phenomenon, reconciliation is key to the healing process that prompts peace and forgiveness, which is why we need to set an example in accepting neighbours, strangers, and all who are suffering.[7] Setting the example involves speaking against racism, sexism, xenophobia, and any other form of social injustice. In other words, we as the church are

---

7. K. T. August, *The Quest for Being Public Church: The South African Challenge to the Moravian Church in Context (1737–2004)* (Bellville: Print Man, 2009).

challenged to promote peace, to bring about peace, and to keep peace. We must seek to reconcile the self with the other and partake in God's redemptive plan of reconciliation. This means that the answer to disunity lies in the peace God gives us, which is like an infinite ocean and a well that never dries up. It is utterly inexplicable – incomprehensible even – but this peace allows us to keep our eyes fixed on Christ, on the hope of eternal life, and on the promises of God. God gives us his peace in abundance so that it can calm our hearts and then overflow to those around us. Of the four biblical constants, *missio Dei* and *visio Dei* bring to light our reconciling ministry of promoting peace and forgiveness through involvement in God's mission of restoration and holistic transformation.

Constant III – Missio Dei: Participating in God's integral mission

The thrust of transformational development is integral mission, God's restorative plan in Christ. As the church we are therefore called to serve the purpose of God by participating in this redemptive plan, which is *missio Dei*, a Latin term meaning the mission of God. The *missio Dei* presents a God who works creatively, redemptively, and lovingly in the world. *Missio Dei* gives a deeper understanding and a new orientation to the practice of missions by the local church. In this view, *missio Dei* is a movement of God toward the world. It evokes the idea of a God on the move whose purpose is to find and restore lost humanity. Thus, integral mission belongs to God and emanates from God, which shows that our mission as the church in the world is not only about evangelism and church planting, but also about the proclamation of the gospel through works in response to the concrete needs of those who have been pushed to the margins. In brief, the call to turn to God is coupled with a call for social justice.

There is a coherent link between *missio Dei* and transformational development. First, God's work in this world – *missio Dei* – is the work of *shalom*. The renowned South African scholar Steve de Gruchy points out that the Hebrew word *shalom* means "just relationships," and it is manifested in four areas: *shalom* between humans and God, *shalom* between humans, *shalom* between humans and nature, and the *shalom* of humans with themselves.[8] Second, Jesus incarnated this work of God, and he manifested it by bringing salvation to the poor, the sick, the blind, the prisoners, and the marginalized.

---

8. Steve de Gruchy, "A Christian Engagement with the Sustainable Livelihoods Framework," *Missionalia* 33, no. 1 (1 April 2005): 58.

The whole of the Christian body today is unanimous in affirming that we have a mission and a role to play in this present generation. We continue to believe in our vocation and calling, that as a church we are both missionary and missional by nature, and our *raison d'être* is to be active in the world. The church ceases to be the body of Christ when we stop proclaiming the good news of salvation of which we ourselves are a sign. The proclamation of the gospel in the world defines our mission and purpose, and it is only in missional dynamics that we know what we are as the church, why our community exists, and where we are going. Outside this missional framework, we lose our identity and our own essence as the church, and we are no longer credible.

We are called to worship God as a gathering of believers, to help build members, and to have a ministry of compassion and proclamation. The words of Jesus, "As the Father has sent me, so do I send you" (John 20:21), and "Go therefore and make disciples of all nations" (Matt 28:19) are key examples for understanding integral mission, as indeed the acts of the Father sending the Son and the Son leaving the Holy Spirit to continue his work are essential to understanding the mission of God. The first act of God to reconcile human beings to himself is seen in Genesis when he sought for Adam after the fall (Gen 3:8–9). This was God's first missional initiative to restore his image. Thus, there is a coherent link between the constant of *missio Dei* and the constant of *imago Dei*. As the church, when we obediently join in the *missio Dei*, we become instruments that God uses to restore his *imago* in Christ. That is to say, our mandate is to participate in the process of restoring the image of God to its originality. This means the local church that participates in integral mission is actively involved in God's redemptive work. As the church we must migrate toward the other in order to proclaim with absolute relevance the saving work of Christ and the justice of God for all nations. In Matthew 28:19, Jesus commands all believers to leave their comfort zones and go to "all nations" in order to transform lives holistically. This ecclesial migration is done for the purpose of participating in the *missio Dei*, God's integral mission. The Great Commission is thus the migration of the self into the world to meet the holistic needs of the other – which is pivotal for transformational development.

The constant of *missio Dei*, therefore, is a grand tenet of the church in our ministry of reconciliation because it emphasizes what God is doing in the world through us. It is God's desire that social structures and systems reflect justice and promote peaceful coexistence.[9] Thus, the mission of the church is

---

9. W. G. Bragg, "From Development to Transformation," in *The Church in Response to Human Need*, ed. V. Samuel and C. Sugden (Grand Rapids: Eerdmans, 1987), 39.

in essence the mission of God. Active participation in *missio Dei* is at the heart of the ministry of reconciliation. Here, we are sent out and partake in God's redemptive plan. In view of this, transformational development is essential to *missio Dei* because it emphasizes our participation in God's salvific plan in a way that loosens all human constructions that divide the self from the other. As the church, when we are involved in the *missio Dei*, we challenge human structures and tendencies that dehumanize the other,[10] which is why Bosch describes the *missio Dei* as God's movement into the world through the church.[11] In other words, it is God who moves in the world by using our communities of faith as a channel. Therefore, we exist as the church because of the *missio Dei*.

When we grasp the essence of *missio Dei* as a constant of the church, our perception of church missions changes. We start understanding mission based on the premise that we cease to be a church the moment we stop being a church after the *missio Dei*. This understanding shows that *missio Dei* is not an outreach activity that we as a church undertake or an evangelistic programme we aim to achieve. Such missionary activities carried out by a church are what missiologists call *missio ecclesiae*, which is the doing of a church.[12] The *missio ecclesiae* is the activity of the local church, and it derives its existence from our participation in the *missio Dei*, which is God's activity and initiative.[13] The *missio Dei* involves vertical and horizontal relationships. Its main purpose is to translate the attitude of God toward humanity into service toward the other, which signals the essence of the community of faith as partakers of or participants in God's salvific work. From this perspective, the *missio Dei* is a constant in transformational development and serves to amplify our natural identity as the church.

The constant of *missio Dei* is therefore participatory because it has a holistic approach. As the followers of Jesus Christ who engage in social action, we never choose between satisfying physical hunger and spiritual hunger or between healing bodies and saving souls because the *agapé* love of God leads us to serve holistically.[14] In this instance, *missio Dei* is the holistic practice of God through us, the church. Transformational development is now understood

---

10. Groody, "Crossing the Divide," 653.

11. D. Bosch, *Transforming Mission: Paradigm Shifts in Theology of Missions* (Maryknoll, NY: Orbis, 1991), 121.

12. Bosch, *Transforming Mission*, 130.

13. Bevans and Schroeder, *Constants in Context*, 290.

14. August, *Quest for Being Public Church*, 52.

from the perspectives of both the Scriptures and the daily circumstances of life, which is why transformational development is practical and contextual. *Missio Dei* gives us a cutting-edge by situating the biblical reality in our context with utmost resonance. It is this reality that causes us to find eternal relevance in social affairs.

Understanding the *missio Dei* from God's revelation makes us consider the fact that the Bible is a missionary book par excellence. For instance, in the first two chapters of Genesis, God presents himself as the Creator of all things and one who has a life project for humanity. However, because of free will, human beings eventually disobeyed the commandments of God, and this disobedience had negative impact on the rest of the creation. Genesis 3 to 11 draws a picture of the consequences of this human act on creation. The pericope highlights both the wickedness of human beings and the intervention of God. In spite of the dark reality, God did not abandon his creation; on the contrary, he saved it. From the fall of humans onward, God presents himself as one who saves, and as one who even goes looking for lost souls (cf. Gen 3:6–9). His project of life and blessing has not changed despite our rebellion against his perfect will. The whole of the Bible tells the story of redemption and restoration, which is the foundation upon which the church rests.

Thus we see that *missio Dei* has a theocentric basis, an ecclesiocentric purpose, and an anthropocentric focus. It emphasizes God's action in history and how this action was conducted in the past, is conducted in the present, and will be conducted in the future. *Missio Dei* also assumes a universal approach in God's action. That is to say, God's mission touches all the elements in the world including the church. God manifests his love for the world and his church in very inclusive ways, which is the reason Jesus's ministry was equally inclusive. His ministry broke down erected boundaries to include everyone. Through the *missio Dei*, we reach out to those whose dignity has been damaged and hope has faded, and bring them into the community of faith for protection in the sanctuary.

Constant IV – Visio Dei: *Transforming lives through God's vision*

Transformational development is about taking what is and turning it into what it should be.[15] Such a process leads to reconciliation and promotes peaceful coexistence. The oppressor and the oppressed need to be reconciled; those who come from war-torn countries need to be reconciled; the victims of violence

---

15. Bragg, "From Development to Transformation," 39.

and survivors of all sorts of abuse need to be reconciled; and refugees and host communities need reconciliation, too. It is our task as the church to preach the grace of reconciliation for peace to reign between two parties. This is God's vision of holistic transformation. In other words, the *visio Dei* for humanity is that lives be holistically transformed as he intended them to be in an ideal *shalom* community, which is a community characterized by human flourishing – harmonious living, peaceful coexistence, healthy well-being, prosperous lifestyle, and just relationships.

Thus *visio Dei* gives us a better perspective on how to participate in the *missio Dei* and restore the *imago Dei*. When we use the *visio Dei*, we will be actively involved in holistic transformation to change the lives of those who have been dehumanized by structures of this new age.[16] Through the constant of *visio Dei*, we imitate our founder and serve everyone regardless of their background or origin because when we do so, we see all creation as God does. The *visio Dei* is not based on the geography of the self or the religion of the other but on the divine initiative and openness of heart which leads to a perception of the other as the *imago Dei*. When we welcome someone as the *imago Dei*, we do so because we have visualized them with the *visio Dei*. This act of visualizing the other through God's eyes seeks to correct evil structures and systems. Therefore, the constant of *visio Dei* challenges us "to move beyond a narrow sense of national, racial, or psychological territoriality through the positive dimensions of globalization that foster interconnection."[17] As a result, we are able to open people's eyes so they can visualize others using the *visio Dei*, which is vital because it restores the sight of those who have lost the sense of appreciation for the *imago Dei* in themselves and in others. This restoration of sight is made possible through the finished work of the *Verbum Dei*. In other words, the work of salvation is reconciling, and this salvific reconciliation starts by breaking the barrier that divides the self and the other to create a bridge of understanding between them.

Thus God's vision is that those who have been pushed to the margin be brought to the centre. Because of this vision of God, Jesus stood in solidarity with the poor and was committed to fight poverty on their side. He had a special preference for them. In fact, he was always closer to those who were materially poor – the oppressed, the hungry, the sick, and the refugees. We see his commitment in the discourse at the beginning of his mission: "*The Spirit of the Lord is upon me, because he has anointed me to bring good news to*

---

16. Groody, "Crossing the Divide," 661.
17. Groody, 663.

the poor. He sent me to proclaim release to the captives and recovery of sight to the blind, to set the oppressed free, and to proclaim the year of the Lord's favor" (Luke 4:18–19). Jesus did not just say these things; he actually did them. He brought his acts and his words together. He healed the sick and the disabled; he opened the eyes of the blind; he opened the ears of the deaf; he made the person with paralysis walk; and he raised the dead. When John the Baptist sent his disciples to inquire whether Jesus really was "the one to come" or whether they should "wait for another," Jesus answered, "Go and tell John what you have seen and heard: the blind receive their sight, the lame walk, the lepers are cleansed, the deaf hear, the dead are raised, the poor have good news brought to them" (Luke 7:20, 22–23). Jesus started sharing the good news with the poor in order to restore them to life in fullness – the life that God gave to human beings at creation, which is God's vision for humanity.

God's vision for humanity includes those who have been pushed to the margins of society as a result of forced migration. It should be remembered that migration has always been part of human history, and God has always been concerned about people who have had to leave their homes for one reason or another. This concern explains why the refugee phenomenon is one of the most important fields of mission for the church because it calls us to practice both the centrifugal mission and the centripetal mission. The people of God in the Old Testament practiced the model of "come and see," which is in essence centripetal. They did so because Israel was a priestly nation which was to present God to the nations (Exod 19:5–6). Given this role, the old covenant texts speak little about reaching out to the unreached. Foreigners were literally expected to come to Israel, and Israel made little effort to reach them. This drawing in is the centripetal model of mission.

The centripetal mission is analogous to the pull factor as it tends to pull toward the centre, and the centrifugal mission is analogous to pushing from the centre, thus illustrating a push factor. In the Bible, the nation of Israel in the Old Testament provides us with a good example of the centripetal mission, while the mission of Jesus and his disciples best demonstrates to us the ideal of balancing the centripetal essence of mission and the centrifugal necessity. The term "centripetal" means moving to the centre. Thus a centripetal force attracts objects towards the centre like a magnet pulling on a piece of iron or a flower attracting bees. On the other hand, the term "centrifugal" means moving from the centre, therefore is the opposite of a centripetal force. The plan of God's centripetal mission was for Israel to attract other nations to faith and worship. The centrifugal mission is exemplified by a messenger who crosses borders to go and convey the good news to those who are far away and attracts them towards the person at the centre. God's plan then was to reveal his character to the nations by placing Israel strategically and providing them with every facility to become the greatest nation on the face of the earth.

The results of the centripetal mission are shown in the reign of King Solomon for example. His knowledge and gift of wisdom led ambassadors from all the kings of the world to listen to him (1 Kgs 4:33–34). The Queen of Sheba even came from a land far away in Africa and admitted that the report she had heard from her own land regarding Solomon's achievements and wisdom was true. She stated,

> I did not believe the reports until I came and my own eyes saw it. Not even half of the greatness of your wisdom had been told to me; you far surpass the report that I had heard. . . . Blessed be the LORD your God, who has delighted in you and set you on his throne as king for the LORD your God. Because your God loved Israel and would establish them forever, he has made you king over them, that you may execute justice and righteousness." (2 Chr 9:6, 8)

This attraction of the Queen of Sheba to the God of Solomon by his wealth and wisdom illustrates a centripetal model of mission. So Israel's centripetal role was to be a light to the nations and to live their lives in such a way that the nations would see the true and living God and be drawn to their life and their God.

In the New Testament, however, the strategy changed when the call became "go and tell" (Matt 28:16–20; Acts 1:1–11), which is a practice of a centrifugal model of mission. Thus in the book of Acts, Jesus sends his disciples from Jerusalem to the ends of the earth as a centrifugal force. The main focus of the book of Acts is not the centre but the periphery, that is, not Jerusalem but the nations. While during the old covenant times the nations were to draw centripetally to God, now we are expected to reach out to the nations centrifugally. However, because Christ did not come to do away with the old covenant but to complete it, it is therefore proper to deduce that the centrifugal and centripetal models are two sides of the same coin in church mission. Thus, the vision of God is to transform communities using both centripetal and centrifugal means. So, our nature as the church is centripetal, but our function as the church is centrifugal.

To reach out to those who are vulnerable, we must go to them with the vision of God. Indeed, we must be an incubator of the love of God as the church so that the strength of those who are tired on this journey can be renewed.

However, our calling is primarily to be an army of ambassadors who reach out to those who are spiritually and physically vulnerable to systemic plans that do not honour God. Because we have the Spirit of Christ, we have an additional strategy that provides guidance on how we are to accomplish the integral mission. Thus ours is not only a "come and see" message, which often weighs heavily on the person burdened by abject poverty and unspeakable vulnerability to take the first step. As men and women whom God has sought and called, we are also a people whose mission is to reach out to others with love because of our centrifugal propensity.

The vision of God for us the church is to reach out not only to the lost but also the deprived, the depressed, the hopeless, the excluded, the abandoned, the marginalized, and the victimized. This was the case in the first-century church, and it is the case in the twenty-first century church. The role and place of the local church is of vital significance considering the complex development of the refugee phenomenon in sub-Saharan Africa. We are expected to provide refugees with both spiritual care and psychosocial support among other supports of existential relevance. In this context, we are also expected to promote the integration of refugees into mainstream society to enhance their belonging because integration builds a society where every individual is an active member of the community and responsible for the well-being of the other.

Holistic transformation becomes a possibility when as the agents of development we see the community in need of transformation through God's eyes. To see the other through the eyes of God, the observer must have the vision of God or the *visio Dei*. So, *visio Dei* introduces the theological notion of anthropomorphism and alludes to the concept of corporeal deity. The Bible is loaded with anthropomorphic terms that describe God using various parts of the body to give him a possible human shape, for example the hand of God (Ps 89:13; Prov 21:1), the eyes of God (Ps 33:18; Hab 1:13), the heart of God (1 Sam 13:14; Acts 13:22), etc. The notion of corporeal deity does not mean God is a physical being with a physical body. It only shows that humans are not capable of grasping the fundamental nature of the divine, but we can still participate in the divine activities. The participation of humans in the divine activities is made possible through the *visio Dei*. The *visio Dei* is, in this instance, the seeing, the encounter, or the anthropomorphic visualization of God. One must have had an encounter with God to be able to see others with the vision of God.

This visualization of the divine is spiritual. It is a beatific experience that leads to spiritual insight. In other words, the *visio Dei* experience is a spiritual encounter between the human and the divine which brings spiritual relevance to the life and ministry of the church. The constant of *visio Dei* is transformational because a human being cannot see God and remain the same. The constant of *visio Dei* is founded on the Matthean beatitude: "Blessed are the pure in heart, for they will see God" (Matt 5:8). Unless we have had an encounter with God – that is, unless we have the *visio Dei*, the other three constants, namely the *imago Dei*, the *Verbum Dei*, and the *missio Dei*, will have no spiritual implication. The *visio Dei* is such a basic requirement for us as the church. Therefore, "the chief end of church ministry to refugees is not to seek the *visio Dei* in heaven but to see things . . . as God sees them here."[18] When the church sees things as God does, the church has the *visio Dei*. This *visio Dei* will bring about holistic transformation and "influence the way we understand migrants and refugees [because] a theology of migration seeks to articulate a renewed vision of God" and human life.[19]

Because the local church is a community of faith, each member of this community is to see the other as the *imago Dei* using the *visio Dei* in order to faithfully participate in the *missio Dei*, which the *Verbum Dei* continues through church missions. Considering these four constants and two contexts, we are called to contextualize Christianity by theologizing along the lines of African spirituality and keeping Christ as the only constant. Such a theological practice is inculturation. The practice of inculturation helps us to understand better the ethos of Ubuntu, which encourages the fellowship of one another. In turn, the fellowship of one another strengthens unity in diversity. Early Christians lived in unity while maintaining their diversity. That is to say, they lived communally, selling what belonged to the individual self and sharing the income with the individual other to meet the needs of everyone.

Discussion Questions

1. How is the church a sanctuary and a reconciler?
2. In what ways are *missio Dei*, *imago Dei*, *Verbum Dei*, and *visio Dei* calls to participate in God's salvific plan?
3. When do we say that mission to refugees is centrifugal or centripetal?

---

18. Groody, "Crossing the Divide," 660.
19. Groody, 661.

4. Read Matthew 25:31–46.
   - What does this passage tell us about how we as the church should care for those in need?
   - How can we transform the situation where people in our communities are excluded or their needs are ignored, and ensure that everyone can participate fully in the life of the community?
5. Read Deuteronomy 1:16–17; 16:11; 24:14–15, 17–19; 26:12; Leviticus 19:33–34; 25:35; Numbers 35:15; Jeremiah 22:1–5.
   - List the rights and duties mentioned in these texts
   - Which of these rights and duties are new to you?

   Jesus takes the way people care for strangers seriously. Read Matthew 25:34–36.
   - What does Jesus say here about the treatment of strangers?
   - How does this passage describe how we are to respond to refugees?

4

Transformational Community Development as Ubuntu in Action

After living in the Nyarugusu camp for almost five years, life became more and more unbearable. Some of our friends who had left the camp for Mozambique, Zimbabwe, and South Africa had started sending letters and photos as proof that life was better elsewhere than in the Tanzanian camps, including Nyarugusu. My father who had always wanted me to study organized that I leave the camp and go to Lubumbashi, in the DRC, where I was to pursue my studies at the university level. He had already spoken with some relatives who would have accommodated me while in Lubumbashi. However, my older brother who was already in Durban, South Africa, insisted that I join him so that I could seek to study in South Africa instead. During this meeting with Dad, I indicated a few factors to consider Durban rather than Lubumbashi and managed to convince him that South Africa was indeed the best option, especially as I had the vision to pursue my studies further. Unlike in most African countries, refugees in South Africa did not and still do not live in camps. They have the freedom of choice to live wherever they want in the country like everyone else provided they are documented. This freedom was another pull factor for me. So, the trip to Durban, South Africa, started a few weeks after this meeting. I was with two other friends. It was a long journey. We used bicycles, motorbikes, buses, trains, and taxis, and on many occasions, we walked on foot. We also got robbed, etc.

We arrived in Maputo, Mozambique, six days after we left Nyarugusu. We had run out of money, so we went to Bobole, a refugee transit camp located in Maputo. We stayed in Bobole for a few weeks and then proceeded to Durban. The transport we took from Maputo, which was to take us to the border of South Africa, dropped us half-way. We later realized that the mini bus was not going to the border side, and we got lost. It was a few minutes past 1:00 pm. We asked some passers-by the way to the border with South Africa, and they showed us the "shorter route" through the forest. So was the beginning of our long walk to Durban. As we proceeded with the journey through the Maputaland forest on the Mozambican side, we saw a guy along the way going the same direction. Upon asking him the direction to the South African border, he told us that it was a bit far, but we could walk together since his house was just a kilometre away from the borderline. He became our walking companion. At some point, we needed to cross a certain river; this gentleman got us a small wooden boat which we used for crossing. When he got to his home, he showed us a path that led to the borderline, which we followed. Immediately after crossing the fenced borderline of South Africa, at that unconventional crossing point – luckily the fence was no longer electrified as it used to be – we got completely lost. We did not know which path to follow as there were quite a few of them. We continued the journey through the Maputaland forest on the South African side without knowing if we were heading in the right direction. There was no one to ask, so we walked in the dark, praying that no wild animals would have us for dinner. The Maputaland forest covers the southern part of Mozambique, the eastern part of Swaziland, and the northern part of the province of KwaZulu-Natal in South Africa.

We had started walking at 1:00 pm, and around 7:00 pm we met a gentleman who asked us where we were going. We told him that we lost our way, but we were going to Durban. The man invited us to his home and asked his wife to give us some food to eat. His wife cooked a meal, and we ate to our satisfaction. The gentleman then proposed that we not proceed to Durban but instead live with them in that village, in the middle of the forest, and he would give us land we could cultivate and build our future home. We politely declined the offer and maintained that we still wanted to proceed to Durban. The gentleman then contacted one of his friends who had a car and asked him to give us a lift. His friend came and told us that the buses to Durban only pass early in the morning. It was already 10:00 pm. He then suggested that we sleep over, and he would drive us to the main road where buses to Durban pass early in the morning. We went to his place and early in the morning, around 4:00 am, he woke us up and took us to the main road in his small pick-up. At 5:00 am, the first bus from Swaziland to Durban passed, and we got into it.

The help we received on this journey is a typical example of Ubuntu, a radical denunciation of selfishness, egotism, xenophobia, and any other form of individualism and intolerance more or less pronounced. Someone who lives in line with and practices the social ethos of Ubuntu, like these gentlemen in the Maputaland forest and their families, is always welcoming, open, and available to others, dedicated to others, and does not feel threatened by others but rejoices with others. The way these families treated us, the strangers, is a great illustration that Ubuntu expresses the awareness of individuals who define themselves following the human context they live in and by their relations with other humans. These experiences were practical evidence that indeed Africans have abundant inner resources that make them live in Africa as Africans. We learned that Ubuntu is the source of hope for Africa because it asserts that as long as Africans trust one another and as long as there are resources in one community, even those who have nothing in the community will not be doomed to starve.

An anthropologist is said to have proposed a game to the children of a tribe in sub-Saharan Africa. He put a basket full of fruits near a tree and told the children that the first to arrive would win all the fruits. When he told them to run, all the children jumped at the same time, joined hands, and ran to the tree. Then they sat together to enjoy these delicious fruits. When the anthropologist asked them why they had run that way when one of them could have had all the fruits to themselves, they replied, "How can one of us be happy if all the others are sad?" Essentially, the children were led by the spirit of Ubuntu and did not imagine how one of them could benefit from eating the fruits while the others did not. Their response is also an indication that someone who is guided by the spirit of Ubuntu is never satisfied when others are not satisfied. They feel belittled when others are belittled; they feel humiliated when others are humiliated; and they feel oppressed when others are oppressed because Ubuntu emphasizes communal living and that people are said to be human through their connectedness to others. In the spirit of Ubuntu, the universe of each is related to that of the other. We are who we are because of who others are. This Ubuntu interconnectedness is of great importance in transformational development. Ubuntu is summed up in the popular saying, "I am because we are, and because we are, I am." This is the philosophical foundation of this source of courage, and Ubuntu is really what gives Africans the courage to hope. I think if we develop this idea, if we interpret it and translate it into our lives and into our communities, we will be able to accomplish much more and create a better Africa.

Ubuntu as Beatitudinal Care

More than ever before, our time is deeply marked by what has been called the migration crisis and international mobility, whether chosen or imposed by different events. Socioeconomic, geopolitical, or religious issues or even ecological disasters are the source of wars, conflicts, and persecution of all kinds which inevitably force masses of people to leave their homes and their country and seek asylum elsewhere. In most traditions of sub-Saharan Africa that rely on Ubuntu as an organizing ethic of their being in the world and of living together in the community, the primary *raison d'être* of humanity is to manifest who they really are.[1] Having lived through the realities of foreignness as a refugee since my childhood, I am able to understand what refugees go through. I know from experience that the first needs for immigrants are to be welcomed, to be safe, to be accepted, and to be integrated into their new community.

All the evidence indicates a common origin and destiny of humanity. Rather than history being the theatre of class struggle, it is a story of globalization and a quest for unity. Africa, the cradle of humanity, must take the lead in promoting unity and not fragmentation. This unity cannot be based solely on transitional systems like economics and politics, but must include deeper values and norms rooted in belief systems. Indeed, there can be no true global ethic if others do not take seriously our rich ancestral heritage as Africans, which is a fundamental requirement not only to be complete from a geographical point of view, but more importantly to achieve the necessary ethical depth. For many years, African traditions and values have been marginalized in the dominant discourse. Ubuntu is not limited to our African behaviour. It is rather part of an African vision of the cosmos focused on relationships and interrelations, which means the implications of Ubuntu transcend African conduct. Its underlying cosmological assumptions entail that, to be ethical, people must consider themselves connected and intersected with the others, the natural environment, the present, the past, and the future. In other words, Ubuntu is a way of life. It is the essence of being human, which means you cannot exist as a human being in isolation. It reminds us of our interdependence as human beings.

In my case, I looked beyond the origins of my restricted family so as to become aware of my multiple affiliations. I could not imagine myself as just

---

1. L. Mpetsheni, "Ubuntu – A Soteriological Ethic for an Effaced *Umntu* in a Post 1994 South Africa: A Black Theology of Liberation Perspective" (Unpublished PhD Thesis, University of Pretoria, 2019), 152, https://repository.up.ac.za/handle/2263/75269?show=full.

my parents' son because I am also the son of my continent, of my country, of my clan, of my territory; in short, of my many encounters. I am who I am and Ubuntu is my culture. I would say the Ubuntu culture is based on a correct knowledge of human relationships and all the other elements of life in the universe. For me, Ubuntu is an eminence or excellence in being, with a vital force exerting a vital influence. To live better with oneself, a human being must be in harmony with their peers and with the rest of the creation. I am human if my life is built on healthy, symbiotic relationships and values such as helpfulness, generosity, trust in others, sharing, and a sense of community, in short, any act of kindness. This spirituality of Ubuntu was passed down to me from my childhood, and it has helped all along my wayfaring. Thus my birth, my growth, my education, my belonging, and my whole becoming have been made possible by others. So I do not see myself existing without others or outside of all my relationships. I am the crux of my relational ties, which means I have a relationship of being or of life with all my encounters.

Ubuntu has a diversity of interdependent concepts. For instance, it opposes revenge and is inextricably linked to values that attach great importance to dignity, compassion, and respect for the other. Ubuntu imposes a change from confrontation and hostility to mediation and reconciliation. It promotes positive attitudes and shared concerns, the restoration of harmony in relationships, and restorative justice that restores rather than distributive justice that takes away. Ubuntu operates in a way that favours conflict resolution rather than hostility and discord. It promotes mutual understanding rather than vengeance and civility and courteous dialogue without hypocrisy based on mutual tolerance. Ubuntu is also a practice of spirituality that can be discussed in the context of its relationship with some biblical values. In African thought, being deprived of your Ubuntu is a vice because Ubuntu constitutes one's spiritual awareness of belonging to a common humanity.[2] As a form of spirituality, Ubuntu informs us that all of human life is connected to ours. The need to connect with others is deeply rooted in us and gives meaning to life as we conceive it because an African is without a doubt a relational being. The very *raison d'être* of an African depends on his or her relationship with another. Apart from relationship, it becomes difficult for an African to self-define. One of the characteristics of Ubuntu is interdependence because we need other

---

2. M. L. J. Koenane, "*Ubuntu* and Philoxenia: *Ubuntu* and Christian Worldviews as Responses to Xenophobia," HTS Teologiese Studies/Theological Studies 74, no. 1 (10 April 2018), https://hts.org.za/index.php/hts/article/view/4668/11090, 56.

humans to be human ourselves. We only realize our humanity through other human beings.

In view of these characteristics, and seeing that Ubuntu is above all a state of mind, we will deduce that Ubuntu is therefore the capacity, in African culture, to express compassion, reciprocity, dignity, solidarity, harmony, and humanity for the sake of building and maintaining a community with justice and mutual concern. In other words, Ubuntu is not only an African philosophy, but also an African spirituality and an art of living.[3] Due to globalization, we are living in a context of multiculturalism where all cultures are interdependent. Ubuntu brings meaningful coexistence to communal living in multicultural situations and exhumes remarkable beatitudinal values.

Of course, there is no precise and simple definition for the term "Ubuntu," but it is a broad concept of African spirituality which touches at the same time on politics, ethics, philosophy, metaphysics, and other values that animate the African person.[4] Ubuntu in its political dimension opposes discrimination and promotes national reconciliation and living together. It is the idea that the human community is one and indivisible. We cannot oppose one another or make any distinction based on ethnicity or belonging. Wanting to stand out or separate from others is a dead end, a game with harmful consequences for everyone. Behind this idea, we understand that rejecting others amounts to rejecting oneself. To hate others is to hate oneself personally, since the fate of each is linked to the fate of all. In its political sense, Ubuntu has a dynamic aspect: it is a momentum for reconciliation, an outstretched hand which carries within it the capacity to accept, understand, love, and forgive, in order to rebuild the human community with the help of all. In the end, political Ubuntu carries a project of inclusion, solidarity, and the search for consensus, humanity being seen as a community of life and destiny.

Ubuntu in its human dimension is an ethic of life. More precisely, it is a state of mind or an art of living that describes the fact of going spontaneously toward the other. In my ancestral Babembe village when I was young and went to visit my grandfather during the holidays, I had noticed that wayfaring strangers who passed and stopped in the village did not need to ask for food or water. When they rested alongside the road, people would welcome them

---

3. R. Khoza, *Ubuntu: African Humanism* (Johannesburg: HSRC, 1994), 21.

4. P. Couture, "Human Dignity, Injustice and Ubuntu: Living the Metaphor of *Bwino/Bumuntu*/White Lime in the Democratic Republic of Congo," in *Practicing Ubuntu: Practical Theological Perspectives on Injustice, Personhood and Human Dignity*, eds. J. S. Dreyer, Y. Dreyer, E. Foley, and M. Nel (Pretoria: LitVerlag, 2017), 12.

in and give them food and water. If there was no food in the house, there were always mangoes to give which they would eat and drink water before they continued with their journey. This is one aspect of Ubuntu, but there are many more. Ubuntu is therefore a way of being, a practice of fraternity on a daily basis. It is going to the other before the other even asks. Ubuntu goes beyond compassion in that it is anticipating, caring, and understanding of the other. It is constant benevolence and spontaneous and unconditional solidarity based on the ability to put oneself in the other's shoes. In this prospect, Ubuntu relies on the intuitive or reasoned awareness that we are the other, and it goes beyond the simple reciprocity of human relations. As such, Ubuntu differs from Western humanism because the latter is based on respect – for example, not encroaching on another's territory, limiting the exercise of one's own freedom in relation to that of others, etc. – while Ubuntu is based on a deeper form of solidarity. To practice Ubuntu in this humanist dimension is therefore to break the illusion of separation in order to recognize oneself in the other. Selflessness, confidence, and generosity are the foundations of the spirituality of Ubuntu in its humanistic aspect, far from any individualism.

Ubuntu in its metaphysical dimension is cosmic because it affects our very being and the way we are present in the cosmos. In this sense, Ubuntu is based on the idea that everything in the cosmos is united and linked. Everything is interdependent. In other words, nothing exists in itself; nothing is truly autonomous and separate from the rest. Everything in nature is connected. For example, humans and animals feed on plants, which in turn feed on solar energy, which means that to some extent we are connected to the sun. We are connected to water, matter, and oxygen; we are influenced by an endless number of elements and factors that make up who we are today. We are at the crossroads of all influences in the universe, the meeting point of all cosmic energies. Likewise, our personality is the result of the education we have received from others, of our encounters, and of what we have been given. However, the difficulty comes from the fact that we often have the impression of being separated from the whole. Our ego prompts us to imagine a tight wall between ourselves and the rest of the world. Individuality in Africa is a borrowed value that creates the illusion of self-interest and renders us incapable of grasping the true workings of the world. Living in this illusion leads to rejection and hatred, feelings from which we will be the first to suffer. Conversely, realizing that our existence depends on everything that surrounds us naturally leads us to take care of people, animals, and all of nature. So to practice the spirituality of Ubuntu in its metaphysical dimension is to realize that we all live with one life in one world, and that our existence depends on that of others. Ubuntu therefore invites us to experience duality in a different way – not as a separation or a threat, but as the opportunity for an encounter, a meeting of existential beings – it is an opportunity for reconciliation. In other words, the spirituality of Ubuntu is a reincarnation of the unitary cosmic energy we call love.

We could also translate Ubuntu as a force that sustains existence because it is a vital energy that circulates in everything.[5] For Africans, Ubuntu is therefore the spiritual power that helps bring everything together and above all describes how to welcome others, pay attention to them, and care for them. It is an openness to others that requires an always benevolent attitude. Ubuntu begins with a greeting coupled with a smile and a real handshake that establishes a positive rapport and constructive relationship. It is knowing how to give without expecting anything in return. In this sense, the spirituality of Ubuntu reincarnates brotherhood or sisterhood and mutual aid. Thus paying attention to others and caring about their well-being consists in putting oneself in their place and considering them as equal to oneself. However, the spirituality of Ubuntu goes beyond the simple notion of equality or reciprocity because it is based on the realization that I am the other. Concretely, there is no longer any distinction between me and others: what I do to others is as if I were doing it to myself; what other people feel is what I can feel myself; my destiny is linked to that of my neighbour. There is no fundamental difference between me and others: we share the same needs, the same desires, and the same interests. Thus the spirituality of Ubuntu brings out what is most universal in every human being. So it is a spirituality that invites humility and responsibility.

Peace, quiet, and tranquility define the spirituality of Ubuntu because they greatly reduce the risk of conflict.[6] In this case individualism and ego naturally fade away, and the values of tolerance, understanding, and acceptance prevail. The consequence is a harmonious, peaceful society in which conflicts are settled with calm, patience, and consensus. This approach is quite different from Western humanism, which is based on the right of everyone to exercise their freedom within the limit of respect for others with the promise of sanction in the event of infringement or trespassing someone else's territory, thus creating a separation between individuals who are each striving and thriving on their own. Conversely, Ubuntu emphasizes the universal bond that binds all human beings together. Also, well-being, happiness, and *joie de vivre* define

---

5. J. Hailey, *Ubuntu: A Literature Review* (London: Desmond Tutu Foundation, 2008).

6. T. Metz, "Ubuntu as a Moral Theory: Reply to Four Critics," *South African Journal of Philosophy* 26, no. 4 (2007): 376.

the spirituality of Ubuntu because no one is left by the wayside; everyone can thrive on their own and through others. Caring for others is taking care of oneself, and vice versa. Everyone finds their place in the human community and can thus cultivate confidence and hope. In African thought, this social harmony translates into a certain sweetness of life.

Ubuntu's spirituality is based on the fundamental cosmic law of oneness. The point is that all things and all beings are interrelated, since they are part of the cosmic whole, a cohesive and harmonious whole. The law of unity can also be called the law of love as indicated earlier. Love is indeed the force which embraces, gathers, accepts, and welcomes everything. It is the energy that attracts and connects everything and everyone to their source, that is, to the cosmic centre. The spirituality of Ubuntu endows us with centripetal power which attracts others to us.[7] This centripetal ability leads us to respect all beings as well as nature on which we directly depend in its entirety. To practice the spirituality of Ubuntu is therefore to recognize and use this positive centripetal energy; it is to place oneself in cosmic harmony. It is a way to achieve wisdom, perfection, and full self-realization. It is an opportunity to open one's consciousness while fitting into the present, beyond the illusion of separation. Ultimately, Ubuntu is the art and spirituality of attracting each person to oneself. It is the centripetal way of goodness, unity, happiness, and human flourishing.

Ubuntu is arguably God's design for human living because it puts emphasis on togetherness and the humanity of every member in the society. When people live by Ubuntu ethics, they constitute the *shalom* community because all that lives or exists on earth is interdependent. In other words, if I exist, it is because you exist. If I write, it is because you read. Besides human interdependence, Ubuntu extends to all that exists, which brings in the whole idea of ecology, preservation of the environment and biodiversity, as well as safeguarding our planet. Thus Ubuntu is an invitation to humility and responsibility. The African worldview is basically reflected in various ways, but there are some common traits with regard to values, beliefs, and practices that mirror what it means to be human as an African. These values form part of the Ubuntu spirituality and explain why, albeit by people from different backgrounds, much is shared in common among Africans. For example, obvious African values include family ceremonies, hard work, respect for senior members of the society, placing a high value on the extended family, a sense of religiosity and worship of a Supreme Being, the importance of having a family plot in the village, and

---

7. Mpetsheni, "Ubuntu – A Soteriological Ethic," 101.

the importance of communicating in the mother tongue. We share similar worldviews about the universe and understand life and death almost the same way.[8] In short, the African family is the centre of coexistence.

The spirituality of Ubuntu also explains the African belief in a Supreme Being who controls all and who is able to protect us and to uplift us when we are devastated by disaster.[9] In other words, Ubuntu recognizes a powerful bond between humanity and the Supreme Being. For example in the Babembe tribe, we believe in *Abéca-Pùngù*, a deity whom we consider to be the living God, creator of the heavens and the earth. To recognize the omnipotence, omniscience, and omnipresence of *Abéca-Pùngù* and to show him respect and veneration following his work of creation, we precede his attributes with the prefix *Mwene*, which suggests "the owner of." Thus we will say *Mwene-malango* (owner of all households, hence the universe), *Mwenembùka* (owner of the homestead), *Mwene-Ikùlù* (owner of or the one who lives in the heavens), *Mwenebyose* (owner of all that exists), *Mwenebatù* (the one to whom all human beings belong), *Mwenebitù* (owner of all things), and *Mwene-Ombe* (the God of all). We make offerings to *Abéca* (short for *Abéca-Pùngù*) through prayers that we call "*Iyela*" or "*Lo'elo*" when famine or disease arrives in the village.

The Babembe have always built the *Lùbùnga* inside their homestead, which is a round straw hut called "Msonge," where family matters are discussed and community issues are resolved. The concept of *Lùbùnga* is what would be called "the Assembly of God." Here, the notion of Assembly of God has a different meaning from that given to it by the charismatic churches in Africa. For charismatic Christians, this expression can be translated as "community of believers" and implies people who share the same faith in Jesus Christ apart from any ethnic affiliation. In the context of the Babembe, Assembly of God means "Assembly of the chosen people of God." To this practical meaning of *Lùbùnga* in our spirituality as a people is added the important religioethnical dimension of the "Judaization" of the Babembe. The belief in the Judaization or Israelization of the Babembe people is a spiritual belief according to which we the Babembe are a lost tribe of Israel. In other words, the practice of Ubuntu spirituality among the Babembe people commands our belief in one Supreme Being, *Abéca-Pùngù*, to whom we ascribe various other attributes, and which leads us to self-realization and self-awareness as a people. We project this self-knowledge in the way we live every day.

---

8. T. Murithi, "Practical Peacemaking Wisdom from Africa: Reflections on Ubuntu," *Journal of Pan African Studies* 1, no. 4 (June 2006): 29.

9. Khoza, "Ubuntu," 34.

Thus the spirituality of Ubuntu requires us to recognize and respect the sociocultural dimensions of others, to discover each other's strengths and beauty, to take care of oneself, to take care of the other, to rely on the group, to welcome in oneself the resonances of the stories that we listen to, and finally to accept the other in their difference.[10] In the spirituality of Ubuntu, it is always too early to give up on life. In a moment of great distress, an African can be tempted like everyone else to end his or her life, but the act of suicide is perceived as a flagrant violation of the values of Ubuntu which honour the preservation of life. For Africans, life is sacred, and it always transcends humanity. Our life was not given to us only for us; it is there to serve the community. So the spirituality of Ubuntu reaffirms that life is an exclusive property of the Supreme Being who is the creator of all things.

The sharing of common values is part of the ability of Africans to coexist, and being African is determined by one's ability to coexist. Such coexistence creates a balanced way of life and explains the embodiment of Africans' togetherness and solidarity. Having the spirituality of Ubuntu is therefore living as a human being as God intended. Both the personality and the humanity of an African person are shaped by the spirituality of Ubuntu, which explains O'Donovan's assertion that life in Africa is shaped by the values and spirit of Ubuntu because "the life and well-being of the extended family is all important to the life and well-being of the individual."[11] Therefore, the individual has unconditional loyalty to his or her extended family, clan, and tribe. O'Donovan's statement verifies the famous Nguni axiom *umuntu ngumuntu ngabantu*, which can be loosely translated as "a person is a person because of other persons." This means a person exists because other people exist, that is, because he or she is surrounded and thus supported by others. It also means a person exists for others, that is, to be around others and thus support them. This coexistence rationalizes African communality and explains the beatitudinal values exhibited by the gentlemen we met in the Maputaland forest even though we were wayfaring strangers. It can be argued that Ubuntu goes beyond socioeconomic dynamics in spite of the challenges that Africa faces such as poverty and unemployment. It is a way of life that upholds the virtues of humanness and regards a human being as having higher esteem than any other factor.

---

10. Murithi, "Practical Peacemaking Wisdom," 29.

11. W. O'Donovan, *Biblical Christianity in African Perspective* (Carlisle, UK: Paternoster, 2000), 156.

The spirituality of Ubuntu therefore makes possible several human attributes such as empathic openness to others, the state of grace in human relationships, helpfulness, generosity, solidarity, benevolence, trust in the other, respect for oneself and others, compassion, forgiveness, reconciliation, hospitality, humility, harmony with all beings of nature, and responsibility to oneself, the world, and others.[12] All of these attributes are reminiscent of the spirituality of Ubuntu. In addition, the spirituality of Ubuntu commands the virtue of beatitudinal care for one another. Caring for others is an Ubuntu gesture that translates into consideration and kindness. Indeed, it is impossible to respond to the distress of the other if you divert your attention from them.

Beatitudinal care consists of paying attention to someone's vulnerability and taking action.[13] Ultimately, the actions of Ubuntu would be my response to vulnerable situations that someone may go through at some point in life. As the church we must create a paradigmatic link between the concept of beatitudinal care and that of Ubuntu in order to help the vulnerable find themselves and pick themselves up again. In my context as a refugee migrant, I recognized my inner beauty because someone enabled me to. It is in my inner beauty that my ability and willingness to care for others lies. So by attentive presence, understanding listening, non-judgement, etc. we are able to call by our own beauty the beauty that lies in others. The spirituality of Ubuntu entails that we see the beauty of people who suffer beyond their vulnerable situation.[14] When people feel understood, listened to, and valued, they will be able to discover their own beauty despite situations that have made them feel like lesser beings.

Considering that Ubuntu promotes a value system that more highly regards communal welfare than the welfare of an individual, the transformation of one community depends on the transformation of another community. The improvement of one becomes the improvement of the other. Bevans and Schroeder perhaps explain this best in their observation "when one crosses into another context – cultural, racial, religious or gender – one inevitably learns not only about the other but – and perhaps most important – about oneself."[15] To this they add that the story, the struggles, and the joy of the other are actually a part of the self's own story, struggles, and joy.[16] This means Ubuntu leads to

---

12. Murithi, "Practical Peacemaking Wisdom," 29.
13. Koenane, "Ubuntu and Philoxenia," 56.
14. B. Lewis, "Forging an Understanding of Black Humanity through Relationship: An Ubuntu Perspective," *Black Theology: An International Journal* 8 (1 April 2010): 73.
15. Bevans and Schroeder, *Constants in Context*, xviii.
16. Bevans and Schroeder, 16.

intercultural interactions and caring for one another. Ubuntu is therefore a strong basis for a participatory development that focuses on the community because transformational development processes ought to resonate with the cultural values of the community in need of transformation.

There is a correlation between Ubuntu, which is anchored in coexistence and communal living, and the church, which is a community of faith made up of people who coexist. This coexistent living entails communal living. Therefore, a "church" in an African context is a community of people who uphold the spirituality of Ubuntu within set boundaries of beatitudinal values specific to the Christian faith. Thus, to understand the depth of the concept of church in Africa, it is important to appreciate the spirituality and the value of community life as expressed in the Ubuntu way of life. It is by appreciating this spirituality of communality that one can understand the connectivity between the self and the other. So, when Ubuntu is lived within the boundaries of Christianity, it becomes a practical fusion of solidarity and cooperation. The practicality of this spirituality entails that one's relational ties spring from the closest family to the whole community, which explains why Ubuntu is more practical than theoretical and more holistic than atomistic. Community development that is holistic and transformational calls for compatibility with the Ubuntu way of life to create an attitude of trust in the church and a spirit of wanting to live and work together.

Johan Cilliers takes the concept of Ubuntu a bit further when he points out that Ubuntu is about trust, helpfulness, respect, sharing, caring, and, unselfishness.[17] He also finds that Ubuntu is rooted in interconnectedness and interdependence.[18] Thus when the community of faith upholds the Ubuntu way of life for spirituality, the unity of members becomes affirmed, and the diversity of cultures endorsed. Cilliers further finds that xenophobia is actually "Ubuntu reversed" because "in Ubuntu we face one another [but] in xenophobia we turn our faces from one another."[19] This means that to an African, xenophobic tendencies are inhuman because they go against the ethical demands of the Ubuntu way of life. While xenophobia dehumanizes the other, Ubuntu helps people to value their identity through their relationships with others.[20] There is a coherent link between Christian spirituality and Ubuntu, and this

---

17. Johan Cilliers, *In Search of Meaning between Ubuntu and Into: Perspectives on Preaching in Post-Apartheid South Africa* (Copenhagen: Societas Homiletica, 2008), 7.

18. Cilliers, *In Search of Meaning*, 7.

19. Cilliers, 9.

20. J. Hailey, *Ubuntu: A Literature Review* (London: Desmond Tutu Foundation, 2008), 7.

coherence is a shared identity of the Christian values and the Ubuntu way of life. This shared identity of Christianity and Ubuntu lays emphasis on the identity of the self and his or her ability to relate with the other, which is vital in building societies while "enhancing community relations and promoting social cohesion."[21] It can then be said that Ubuntu has a grand role to play in African Christianity as it is a vital force behind church praxis.

Ubuntu as African spirituality dictates the activities and doings of the self toward the other, which leads to unity in the community and a reconciling compromise between the two parties. Lewis attests to this postulation when he asserts that "the road toward healing and reconciliation must also be taken by all members of the community, which includes the community of faith."[22] The inference of Lewis' statement that Ubuntu is a road toward healing and reconciliation provides evidence that Ubuntu brings wholeness and a sense of unity in the community of faith. It also shows that Ubuntu is an epitome of the *imago Dei* as it makes the self-aware of the other appreciatively. The Ubuntu way of life underpins the dogma of love and beatitudinal care for the other. When the self meets the other, the self sees itself in the other. This means an individual self is affiliated to the individual other. Thus, Ubuntu is a model for devoted and healthy relationships because the self is expected to care holistically about the other, including caring about their past, present, and future in whatever ways possible and caring about their soul, emotions, and body.

I have experienced great vulnerability in my life, but I never gave up because of faith and hope exercised within the context of spirituality. Faith and attachment to Christian values enabled me to overcome the tragedy of the refugee phenomenon according to my lived experiences. Spirituality according to the principles of Ubuntu endows people with the resilience that allows them to survive and emerge even more human despite all efforts to dehumanize them. Despite my status as a refugee or immigrant in several African countries, the communities in which I lived or continue to live mostly advocate a culture of solidarity and mutual aid, which are two essential values of Ubuntu. Thus with Ubuntu, the individual who experiences great vulnerability no longer experiences his or her suffering alone. She or he shares it with other members of the community, which makes it feel less heavy emotionally. Thus with Ubuntu,

---

21. Hailey, *Ubuntu*, 10.

22. B. Lewis, "Forging an Understanding of Black Humanity through Relationship: An Ubuntu Perspective," *Black Theology: An International Journal* 8 (1 April 2010): 72.

a community becomes a network of support which allows someone not to live in isolation.

A healthy relationship between the self and the other is very basic and matters most in both the Ubuntu way of life and Christian spirituality. A healthy and devoted relationship between the self and the other helps both parties to cope with the pressures of life while dealing with the possible failures or temptations they may experience together. The spirit of Ubuntu, therefore, resonates with African Christianity as it brings relevance between Christian spirituality and the African context. Ubuntu as beatitudinal care reflects the values of Christian spirituality because it is the appreciation of the *imago Dei* in the other which results in acts of solidarity and social cohesion. Upholding Ubuntu in the community of faith is a major step toward eliminating socioeconomic discrimination, stereotyping, and dehumanizing attitudes of the self in relation to the other. This beatitudinal care of Ubuntu champions the ideal of human dignity for all, which is the core of Christian spirituality vis-à-vis refugees.

Ubuntu as God's Design for Communal Living

The quest for an African identity by Ubuntu has influenced the socioeconomic programmes of many in Africa. However, it should be noted that if the structures, strategies, and processes of development do not align with the values of Ubuntu, one may run the risk of failure. In Ubuntu, the sense of responsibility is based on the relationship of individuals with their neighbours in the community, rather than on individual autonomy. Whoever has Ubuntu considers the concerns of others in relation to their own. In a society that emphasizes human well-being, as is the case of Ubuntu where people naturally take care of each other, there can be no economic relationships based on a competitive profit race. Ubuntu is part of an African vision of the cosmos that is focused on relationship and interconnectedness. Its implications transcend human conduct. Its underlying cosmological assumptions mean that in order to be ethical, individuals must see themselves as connected and interconnected to the rest – including the natural environment, the present, the past, and the future.[23]

Development practices in Africa have been dominated primarily by foreign imperatives to the detriment of our own African values. Only the integration of the values of Ubuntu in the affairs of the world can give us our

---

23. Couture, "Human Dignity," 18.

African identity back. The Bible draws attention to the refugee phenomenon from the perspective of Ubuntu as it speaks repeatedly about strangers while emphasizing that the laws of host countries are supposed to be the same for both the locals and the foreigners since they are all members of the human community. In other words, beyond the differences that divide the human race there is love and unity, and beyond the differences between the self and the other there is social cohesion and solidarity. From this perspective, the Ubuntu way of life transcends our human selves and exists for the dignity of the entire human race. Ubuntu is a complimentary expression of Christian values; it is how God intended humanity to live – in a *shalom* community set-up, which is a community of peace and justice characterized by *koinonia*, *marturia*, and *diakonia*.

Ubuntu and koinonia

In its broader context, the Greek word *koinonia* means "fellowship"; but it can also mean community, association, or participation. The *Interpretive Lexicon of New Testament Greek* states that the word cannot be defined accurately in English due to the depth and richness of its meanings.[24] However *koinonia* is a rich approach for community building as it describes well the relationship that the early believers had with one another and the kind of community they lived in. Through *koinonia* Christian believers fellowship with one another in love and unity, which reflects the fellowship we have with God. Kuzuli Kossé states that unity in the African context may be defined as "the condition in which something forms as an organic whole" because each individual member must be themselves "in the midst of such unity."[25] Even if several aspects are involved, "the whole is illustrated by internal coherence which also applies to the unity of believers to the extent that they share a common foundation of faith and practice."[26]

Koinonia therefore describes the idea of togetherness through intimate participation, which was often used to describe the ideal state of communion, prayer, and service in the early Christian church. Thus, there is *koinonia* when there is an exchange of encouragement and acts or instances of sharing. The

---

24. G. K. Beale, D. J. Brendsel, and W. A. Ross, *An Interpretive Lexicon of New Testament Greek* (New York: Zondervan, 2014), 23.

25. Kuzuli Kossé, "Unity of Believers," in *Africa Bible Commentary*, ed. T. Adeyemo (Nairobi: WordAlive, 2006), 1288.

26. Kossé, "Unity of Believers," 1288.

Lukan literature chronicles the "koinonic" lifestyle of the early believers describing how they "devoted themselves to the apostles' teaching and to fellowship" (Acts 2:42). This is one of the scriptural points of reference for *koinonia* as Ubuntu. The context of Acts 2:42 explains *koinonia* as an example of Christian believers living as a community in fellowship with one another and with God. Thus *koinonia*, like Ubuntu, typifies generosity, hospitality, humanity, and love for the other. Langmead, writing from the perspective of the migration and mission, concludes that *koinonia* is best applied within the context of hospitality when he says, "The metaphor for mission that most readily suggests itself in response to the plight of those seeking asylum is that of hospitality."[27] This means that it is through *koinonia* that unity in diversity is built up within the community of faith because the koinonic virtues of hospitality and generosity are concerned with care and the willingness to help the other. As the early believers "had all things in common," they had a "policy" of sharing their resources – making sure that the needy among them were being taken care of (Acts 2:44–45).

Indeed, *koinonia* is an ethical imperative because it suggests hospitality. Dietrich Bonhoeffer gives theological depth to the reflection on our responsibility towards our fellow brothers and sisters.[28] According to him, hospitality attests to what he calls "the birth of *homo ethicus*" which corrects "the logic of *homo oeconomicus*."[29] The latter is a rational egoist who decides to enter into an intersubjective relationship only when he or she can derive personal benefit from it. Conversely for *homo ethicus*, "the criterion of the relationship is gratuity and not utility or utilitarianism."[30] Indeed, it is on the basis of sincere hospitality that otherness will no longer be a sham, and the other will cease to be an intruder in the community. Therefore, true *koinonia* seeks unity of purpose and hospitality in our diversity of relationships.

Koinonia implies unity. Since Ubuntu expresses the truth that no one is an island and that people need each other, the concept matches what *koinonia* entails. However, it is important to note that community according to the Bible goes much further than sharing common goals, even if it involves that. The biblical community is first of all the sharing of common life in Christ. When

---

27. R. Langmead, "Refugees as Guests and Hosts: Towards a Theology of Mission amongst Refugees and Asylum Seekers," *International Association for Mission Studies* (15–20 August 2012): 5.

28. Dietrich Bonhoeffer, *Sanctorum Communio: A Dogmatic Research on the Sociology of the Church* (London: Collins, 1963), 101–102.

29. Bonhoeffer, *Sanctorum Communio*, 93.

30. Bonhoeffer, 99.

we grasp this truth, we are able to understand true community as God intends. While as the church we should cherish the unique depth of *koinonia*, we should also seek to live at peace with everyone (Rom 12:18). From a *koinonia* perspective, it is our responsibility as the church to promote the principle of interdependence without giving up the uniqueness of *koinonia*. Common ground can be sought to enable us live together in peace, and this common ground can be propagated as a cornerstone for our African nations.

Petrine literature emphasizes the virtue of hospitality by encouraging us to sincerely love one another and to open our homes happily and without grumbling to serve others (1 Pet 4:8–10). As Africans we are social beings who generally recognize and respect those who are culturally different.[31] The education received at home gives us the ability to integrate the stranger who comes to us. Hence hospitality is a pillar of our meeting with the other. Carroll affirms that "hospitality to the stranger is a virtue."[32] Christian believers are therefore expected to live in *koinonia* with everyone by being hospitable and sharing food with others including the less fortunate in society. It should be noted that hospitality to refugees requires the transformation of the self, and that this transformation is related to repentance and conversion.[33] The letter of Hebrews reminds believers to always welcome strangers because by so doing, people of old had welcomed angelic beings unknowingly (Heb 13:2). This passage eliminates the vice of stereotyping and clearly shows that not all strangers are criminals or come with bad intentions, but that some of them are actually angels. Langmead asserts, "the simple act of hospitality in the home is based on creating a safe and comfortable space for guests."[34]

Last, apostle Paul exhorts koinonic living and beatitudinal purposes when he urges believers to practice hospitality by sharing what they have with the needy among them, living in harmony with one another, and associating even with those who are at the lowest position in the societal hierarchy (Rom 12:13–16). Paul's exhortation points to the fact that the Israelites were hospitable, and their welcoming attitude towards refugees was part of their ethical life.[35] In fact, Carroll argues that living a *koinonia* life "was part of the ethos of what it

---

31. Mpetsheni, "Ubuntu – A Soteriological Ethic," 66.

32. Carroll, *Christians at the Border*, 93.

33. P. R. Keifert, *Welcoming the Stranger: A Public Theology of Worship and Evangelism* (Minneapolis: Fortress, 1992), 59.

34. Langmead, "Refugees as Guests and Hosts," 6.

35. Carroll, *Christians at the Border*, 71.

meant to be the people of God."[36] The attitudes and actions of Abraham toward the three visitors he received is definitely an Ubuntu practice because it shows the extent of hospitality in its broadest sense (Gen 18:1–8). This story is a call for social cohesion and communal living – a call for *koinonia* as Ubuntu in our communities.

All of these biblical passages emphasize the command of Jesus to love one another (John 13:34–35). As *koinonia* is God's mandate for Christian living, so is Ubuntu. As Christian believers, we are called to live communally, to love others, and to associate with them. Carroll rightly sums up this call by pointing out that the engagements and attitudes of Jesus go beyond cultural identity and "help define what it means to be his follower."[37] Like Ubuntu, *koinonia* is communal life which reflects unity in diversity and where the image of the self is intertwined with that of the other. Ubuntu in a community of faith is a koinonic practice because it promotes within believers a kind of unity nurtured and made possible by the work of the Holy Spirit. After all, it is the Holy Spirit who "transforms believers into brothers and sisters in Christ," and it is the same Holy Spirit who transforms believers "into brothers and sisters to each other," as Kuzuli Kossé further adds.[38] A Christian is someone who follows Christ and believes that the Bible is the living word of God. The Bible guides Christian believers in all aspects of life and all matters of faith since it contains values that are relevant today. These values exemplify the way a Christian should live. As Christians we draw from the Bible a pattern for how we should live in context. Not living according to these values violates God's mandate for Ubuntu as God's design for communal living in line with the principles of *koinonia*.

Ubuntu and marturia

The nature of Christian living is *marturia*, which is a Greek word meaning witnessing. It is through *marturia* that we proclaim the gospel in both words and deeds. *Marturia* as an act of church missions is performed through the proclamation of the gospel by words (i.e. *kerygma*), deeds or service (i.e. *diakonia*), and worship or fellowship (i.e. *koinonia*). Therefore, these missional dimensions of the church are not just interrelated but carried out within the context of *marturia*. That is, they give power to the nature and function of our

---

36. Carroll, 98.
37. Carroll, 125.
38. Kossé, "Unity of Believers," 1288.

witness as the church. The notion of the church as a *marturia* is ever present in the Johannine literature as the apostle John provides pointers on how to testify in public as a true witness of Christ. John's texts are an indication that *marturia* is a public declaration about something that took place – and this public declaration can be done using words or through social actions. So as *marturia* refers to testifying or being a witness, this witnessing can be done by putting the message of the gospel into action. Thus social actions are acts of *marturia* because they reinforce the idea of being a witness in our way of life and acts of goodwill. Therefore, the church as a witnessing community is called to declare publicly the truth of Christ's death and resurrection to the world. It is in this context of being a witness that we exist as the church, and it is in this same context that we are considered true bearers of the message of the cross.

The idea of us being witnesses to the message of the cross in words and deeds is both transformational and missional, and *marturia* entails our truest purpose as witnesses. A witness is someone with a personal experience or who has knowledge of things to testify about. It is in this regard that the practice of Ubuntu is biblical since it actuates the biblical principles of *marturia*. When Jesus said "you will be my witnesses" (Acts 1:8), he seemed to have the idea of a court of law in mind. In a court of law, one finds all sorts of people, and most of them have an important role to play when someone is on trial. There is a presiding judge and a panel of judges who make up the jury. There are lawyers or advocates to defend the person who is on trial and try to get the person acquitted of the charges against them. There are prosecuting attorneys who want to prove that the person on trial is guilty of the charges brought against them so that they can face the full might of the law. Often the accuser who brought all the condemnatory charges against the person on trial is present. There are witnesses (*marturia*) who are brought in to testify of what they know or have seen about this whole scenario. Finally, there is an audience. These are just viewers or spectators whose role in relation to the trial is completely passive. They cannot interfere in any way with the court process.

It is in full knowledge of such a background that Jesus emphasizes that as the church we are his witnesses, because our role as Christian believers in this "court of law," which is the world, is to testify – not to be judges or prosecutors, not to be advocates or spectators. With the help of the defending advocate, true witnessing in a court of law can save the life of a person on trial, which is why Jesus calls the Holy Spirit our "Advocate." The imagery of a court of law helps us to understand our role in God's larger plan of salvation. This law court simile also reinforces the idea of *marturia* in the life of a Christian believer in relation to the practice of Ubuntu and our role as the church to those whose hope is in short supply. It is by virtue of the early church being a *marturia* that Jews were united with the Greeks and the free with the slaves. *Marturia* is a uniting force and essential for transformational development. It is also through *marturia* that we make known the inherent worth and truest value of the human race. Thus we Christian believers cannot detach ourselves from Ubuntu as God's design for communal living since the practice of Ubuntu amplifies the principles of *marturia* by showing beatitudinal care for the other.

The contemporary African believes lived experiences more than theories or doctrinal facts. Thus the first form of the Christian mission is to make our Christian life a testimony. Christ, whose mission we continue, is the witness par excellence (Rev 1:5; 3:14) and therefore our model of Christian witness. The Holy Spirit accompanies us on our journey and associates us with the witness he gives for Christ (John 15:26–27). So the first form of *marturia* is the very life of the believer and the actions of the ecclesial community. The believer who, despite all the limitations and human imperfections, lives in the light of the word of God by following the example of Christ is a witness of the cross. All of us as we strive to follow the divine Master can and must bear witness. This is one of the ways to show love and give hope to those in need such as refugees.

Ubuntu and diakonia

A *diakonia* was originally an establishment built near a church building for the care of the poor and the distribution of church charity to the needy. In contemporary theology, the Greek term *diakonia* means serving those in need, which is a call to serve the poor and the oppressed, to care for the elderly and socially disadvantaged, to support migrants and ensure their integration, etc. So *diakonia* is the implementation of the gospel of Jesus through social commitments to those in need. This definition reminds us that since the beginning of the church, concern for those who are weighed down by misfortune or injustice has held an essential place among believers. In the Acts of the Apostles, *diakonia* takes the rather radical turn of a pooling of goods. The account states that "There was not a needy person among them, for as many as owned lands or houses sold them and brought the proceeds of what was sold. They laid it at the apostles' feet, and it was distributed to each as any had need" (Acts 4:34–35). This concern for solidarity directly echoes the concern of Jesus for the poor and the oppressed and explains why elsewhere Luke makes it the central axis of the mission of Jesus (Luke 4:16–22).

So the practice of *diakonia* should give us as the church the opportunity to revisit the theological foundations of our social commitments and give them a spiritual dimension. Revisiting our theological foundations for social commitments is vital because the diaconal action of Jesus was a commitment to the liberation of the poor, of those who are disenfranchised and marginalized, and for justice so that we can all participate in God's salvific plan in the world. *Diakonia* is therefore the ministry of service through which Christian believers get involved in the social affairs of the various communities to bring about active change by putting the gospel of Christ into practice. It is through this ministry that the gospel is proclaimed in deeds and the manifold wisdom of God made known to those in need. Thus the ministry of *diakonia* is the reality of the presence of Christ in us, which is a prerogative for transformational community development. Our impact on people in need is conditioned by the needs arising from the communities. In this regard, the practice of *diakonia* becomes a demonstration of Ubuntu. Thus within our function as the church is the imperative to serve others with love and compassion as Ubuntu entails.

The Bible leads us to being diaconal. Our involvement in *diakonia* requires that the image of God be given preferential treatment over human characteristics. This means diaconal activities are about bringing the presence of the compassionate Jesus and loving God to suffering humanity. In other words, *diakonia* is a service of faith, hope, and love to those who are hurting and broken hearted because central to the biblical teaching lies the truth that human beings were created to be of service to God, to one another, and to the rest of the creation. For this reason, we are to display the centrality of Christ to others through *diakonia*, which is one of the ways of living according to the principles of Ubuntu. The life, words, and deeds of Jesus were an expression of *diakonia* in its broadest sense. One of the diaconal accounts of Jesus is the washing of his disciples' feet as recorded in John 13:1–17. Jesus, the diaconal King, served people of all backgrounds including the poor, the marginalized, and the outcast; and he served all with compassion and love. In other words, Jesus puts no limits on his compassionate love because true love is unlimited and all inclusive.

In the early church, attention to the most vulnerable represented a nonnegotiable component of the Christian life because "the Son of Man did not come to be served but to serve" (Mark 10:45). It makes sense, therefore, that *diakonia* is one of the main terms used to define the *missio ecclesiae* or the mission of the church as opposed to the *missio Dei*, which is the mission of God. In the New Testament, *diakonia* does not only imply charitable commitments or acts of solidarity. Rather, the term also suggests the whole relational dimension of the Christian condition, and it is the whole ecclesial life, *ad intra* and *ad extra*, that is called to become diaconal. *Ecclesia ad intra* and *ecclesia ad extra* are two Latin terms used to indicate contrasting directions of the church, the first relating to the inner workings of the church, and the second relating to the church's connection with the outside world.[39] Thus *diakonia* concerns both the internal and external functioning of the church.

Another aspect of *diakonia* which is prominently found in the Ubuntu way of life is humility. The virtue of humility is an essential attribute for the genuineness of *diakonia*. Because Jesus Christ is a humble servant, the character of Christian believers involved in diaconal activities should be of humble service. Therefore, *diakonia* is servanthood and hospitality practiced in humility to the hungry, the refugee, the homeless, the sick, and all those in hopeless situations. This is the wisdom of God expressed in love, which is essential for transformational community development. Thus *diakonia* is the guiding principle of all matters of faith with regard to the transformation of socioeconomic structures. The notion of *diakonia* calls for church action and practical engagement to transform the lives of the less fortunate such as refugees. *Diakonia* is inseparably attached to the essence of the church and is therefore a mark of true discipleship. *Diakonia* epitomizes the redemptive power of Christ because we become agents of holistic transformation in communities when we respond to people's needs through diaconal activities. So *diakonia* is the ultimate way to further the gospel of Christ through deeds in response to people's needs. This gospel action often takes the form of the charitable services we render in society, but it goes beyond to as far as changing the unjust structures established by human systems.

Diakonia reminds us that the good news is relational and that social actions are both ethical and theological. They are ethical in the sense that those who are suffering are given an opportunity to rediscover themselves according to the purpose of God. They are theological because the poor, the sick, and the destitute will have an encounter with the Source of true life. *Diakonia* therefore allows us to renew our commitments to social actions – whether they take place in an ecclesial setting or not – and view them as a spiritual encounter with those in need. *Diakonia* is also a reminder that we as the Christian community should not forget those who are in distress or sickness, or are threatened by all kinds of injustices. We must always be sensitive to their presence and their distress in order to give them a prominent place in our prayers and our actions.

---

39. John Daniel Dadosky, "Ecclesia De Trinitate: Ecclesial Foundations from Above," *New Blackfriars* 94, no. 1049 (2013), https://lonerganresource.com/pdf/contributors/LC2001-07_Dadosky-Ecclesia_De_Trinitate.pdf, 68.

Ubuntu is therefore grounded in the Scriptures as it is related in practice with the biblical concepts of *koinonia, marturia,* and *diakonia*. Ubuntu is God's original and ideal plan for living in community as one human family. It is God's master plan through which we as Christian believers live in service to God and one another through words and deeds. In other words, Ubuntu as beatitudinal care and God's design for communal living encourages solidarity, hospitality, love, and caring for one another. It is a perfect example of unity in diversity, which is better understood when put into practice, and God's call for spiritual renewal.

Thus Ubuntu helps to Africanize Christianity rather than Christianize Africa. In other words, it serves as a lens through which we theologize, practice, and appropriate Christianity for ourselves in our own local contexts. This approach contrasts with the Western method of European missionaries who came to evangelize Africa and considered anything of African value, including artefacts, religious rites, objects of worship, and modes of worship, to be a sin.[40] They did so because their aim was to Christianize Africa at the expense of everything that belonged to Africa rather than Africanize Christianity. Thus to practice the spirituality of Ubuntu is to undertake a journey towards self-discovery. For example, hospitality has been an evangelistic method used centripetally by Africans for centuries which is one of the main characteristics of the Ubuntu spirituality. This example tells us that the Babembe people have walked and worked with God for centuries. The Babembe, like all Africans, are a people of faith. Faith is what sustains us. Faith is part of our Ubuntu in the ordinary and everyday life. It is in the context of faith that we are reassured of the presence of a God who dwells among us, a God who walks and suffers with us. It is interesting to note that the Babembe people never accuse *Abeca-Pùngù* of wrongdoing or being the author of our suffering. Theodicy is therefore not part of the philosophy of our religion as a people. We believe that evil does not just happen like that, of course, as every effect has a natural cause, and this cause is never *Abeca-Pùngù* but rather evil forces are beyond human comprehension. From this example of Babembe, we will therefore deduce that we Africans walked with God a long time ago and were living in faith. Our cosmological notion links our past, our present, and our future.

To conclude this chapter on Ubuntu, I would like to quote this African proverb which illustrates the cultural depth of traditional African thought on living together: "In the forest, when the branches of trees quarrel, their roots

---

40. Couture, "Human Dignity," 18.

kiss."[41] The branches represent the diversity of the tree because they differ in their singularities and uniqueness. The roots that kiss are the intangible, the deep values that unite – our Ubuntu. The challenge for the vitality of the whole societal tree is therefore not to cut down, eliminate, or hide the diversity of our trees but to live together so that as our deep-rooted values kiss, they can in turn nourish the quarrelling branches. The truth of this African wisdom is imperative if we are to ensure unity in diversity within our African communities. Besides even if we cut this tree, it will continue to grow because according to Job 14:7–9, a tree has hope. When it is cut down, it grows back at the smell of water and still produces tender shoots and branches like a seedling. So a refugee is like a tree that has been cut; but there is hope for the refugee. We the church must bring refugees the water of life to restore their situation holistically, and each refugee will be like a newly planted tree, producing tender shoots and branches. This passage in Job is essential for understanding the importance of hope in holistic transformation. The next chapter will go further and discuss the role of hope as a tool for transformational development when put into action.

Discussion Questions

1. How is Ubuntu beatitudinal care? Why is Ubuntu said to be God's design for human living?
2. What are the similarities between the theological concepts of *koinonia*, *marturia*, and *diakonia* in relation to Ubuntu?
3. Read Nehemiah 1:1–11. Nehemiah was a refugee. Some of his fellow Jews returned to Judah after their oppressors, the Babylonians, were overthrown by the Persians. But many Jews – including Nehemiah – felt settled and therefore stayed in Babylon.
    - What does this passage tell us about the relationship between Ubuntu and integration in a country of asylum?
    - How does the passage challenge us in our relationship with the refugees living among us and in our response to their needs?
4. Refugees are accused of many things, including crimes, although often there is no substantial evidence to support these claims.

---

41. Mpetsheni, "Ubuntu – A Soteriological Ethic," 101.

- How would you feel if you were called a criminal for a crime you did not commit?
- What Ubuntu principles can we apply to change such a narrative about refugees?

5. How can we use Ubuntu when responding to the needs of refugees in our community?

5

Transformational Community Development as Hope in Action

When I arrived in South Africa, life was not easy, and all hopes seemed to evaporate. While I was still in Tanzania, my dad had suggested that I go to study at the University of Lubumbashi in the DRC, and I managed to convince him that studying in South Africa was a better option. When all prospects for furthering my studies seemed to fade, he started calling me back so I could go to Lubumbashi if things were not working for me in South Africa. At that time, I was working as a security guard, and I had already spent almost five years in South Africa with no prospect to study in the near future. For some reasons, I kept hope alive knowing that one day God would open academic doors for me. One day in April 2005, a certain pastor called John from Port Elizabeth, a South African city roughly one thousand kilometres from Durban in the Eastern Cape province, contacted another pastor in Durban called Paul saying that he was looking for me. Pastor Paul could not locate me instantly since he did not have my number. He managed to get the number of my cousin Jérémie who was my roommate at the time. Early in the morning as soon as I arrived home from my night shift job, my cousin told me that Pastor Paul had called and left the number of a person I should urgently call.

I took the number that Pastor Paul left, went to the nearest calling booth, and called. On the other side of the call, Pastor John answered. He was very happy to finally talk to me. He told me he had been looking for me for a very long time, and he was glad we could connect. Honestly, I had no idea who he was. He said he had seen me leading praise and worship in the church where Pastor Paul was the minister, and I left a strong impression on him through my ministration. I still did not recall who he was as many visitors come and go, including pastors, and one cannot remember all of them. Anyway, he then said that he had started a church in the Eastern Cape, and he would like me to go there and assist him in building the worship team. After I prayed about it, God showed me to go. I then resigned from the security job I had and left for Port Elizabeth, a land unknown to me, to assist a person unknown to me.

I took this step of faith because I had hope that God had a better plan for me – and all I had to do was to leave Durban. This I did despite being discouraged by family members and friends. Pastor John bought me a bus ticket, and I travelled to Port Elizabeth. As soon as I arrived, I started ministering in Emmanuel Christian Church (ECC) alongside Pastor John. It was during my ministry at ECC that I received my calling for theological training, so I can train African pastors. Had I not put my hope into action by taking that step of faith, I would not have been where I am today in terms of education and Christian ministry.

I left Durban and moved to an unknown location to serve with an unknown person. It was hope in action against all hope. Many refugees use hope as a coping mechanism in a variety of situations. The decision to leave home is never easy. Sometimes it is not even a decision at all. A common consequence of forced migration is that refugees lose contact with their loved ones. This experience explains why refugees have the ability to actuate a ray of hope in order to meet their own needs. Hope becomes their major asset for holistic transformation, while putting hope into action becomes for them a process leading to transformational development. So there is growing interest in the well-being of refugees, particularly the strategies and coping mechanisms they employ in their quest for improved livelihoods. This chapter addresses this matter by providing evidence that refugees put their hope into action as a strategy for holistic transformation and as a coping mechanism vis-à-vis various challenges they face.

Development as an Expression of *Missio Ecclesiae*

If our mission is to implement God's plan in the world, we inevitably need a contextual methodology because we are utterly incompetent and unable to fulfil the *missio Dei* in its entirety. However, our inability to execute the full mission of God does not exclude us from participating in it. Our role in the *missio Dei* is to do what God has told us to do. In other words, our part as the church is the *missio ecclesiae*, which is the mission of the church. We need the *missio ecclesiae* if we are to participate in the *missio Dei*. This theological truth explains why as the church we often express ourselves through interventional social actions to ensure the transformational development of the communities in which we live and even beyond.

We should remember that the church is a gathered people, or as Hughes and Bennett put it, "a special people assembled by God" for devotion to him in a very special way.[1] As such, the church "must not be identified with any particular culture, social or political system, or human ideology" because we are a community of a faithful people united in Christ alone.[2] That is to say, the church is neither a place to go on Sunday for worship, nor a building where people come in to observe some religious rituals. Instead, the church is a community of people sent out by God to live for him under his kingly rule. The church is in essence the salt of the earth meant to influence, and the light of the world meant to shine. It is within this missional nature of the church that transformational development is limited in an attempt to rebuild hope in the lives of people.

The role of the church is unique since the church is established at the centre of local communities yet has global relevance. In other words, as the church we are locally based yet far reaching. This global reach provides us with the ability to play an influential role in advocacy, public awareness, and building partnerships with other role-players. Our presence as the church in communities, even in the farthest places of a country, puts us in the position of taking actions that benefit the local community the soonest in cases of emergency, such as the refugee phenomenon. A local church is often among the first to respond to the needs of affected people when a humanitarian crisis arises, although in some instances, we become "the sleeping giant" as the church when we do not live up to our full potential.

For us to fully realize our potential, we need to implement a praxical approach that merges theory and practice. Anne Morisy refers to such a praxis as a way of "linking action and reflection."[3] However as David Bosch warns, it is only when we have read the Scriptures that we are able to develop a theology of church mission.[4] It is for this reason that the church is said to be "a company of strangers" engaged in evangelism "defined by its centre than by some criteria of who is in and who is out; who is a part of the family and who is

---

1. D. Hughes and M. Bennett, *God of the Poor: A Biblical Vision of God's Present Rule* (Carlisle: OM Publishing, 1998), 73.

2. *The Lausanne Covenant*, Section 6: "The Church and Evangelism," The Lausanne Movement (1974), https://www.lausanne.org/content/covenant/lausanne-covenant#cov.

3. A. Morisy, *Beyond the Good Samaritan: Community Ministry and Mission* (London: Continuum, 1997), 45.

4. Bosch, *Transforming Mission*, 15.

not."[5] Thus as the church we need to do mission even to refugees because the refugee phenomenon characterizes and discloses the world's inequalities and conflicts and reveals a world distinct from the one in which people realize that "If one member suffers, all suffer together with it; if one member is honored, all rejoice together with it" (1 Cor 12:26). Love and support are to be afforded to all people including refugees with respect and dignity proper to the *imago Dei*.

The Scriptures provide an illustration. We read in 2 Chronicles 2:17–18 that King Solomon took a national census of all refugees residing in the land of Israel and gave them jobs to enable them to survive, which was an act of rebuilding their hope. According to the chronicler, it is obvious that King Solomon counted all of the foreigners in his territory in order to monitor their existence, manage their stay in the country, and allocate work to them. Thus, "Seventy thousand of them he assigned as laborers, eighty thousand as stonecutters in the hill country, and three thousand six hundred as overseers to make the people work" (2 Chron 2:18). Indeed, Solomon realized that resident foreigners are an important addition to the human resources that the host country needs, and he needed to create space for them to put their hope into action. Solomon even assigned them supervisory responsibilities to manage Israel's public works projects. This account is a good example for us to be involved in transformational development activities in order to promote integral mission, which makes us a catalyst for change and socioeconomic growth. As refugees continue to be on our church thresholds, we are expected to reach out to them with love and compassion. Integral mission is not necessarily about going miles away for evangelistic purposes; it is also about being what God intended us to be – a people gathered by God, for God, and under his kingly rule. The strategies and approaches of transformational development affirm the dignity and the value of people as *imago Dei*. Thus, transformational development as hope in action is redemptive and reconciliatory. Indeed, the interventions we use for transformation purposes must be appropriate and sustainable.

We exercise our God-given gifts within the community of faith and glorify God by being salt and light, which means influencing the society so that it becomes inclined toward a structure that is more just, compassionate, and godly. As God's people, we are to serve beyond the boundaries of our confined buildings by strengthening the knowledge and skills of those who are in positions of powerlessness. We are to help institutions alter their structures

---

5. Keifert, *Welcoming the Stranger*, 91.

in order to meet the expectations of those at the grassroots sustainably. The question of refugees is often perceived negatively and is commented on in different ways from different perspectives. Hordes of accusations weigh heavily on refugees when they are blamed for environmental degradation including spoiling the ozone layer and causing air pollution. They are also judged as being a heavy burden on the hosting government. Throughout the Bible are images of displaced people and a mobile God which illustrate the ethical imperatives of hospitality toward those seeking a home for protection.

Abraham left his home in the Ur of the Chaldeans and migrated to Haran (Gen 11:31), then left Haran and migrated to the land of Canaan (12:5). He again left this Canaanite land to migrate temporarily to Egypt (12:10). After being expelled from Egypt, Abraham returned again to Canaan (12:19–20). Later on, he migrated to the Negev (13:1), then left the Negev to settle somewhere "between Bethel and Ai" (13:3). Later in his life, Abraham went to live between Kadesh and Shur at a place called Gerar (20:1). Similarly, Moses fled Egypt and found refuge in Midian (Exod 2:15). He returned to Egypt (Exod 4:20) and migrated into the desert on the way to the promised land with the people of Israel (14). Unlike Abraham, Moses did not enjoy the promised land, but only saw it from afar (Deut 34:1–4). Both Abraham and Moses died as migrants (Gen 25:8; Deut 34:5; Heb 11:8–13). These Old Testament accounts of the migrations of the patriarchs of the faith, Abraham and Moses, among many other accounts not mentioned here make migration a space of faith in God.

Similarly, forced by an imperial foreign ruler, Joseph and Mary had to leave Nazareth for Bethlehem (Luke 2:1–7). For fear of persecution, Joseph and Mary fled again, this time with baby Jesus, to Egypt – becoming refugees (Matt 2:13–15) – until they were able to return home (Matt 2:19–23). Jesus later spent his adult life as an itinerant preacher with no fixed abode (Luke 9:58). The account of Jesus in the New Testament – including many other accounts of his disciples not mentioned here – is characterized by episodes of displacements, sometimes forced, hence his ability and willingness to identify with migrants in their situation.

This biblical content suggests that transformational development as an expression of church mission is faith-grounded and people-centred. This twofold nature of transformational development as an expression of church mission can never be fragmented. Thus we cannot engage in transformational development practices as faith-based interventions without those practices being people-centred.

Missio ecclesiae as faith-grounded development

The *missio ecclesiae* integrates acts of social intervention with evangelization. As the church, we are called to participate in the redemptive mission of God – *missio Dei* – in order to continue the restorative mission of Christ – *missio Christi* – as stated in Luke 4:18–19, which is possible as we join the mission of the Holy Spirit – *missio Spiritus* – and surrender our lives to his guidance and power. In other words, Christ entrusts the Holy Spirit with the *missio Christi*, and the Holy Spirit continues the *missio Christi* in the context of the cross through us, the church. So beyond the role of the Holy Spirit in creation, redemptive history, and eschatological fulfilment, the mission of the Holy Spirit in the world – *missio Spiritus* – is to continue the mission of Christ through us, the church. Because the continuation of the mission of Christ is primarily the mission of the Holy Spirit, our *missio ecclesiae* is the work of the Holy Spirit through us. The presence of the Father in mission – through *missio Dei* – of the Son – through the *missio Christi* – and of the Holy Spirit – through the *missio Spiritus* – makes the *missio ecclesiae* a Trinitarian initiative grounded in the Christian faith.

So the Holy Spirit acts through the church, and by this action the good news penetrates human consciences and hearts. Thus the New Testament attests to a pluralism in the fundamental unity of the mission of God, *missio Dei*, which reflects different experiences and situations in the first Christian communities communicated by the Holy Spirit himself. The *missio ecclesiae* is in this regard a cooperation with the promise of Christ: "And remember, I am with you always, to the end of the age" (Matt 28:20). This premise explains why the mission of the church is not based on human capacities, but on the power of the Risen One and the guidance of the Holy Spirit. So the *missio ecclesiae* is the work of Jesus Christ by the Holy Spirit through the church. After the resurrection and ascension of Jesus, the coming of the Holy Spirit turned Jesus's disciples into witnesses, which prompted them to pass on to others their experience of Jesus and the hope that animated them (Acts 1:8; 2:1–40). The Holy Spirit therefore gives us the capacity to bear witness of Jesus with assurance.

In Acts 13:46–48, the Holy Spirit sends Paul and Barnabas off to the gentiles, which raises questions on how should converted pagans live out their faith in Jesus. At the Jerusalem Council, the decision was made that it is not necessary for a pagan to submit to Jewish law to become Christian (Acts 15:4–20). From this moment on, the church opened its doors and became the house in which all can enter and feel at ease, preserving their culture and traditions, provided they are not in opposition to the gospel of Christ. So under the impulse of the Holy Spirit, the Christian faith deliberately opened up to nations, and the witness of Christ extended to all. It is the Holy Spirit who pushes us to always go beyond, not only geographically but also beyond ethnic and religious barriers, to accomplish the *missio Christi*. The mission of the church, which first concerned Israel and thereafter the nations, developed at different levels. It started as a mission of the twelve disciples to proclaim the good news as one body. Then the community of believers by their way of living and doing bore witness to the Lord and converted pagans (Acts 2:43–47). Thus the mission of the church is our communal duty and a responsibility of the local church.

Transformational development as an expression of church mission is both a public and Bible-grounded exertion that addresses "the manifold ways in which human dignity is threatened in contemporary culture and society."[6] The "core task" of transformational development is missional. Therefore, practical theology should not be viewed only within the pulpit and pew context since its relevance goes beyond the walls of church buildings. The broader understanding of transformational development is as an applied science. As such, we are led to explore the realities of our societies and determine better alternatives for holistic community transformation. Since as the church we are a divinely instituted body, we cannot be silent before social problems. To bring about transformative change, we have to be proactive rather than just reactive to the ills of society because the refugee phenomenon often grows within socioreligious tensions, *inter alia*, and is mostly grounded in the dynamics of violence and poor leadership of the elite. As the church we play an important role in inspiring biblical values in survivors of terrible deeds, which is the role we ought to play.

Missio ecclesiae as people-centred development

There is no development without people. People are at the centre of all development activities that we carry out as the church. So development becomes an expression of the *missio ecclesiae* when it promotes the social well-being of everyone and considers the material and spiritual growth of people. The mission of the church is people-centred development when we use development approaches that focus on improving self-reliance, social justice, and participatory decision-making. Economic growth in terms of gross

---

6. R. K. Soulen and L. Woodhead, *God and Human Dignity* (Grand Rapids: Eerdmans, 2006), 1.

domestic product (GDP) does not intrinsically contribute to transformational development, which is why we are to call for changes in our sociopolitical and environmental practices. As the church, we face a paradox because the secular world has embraced economic growth as the primary indicator of human progress. Yet as economic production and consumption increase, the number of people forced to live in dehumanizing conditions of deprivation increases, and the quality of life for all but the richest decreases.

Hope for the human future therefore does not rest on the institutions of power, but on the millions of individuals around the world who are awakening to the reality of our collective crisis. Acting out of love, compassion, and a deep sense of responsibility to people and the rest of creation, we must see the human future as a matter of choice, not of destiny, for the purposes of seeking a world that works for all people. Thus the situation, the journey, the faith, and the lives of refugees and their communities set in motion a theology of transformational development which is a scientific appreciation of the faith and hope of refugees. The refugee phenomenon gives us the image of a people on the move. By the ease of transport and fluidity of communications, their movement characterizes the contemporary era. Images of forced migrants crammed into small boats or walking through the streets in large numbers continue to characterize the world and in particular Africa. All of these images have a human face and are proof that the church's development and social actions should be people-centred. Migratory movements are accompanied by hopes and fears and generate either a discourse of exclusion and fear or inclusion and opportunity.

As an expression of *missio ecclesiae*, development becomes people-centred when we integrate practical and spiritual approaches for holistic transformation. Refugees are to experience new and hospitable relationships because hospitality encourages them to contribute to the welfare of their host countries with their skills and their witness of faith when they put their hopes into practice. However, while some refugees integrate easily in the host communities, others live in extremely dire conditions. Sometimes they are even exploited or deprived of their basic human rights. As a result, they engage in behaviours that are detrimental to the society in which they live. In our missional function, we need to bring refugees to the realization that for them to be holistically transformed, they should attend to the values offered by the society in which they live for the purpose of social cohesion without doing away with their own identities.

The rapid and profound transformation that characterizes the world today, especially Africa, exerts a strong influence on the framework of church mission. We are called as the church to side with refugees and work for their transformational development. So it is also the mission of the church in the world to identify the major challenges that people find themselves facing today. If the threat to our future is clearly identified, we will not have an attitude of denial toward some of the pressing issues that confront us. As the church we have a constant duty to scrutinize the signs of the times and to interpret them in the light of the gospel.

Since the migration of Abraham, or even of Cain, the basic storyline of the Bible is about people who leave; who migrate to search for bread, land, and protection; and who wander and come back. In other words, it is a story of perpetual wayfarers – a story of the constant geographical movements of people, families, and nations, such as the wanderings undertaken by Abraham and by Joseph and his brothers. The Bible is also a story of symbolic migration which describes life as a journey, a pilgrimage, a path as described for example by Psalm 1:1. So transformational development is an expression of church mission because within the context of migration, it is based on the biblical narrative which from the beginning presents us with a God on the move, a God who accepts to live in a tent so he can share with his people the experience of being on the move toward the realization of his own promises. Thus our God is a moving God, a wayfaring God, and for that reason the mission of the church is people-centred so as to meet the needs of refugee migrants.

Missio ecclesiae as the basis for human flourishing

With the true shepherd, the sheep have life as well as food, freedom, and security. In the context of the ancient Near East, the shepherd gave life to the sheep in the fold. Jesus paints the picture of John 10 in the context of Ezekiel 34, where the Lord castigates the religious leaders of Israel for being egocentric and greedy shepherds who used the flock for their own comfort and gain, but did not care about the suffering of their flock. The Lord pronounces judgment on these false shepherds and promises to provide the flock with someone who will feed them and be their shepherd (cf. Ezek 34:23). This prophecy was fulfilled by the Lord Jesus Christ, who gives life to the sheep in abundance by being the true and good shepherd of the sheep (John 10:10–11).

In John 10:10, Jesus says he came so that we may have life in its fullness, which means one of his missions on earth was for us to have life fully. In other words, Jesus came so that we could have a flourishing and meaningful life in him. The Greek term translated "more abundantly" (NKJV) or "to the full" (NIV) is translated as well by terms such as "till it overflows" (AMP), "to the fullest" (CEB), "in its fullest measure" (CJB), "in its fullest" (CEV), "in abundance" (GNV), "in all its fullness" (GNT), and "satisfying life" (NLT). In short, it is an amount that greatly exceeds what is expected. Thus Jesus promised us a much better life than anything we can imagine, which reminds us of Ephesians 3:20, that God "is able to accomplish abundantly far more than all we can ask or imagine."

Transformational development has been described as "an expression of shalom."[7] This means it includes sustainable peace because the biblical concept of *shalom* does not only mean total absence of conflicts but also the proportional presence of human flourishing. In my case, my life flourished as a refugee in South Africa when I put hope into action by taking a step of faith to an unknown territory. In other words, transformational development is achieved when there is complete harmony between faith and hope. This harmonious relationship is more evident in our societies if our vertical relationship with the divine, horizontal relationships with others, ecological relationship with nature, and reflexive relationship with ourselves that were once ruptured are restored. Thus transformational development is the act of responding to the call of God and partnering with him in building the kingdom. In transformational development, the needs of the poor and the marginalized are met holistically and sustainably. The church is involved in transformational development when we seek to take care of the physical, spiritual, social, and cultural dimensions of human life as Jesus did.

Jesus sent his disciples to all people and to all nations. Through this sending, the church received a universal mission which knows no limits and concerns salvation in all its richness according to the fullness of life that Christ came to bring (John 10:10). So our mission as the church is to communicate the love of God to all peoples and nations through evangelism and social action. This mission is unique because it has a single origin and a single purpose, but it includes various tasks and activities. Within the unique mission of the church, the differences in activities do not arise from reasons intrinsic to the mission itself but from the various circumstances in which it is exercised.

A particular interest in transformational development as an expression of church mission is going beyond the dichotomy between evangelization and social responsibility. Transformational development as an expression of church mission highlights the connection between respect for God and respect for

---

7. J. E. Alvarez, E. Avarientos, and T. H. McAlpine, "Our Experience with the Bible and Transformational Development," in *Working with the Poor: New Insights and Learnings from Development Practitioners*, ed. Bryant L. Myers (Monrovia, CA: World Vision, 1999), 57.

social justice in today's globalized world. The proclamation of the gospel has lost none of its relevance, but proclaiming the gospel does not relieve us of our responsibility to address the blatant injustices of the world, as well as the human and environmental consequences of profit-driven development that continue to tear our world apart. Our mission as the church is to be fully engaged in the affairs of the world in humility and in the hope that the gospel gives. This vision fully promotes social action locally and globally. Thus, transformational development as an expression of church mission gives primacy to praxis over theory and promotes human flourishing.

It is worth noting that transformational development as an expression of church mission is pivotal to helping refugees put their hope into action because the theme of forced migration is prevalent in the Bible. In the Judeo-Christian tradition, welcoming the stranger is not just an ethical question; it is a consubstantial requirement to faith. Being confronted with strangers can be enriching and challenging, but sometimes it also leads to fear and uncertainty. So transformational development as an expression of church mission mediates reconciliation processes between groups that are different in social class, racial grouping, religious affiliation, or national citizenry. As the church we eliminate stereotypes for the purpose of transformational community development, which shows that transformational development as an expression of church mission is a contextual practice because the very act of doing theology is to theologize in the public domain.[8]

How Ordinary People with Extraordinary Challenges Improve Livelihoods

Dignity, one of the fundamental values of a human being, needs to be respected, defended, and protected. Ferris points out that people leave their countries because they are either "unable to survive or afraid to live there."[9] Her sentiments indicate that for some people, home might be the most dangerous place to live, and asylum could be their sole alternative. However in most African countries including South Africa, refugees strive for local integration into mainstream society regardless of the discriminatory treatment they endure or the constant, looming fear of xenophobic attacks. Some refugees rely on

---

8. August, *Quest for Being Public Church*, 9.

9. E. G. Ferris, *Beyond Borders: Refugees, Migrants and Human Rights in the Post-Cold War Era* (Geneva: World Council of Churches, 1993), 66.

short-term humanitarian aid due to restrictive policies of the host country which limit them from exploring various other avenues for self-reliance.

In South Africa, for example, refugees enjoy freedom of movement and are entitled to various legal rights, but the feeling of vulnerability among them is increasingly high, resulting in compromised well-being and dignity.[10] They are often considered to be parasites who deprive local citizens from enjoying the fruits of their struggle for freedom and as people who exhaust the country's resources and who "should not be in South Africa in the first place."[11] Such intolerance causes refugees to live in renewed fear of xenophobic attacks.

Refugees are ordinary people going through extraordinary challenges which increase their vulnerability and feelings of indignity. Yet even in the face of such challenges, refugees are known to be courageous and have a strong desire and determination to rise above their day-to-day hurdles. They strive to thrive in spite of the insurmountable odds against them. In South Africa for instance, the Department of Home Affairs (DHA) adds to refugees' vulnerability through the many irregularities in their documentation process. Asylum seekers are told to bring in to the agency "any proof of identification from [their] country of origin."[12] It is also the case that most asylum applications are rejected by the Refugee Status Determination Officer (RSDO) because the applicants did not leave their home countries due to persecution. They are accused of having come to South Africa in search of a better life only, so they do not qualify for refugee status. This treatment seems to validate the claims of many refugees in South Africa who say that living in South Africa is difficult because the local population does not like foreigners. Such government rejection not only increases the number of undocumented migrants in the country, but also increases corruption because refugees who fear being rejected are more likely to bribe the officials in order to get their documentation and avoid arrest, detention, and deportation.

Various studies indicate that arresting and detaining refugees because of documentation issues leads to a variety of unlawful practices and gives rise

---

10. D. Buscher, "New Approaches to Urban Refugee Livelihoods," *Refuge: Canada's Periodical on Refugees* 28, no. 2 (2011): 21; R. D. Sutton, D. Vigneswaran, and H. Wels, "Waiting in Liminal Space: Migrants' Queuing for Home Affairs in South Africa," *Anthropology Southern Africa* 34, no. 1–2 (2011): 31; M. F. Belvedere, "Insiders but Outsiders: The Struggle for the Inclusion of Asylum Seekers and Refugees in South Africa," *Refuge: Canada's Periodical on Refugees* 24, no. 1 (2007): 59.

11. Belvedere, "Insiders but Outsiders," 58.

12. See Department of Home Affairs (DHA), "Refugee Status and Asylum," Department of Home Affairs, Republic of South Africa (2021), http://www.dha.gov.za/index.php/immigration-services/refugee-status-asylum.

to increased opportunities for bribery.[13] However, proper documentation is essential for refugees to settle and pursue improved livelihoods within the requirements of the law. So some refugees decide to use a "short cut" to acquire their documents, and this "short cut" is in monetary form. Due to dissatisfaction with the DHA on documentation and service delivery, many refugees express their feelings of vulnerability and of the undignified treatment they receive from the DHA. Remarkably, staying documented demands great courage. For example because most reception centres in South Africa have been closed, refugees in Cape Town or Pretoria must travel all the way to Durban or Musina on the border to extend their permit and remain legally documented. The challenges of documentation also make refugees depend on humanitarian assistance for survival rather than making a living through personal livelihoods. It could be argued that such documentation challenges not only deprive refugees of their human right to asylum and development but also contribute to the increase in criminal activities which some refugees engage in for survival. Refugees benefit from humanitarian assistance mostly when they are still new in the country because this assistance is often reserved for the most vulnerable, the marginalized, and the unaccompanied or orphaned children.

Humanitarian assistance is a short-term strategy that allows refugees to rebuild their lives in the host country. Many refugees use the assistance they receive while they are still "newcomers" both to establish themselves and rebuild their shattered lives and become self-reliant. They strive to thrive albeit with sheer vulnerability. According to the UNHCR, self-reliance is "the social and economic ability of an individual, household or community to meet basic needs in a sustainable manner and with dignity."[14] Being self-reliant improves and strengthens refugees' livelihoods, on the one hand, and reduces their vulnerability and dependence on humanitarian assistance on the other. In their quest for improved livelihoods, refugees agree to work for insufficient payment, and they often struggle to find jobs that earn them sufficient money for survival. Quality livelihoods are essential for the emotional and socioeconomic well-being of refugees. Thus, protecting refugees is concomitant to ensuring their livelihoods.

---

13. See for example R. Amit, "Security Rhetoric and Detention in South Africa," *Forced Migration Review* 44 (2013): 32–33; L. Kiama and D. Likule, "Detention in Kenya: Risks for Refugees and Asylum Seekers," *Forced Migration Review* 44 (2013): 34–35; M. C. Kane and S. F. Kane, "A Last Resort in Cases of Wrongful Detention and Deportation in Africa," *Forced Migration Review* 44 (2013): 36.

14. UNHCR, "Promoting Livelihoods and Self-Reliance: Operational Guidance on Refugee Protection and Solutions in Urban Areas" (2011), 15.

Studies carried out by various researchers confirm that the contexts in which refugees pursue livelihoods are unsupportive and uncaring, although the refugees provide economic inputs in the form of skills and needed labour.[15] This environment could be due to restrictive policies in most host countries. Until recently in South Africa it was illegal for asylum seekers to study, work, or own businesses, and it is still illegal for both asylum seekers and refugees to own property or to access financial services such as loans. Although refugees are now entitled to study and work, finding employment remains a great challenge because refugees compete for the jobs with the majority of the local population who are in most cases prioritized for job openings.[16] This situation makes refugees' resilience fragile and their pursuit of improved livelihoods challenging. Refugee sentiments provide pointers to the government's policy to prioritize civic services to the local population.

A common attitudinal misconception is that refugees are a dependent people surviving at the mercy of either the humanitarian organizations or the generosity of the local community. However, refugees use various available avenues to enhance their livelihoods. The factors that facilitate access to improved livelihoods and build resilience in refugees can be divided into three categories: *internal* factors, *external* factors, and *supernal* factors. Internal factors involve personal qualities such as courage, strength of mind, determination, and skills. External factors involve the support refugees receive from friends, relatives, faith communities, and humanitarian organizations. Supernal factors include religious beliefs and spirituality.[17] All of these factors interact in helping refugees to improve their living conditions by pursuing productive livelihoods, and it is because of the interaction of these factors that most refugees are economically active and productive in their own way. In South Africa, refugees from the Great Lakes region of Africa are generally in the security industry as guards. They also do car guarding, repairing appliances, hairdressing, and barbering. Those from the Horn of Africa mostly own or work in retail supermarkets or *Spaza* shops, mini shops mostly found in black

---

15. See for example Deborah Potts, "Making a Livelihood In (and beyond) the African City: The Experience of Zimbabwe," *Africa* 81, no. 4 (2011): 588–605; Buscher, "New Approaches," 26; D. A. Jacobsen, *Doing Justice: Congregations and Community Organizing*. Minneapolis (Augsburg Fortress, 2001), 585; B. E. Harrell-Bond, "Can Humanitarian Work with Refugees Be Humane?" *Human Rights Quarterly* 24, no. 1 (2002): 51–85.

16. Amit, "Security Rhetoric and Detention"; Belvedere, "Insiders but Outsiders."

17. Mary Hutchinson and Pat Dorsett, "What Does the Literature Say about Resilience in the Refugee People? Implications for Practice," *Journal of Social Inclusion* 3, no. 2 (2012): 59–63.

townships. Thus, the security/car-guarding "industry" and restaurants, for mainly Zimbabweans, are the leading "employers" of refugees.

Most refugees in Cape Town have relatively strong societies which increase their trust and ability to work together and help each other. Such societies are social capital that multiply the refugees' connections and give them access to financial capital. They also use social media to get support from relatives or friends and when they want to send remittances to their home countries. Many refugee-owned financial services in the city of Cape Town facilitate money transfers abroad. These services provide an alternative to the South African banking system whose policies vis-à-vis refugees are very restrictive. Refugees also make contributions to assist those in need, especially during bereavement or any tragedy. Refugees demonstrate enviable solidarity with the newcomers in their midst whom they accommodate from the time they arrive until they find something to earn them a living. Those who own businesses, such as Somalis, introduce the newcomers in the world of business without delay. Refugees are indeed economically productive and have skills that can make them a useful asset to the hosting community if they are allowed to fully explore their potential. The livelihoods of migrants are linked to the acquisition of goods, services, and cash. Unlike other migrants, however, refugees find little opportunity to increase their means of support or sources of revenue. They face realities that thwart their holistic well-being and prevent them from exploring various developmental avenues for self-empowerment.

Refugees' resolve to improve their livelihoods is also demonstrated by the strength of their mind. Their hope for transformation propels them to work harder in order to establish their presence in the host community. The hope of seeing their dignity restored is made concrete in their pursuit of and access to livelihood opportunities. Many end up being their own managers because finding a job is a challenge even for the local population. This situation prompts refugees to put the little hope they have into action, and even when salaried employment is not forthcoming, their financial burdens compel them to engage in some form of self-employment to preserve their dignity and economic independence.

Refugees Resolve to Build Resilience: Waiting for Godot?

The majority of refugees do not want to return to their home countries regardless of the ill-treatment they endure on a regular basis. On the one hand, they do not want to return to the life-threatening situations in their respective countries, and on the other, they see their chances of improving their livelihoods as greater in South Africa than in their countries of origin. Thus these refugees put their hope into practice to achieve what they hope for. Despite the many challenges and the bad treatment that refugees receive from individuals and institutions, most of them are reasonably better off in various aspects of their lives than they were in their home countries. Thus, the holistic development of refugees rests on realized hope. Such hope is not "a kite at the mercy of the changing winds"[18] but "a sure and steadfast anchor of the soul," firm and secure (Heb 6:19). This kind of hope is not easily shaken by the realities of the world.

Brueggemann observes that "hope is a distinctive mark of faith with dangerous and revolutionary social potential."[19] Here Brueggemann implies that hope and faith are closely related. In this regard, refugees can be seen to practice hope as a coping mechanism within the bounds of faith. The existential nature of hope is universal since it "lives in all and is for all."[20] Thus, our communities of faith ought to make known and defend the universal relevance of hope due to "the common human experience of suffering and the dangers [of hopelessness] that it brings forth."[21] The universality of hope makes it a quality of life that no social group can claim as rightful owners. Similarly, "hope is experienced from within and reaches the depths of human soul,"[22] and it is a "necessity," thus "as necessary as light and air to human life."[23] Brueggemann argues that "no single tradition is the designated custodian of hope."[24] With regard to the refugee phenomenon, it is the presence of hope rather than the absence of it that keeps refugees going despite their increased vulnerability and undignified treatment in the host country.

A growing number of people today succumb to despair because the current socioeconomic system is not working fine. Our communities of faith can neither conform to the system nor withdraw from it. Instead, we have to

---

18. R. V. Tasker, "Hope," in *The New Bible Dictionary*, ed. J. D. Douglas (Leicester: InterVarsity, 1962), 535.

19. W. Brueggemann, "Hope," in *Reverberations of Faith: A Theological Handbook of Old Testament Themes*, ed. W. Brueggemann (London: Westminster John Knox, 2002), 102.

20. W. Hryniewicz, *The Challenge of Our Hope: Christian Faith in Dialogue* (Washington, DC: Council for Research in Values and Philosophy, 2007), 9.

21. Hryniewicz, *Challenge of Our Hope*, 68.

22. M. Bielawski, "Thinking about Church with Hope: The Example of Waclaw Hryniewicz," in *The Challenge of Our Hope*, ed. W. Hryniewicz (Washington, DC: RVP, 2007), 284.

23. G. Tinder, *The Fabric of Hope: An Essay*, Emory University Studies in Law and Religion (Grand Rapids, MI: Eerdmans, 1999), 3.

24. Brueggemann, "Hope," 102.

rise to the occasion and provide a transforming framework that changes the status quo for the better and invite society to live in a new way – the way of hope.[25] Our communities of faith must help the inclinations, the desires, and the dreams of those in despair to be rooted anew in faith, love, and hope. In this same vein, the more faith is in harmony with the groaning of people, the more love is in solidarity with them and the more comprehensive the horizon of hope becomes.[26] These "groaning" people include refugees. Without hope, the realities of the world can destroy love and shake the foundations of faith. When hope is put into practice, it becomes concomitant to faith. Thus, rootedness in faith determines the quality of hope and acts as a stimulus for pure love.

When refugees actuate the seemingly feeble hope they have, they seek to find a new identity because identity is a crucial part of their existence. Yet refugees often find themselves in a grey area when it comes to getting a new identity because they are made to wait for extended periods of time before they are attended to. Sutton, Vigneswaran, and Wels find that "the more power, the less waiting; the less power, the more waiting."[27] In other words, waiting is associated with the powerless and not waiting with the powerful. Refugees are often made to wait in long queues, often for days, expecting something, anything, or nothing to happen. However, their waiting is not a waste of time or "being without time" as Günther Anders says of Samuel Beckett's play "Waiting for Godot" in which the two characters, Vladimir and Estragon, wait for a certain Godot who never comes.[28] The two have no idea who this Godot is and do not even know what he wants. At the end of the day, when Godot does not show up, they take care of their disappointments by waiting for him the following day.

Like the waiting of Vladimir and Estragon, the waiting of refugees involves disappointments, frustrations, and despair, but at the same time, it is fanned with a great sense of hope. Their waiting involves frustrations and despair because of their fear that the long wait might not culminate in getting to the top of the queue at the end of the day, and they hope because their waiting is based on their longing for a new identity.[29] Thus, the waiting of refugees is not a hopeless situation but rather a resilient waiting. This waiting in hope is a virtue

---

25. Tasker, "Hope," 536.
26. J. Moltmann, *Hope and Planning* (London: SCM Press, 1971), 49.
27. Sutton, Vigneswaran, and Wels, "Waiting in Liminal Space," 31.
28. G. Anders, "Being without Time: On Beckett's Play 'Waiting for Godot,'" in *Samuel Beckett: A Collection of Critical Essays*, ed. M. Esslin (Englewood Cliffs, NJ: Prentice-Hall, 1965), 140.
29. Sutton, Vigneswaran, and Wels, "Waiting in Liminal Space," 32.

that gives meaning to their existence. For refugees, waiting is a state of being and therefore a quality of life. Refugees live in a constant state of waiting: they are made to wait when in need of services from public offices. They wait for the situation in their respective countries to stabilize so they can return home, In South Africa they wait in long queues at the DHA for their documents to be processed. And they wait in hope for a better tomorrow. Thus, the everyday life of refugees is a waiting story.

Like the resilience of Vladimir and Estragon, refugees keep waiting for their Godot despite the frustrations and disappointments. Their waiting is driven by the assurance of faith, the embrace of love, and the resilience of hope. Unlike Vladimir and Estragon whose waiting was fuelled by nothingness, the waiting of refugees is that of activity, although coupled with a mixture of patience and impatience, belief and disbelief. Indeed, when belief and disbelief conflict, "hope arises from patience and experience, and finally overcomes."[30] Thus, even in their waiting, the hope of refugees for a better tomorrow triumphs over their disbelief and impatience.

Waiting is associated with the virtue of patience. The Greek word *hupomoné* translated "patience" suggests bearing up a heavy load from an oppressor on the shoulder and abiding under difficult circumstances when it is not possible to escape.[31] Waiting is therefore concomitant to long-suffering.[32] Although the waiting for documentation of their new identity is longer than expected for most refugees, they keep on waiting which shows that their waiting is a hopeful enduring and a coping mechanism for survival. In the words of Sutton, Vigneswaran, and Wels, "it is hope that makes the powerless persevere and . . . ultimately makes waiting a phenomenon that is socially productive."[33] It could be said that hope transforms the waiting of refugees into a socially productive and resourceful weapon.[34] Waiting generates strength and the ability to be patient in spite of the fact that prevailing circumstances do not give any reason to do so or even though there are no rational grounds for hope. Refugees wait in "active hope." Thus, hopeful waiting is a strategy to pursue

---

30. Moltmann, *Hope and Planning*, 49.

31. J. Strong, *Strong's Exhaustive Concordance of the Bible* (Peabody, MA: Hendrickson, 2009), #5281.

32. C. Brown and U. Falkenroth, "Patience, Steadfastness, Endurance," in *The New International Dictionary of New Testament Theology*, ed. C. Brown (London: Paternoster, 1976), 765.

33. Sutton, Vigneswaran, and Wels, "Waiting in Liminal Space," 31.

34. Sutton, Vigneswaran, and Wels, 36.

improved livelihoods for their survival. Indeed "we learn to hope anew when we practice hope."[35]

Refugees have a strong desire to be productive in order to take care of their families and pay the bills related to their livelihoods. They could be said to put their hope into practice to attain the hoped-for. Here putting hope into action is what makes the powerless powerful and turns their waiting experience into a socially productive phenomenon. Botman observes that translating hope into action is "a theological grounding to become meaningful" in this twenty-first century.[36] Thus, active hope is central to human living. It is a part of what it means to be human. The prevalence of hopelessness and despair, which is the "groaning of people,"[37] should therefore motivate our communities of faith to get involved in the society in order to birth hope.

Moltmann argues that hope is not only sitting and waiting for the *eschaton*. He espouses the view that theological statements of hope need to express the "present experience of suffering."[38] Waiting ought to be a hopeful experience coupled with activity, rather than passivity as one awaits the hoped-for. For example, the hope for peace and justice in the future must encourage us to work for peace and justice in the present. In the same way, our hope for a better society must be translated into concrete actions which pave the way for the realization of what we hope for.

It cannot be overemphasized that the majority of refugees leave their countries uncertain of their survival in the host country, but they continue to put their hope into action to pursue and improve their livelihoods. To nurse the frustrations and disappointments of the day, they seize every available opportunity to build up new hope for tomorrow. In their quest for a better tomorrow, they rise above dependence on relief and handouts and instead engage in various trades, however insignificant, for their self-reliance. Their hope is not abstract; it is visible through their active involvements and is a positive force with the potential to transform lives. Refugees are victims of circumstances that have inflicted neediness, hopelessness, and misery upon them. They are capable people who are momentarily without resources. Even though they are faced with challenges, refugees put their hope into action to

---

35. F. A. Keshgegian, *Time for Hope: Practices for Living in Today's World* (London: Continuum, 2006), 188.

36. R. H. Botman, "Hope as the Coming Reign of God," in *Hope for the World*, ed. W. Brueggemann (London: Westminster John Knox, 2001), 70.

37. Moltmann, *Hope and Planning*, 49.

38. Moltmann, 18–19.

enhance their chances of improved livelihoods. Their resolve to succeed against the odds propels them to engage in various kinds of trades to earn a living. In so doing, they play a positive role in improving the living conditions of many. Such resolve to improved livelihoods is a commitment to work successfully and reach a certain level of self-sufficiency which would see refugees integrated into the mainstream community within the host society and become open to social change.

So, although refugees are often portrayed as helpless people whose revenue depends on the benevolence of others, refugees are actually agents of change and contribute to the economic development of their host country. They have been shown to employ a whole range of coping mechanisms to ensure improved livelihoods. This they do not only for survival but also to give their life meaning through dignified and sustainable means of support. In spite of the challenges that refugees have to surmount on a daily basis, their narratives express hope for a better tomorrow. Hope is indeed a practical paradigm for transformational development, and the actuation of this hope is necessary for the well-being of a community. Put into action, hope can rekindle the ambitions of the less privileged in the community. The coping mechanisms of refugees constitute an opportunity for new hope as they strive to rise above satisfying basic needs for survival to meeting specific goals. If managed properly, the refugee phenomenon presents an opportunity that can be capitalized upon to bring about the desired transformation that leads to a more productive economy. This will demand that the hope of refugees for a better tomorrow is combined with the hope of the hosting community for holistic development.

Being human is actually a call to be utterly discontented with the ever present predicaments of life that are increasingly causing despair in the world. This call entails helping those in despair to hope anew. It is this discontentment that moves hope toward action. Our attitude toward development should therefore be reflected in our efforts to empower the powerless and restore their dignity. Simply put, transformational development without hope put into action is doomed to fail. Refugees and local citizens should take pleasure in each other's company for a common goal: the welfare and development of the community. As already discussed, millions of people have left their countries and are scattered all over the world due to a range of combined factors, and most of them have no hope of returning home. They chose to become refugees rather than live in a situation that puts their lives in danger. Although official policies welcome refugees and seem to recognize their contribution, refugees are not always welcomed by some members of the local population. The church ought to be the place where refugees can find homely warmth and their situation addressed lovingly since both the nature and function of the church go beyond cultural boundaries.

When reading the Lukan writings, we come across a chapter where Luke speaks of the ministry of Tabitha, also called Dorcas, as doing good and helping the poor (Acts 9:36–41). As we read this story, we realize that Tabitha has taken seriously God's commands concerning the most vulnerable people in society (cf. Lev 23:22; Deut 10:17–19; 24:17–19, 20–2; Prov 19:17; Jas 1:27). Helping the marginalized is one of the characteristics of God. As Psalm 146:8–9 states, "The LORD lifts up those who are bowed down; the LORD loves the righteous. The LORD watches over the strangers; he upholds the orphan and the widow." In biblical times, the term "poor" was used for people who had no means of financial support and who needed protection as well as physical, legal, and financial assistance. In other words, a poor person is someone with constant needs – and being a refugee, orphan, or widow was almost synonymous with poverty.

In a parable about helping the needy, Jesus contrasts the rescue actions of a certain Samaritan to the indifference of other travellers such as the priest and the Levite (Luke 10:25–37). Unlike those members of the priesthood who did not help the man beaten by bandits, Tabitha deliberately sought out the poor and the marginalized and actively sought to see how she could help meet their needs. In the first century when women's activities generally focused on the daily survival of their families, Tabitha met the needs of her community. Her goal was the transformation of her immediate community. Her lifestyle shows that love is an active word and that it seeks to do good to others. Tabitha probably enjoyed her work and loved the people despite their poor living conditions. The response of grief in the community at her death shows how the community was transformed as a result of her ministry to the poor – and the whole community loved Tabitha in return (Acts 9:38–39). This is quite an example for us if we are to be the church after God's mission.

Tabitha, a virtuous woman known for her good works and charity towards the poor, was indeed God's instrument of transformation, and her interventional actions for the most vulnerable in her immediate community prompted the disciples to send for Peter when she died (Acts 9:36–42). Her untimely death did not go unnoticed as she was a woman who always did good and helped the poor, including making clothes for the needy. She was particularly compassionate and tender to their needs and actively and personally served them and others. This example is an inspiration to us as the church today to strive to serve refugees and others with all the talents God has bestowed on us. Since Tabitha's good works were known throughout Joppa, God used her popularity and the event of her death and restoration to life as a means of preaching the gospel and calling many others to salvation. As the church, we are the Tabithas of today, and God wants to accomplish his purposes on earth to transform the lives of those in need such as refugees through us. To do this, we must understand the challenges refugees face by listening to their stories, which are stories of hope and courage.

This chapter has discussed the need for transformational community development to improve our well-being and promote livelihoods. I demonstrated to what extent hope when put into action is an asset for development and therefore an important tool for the *missio ecclesiae*. We have also underlined that development is a living expression of hope in action because it makes our mission people-centred, faith-grounded, and the basis for human flourishing. We further saw that refugees are ordinary people facing extraordinary challenges but who use the glimmer of hope they possess to improve their livelihoods and strengthen their resilience. Finally, we emphasized that as the church, we are called to support refugees and help them renew their hope. The next chapter discusses refugee stories from an empirical study to show how hope motivates refugees' resolve to cope despite their daily challenges. These stories should inspire us to do something like Tabitha, even on a small scale, to make a difference in the lives of the refugees and other vulnerable people in our midst. In doing so, we will have preached the gospel in a great but social way, and we will have left a legacy of hope.

Discussion Questions

1. What does "hope in action" mean, and why do we say that development is hope in action?

2. How is development an expression of church mission, and how does this understanding affect the way we live in our communities?

3. What is the relationship between *missio Dei*, *missio Christi*, and *missio Spiritus* vis-à-vis *missio ecclesiae*?

4. What resources do we need as the church to carry out our mission to the refugees in our community, and how can we use the resources we have?

5. Read Acts 9:36–42.
    - Why was Tabitha's ministry important to the church then, and how crucial is it for the church today?
    - What kind of lifestyle must we lead to be known as always doing good and helping the poor?
6. How can we apply the Tabitha ministry method to reach out to refugees in our immediate community?

6

Narratives of Hope

The decision to leave everything behind was indeed a painful ordeal for my family and me but we had to free ourselves from a situation that left us without hope for the future. The hope of being able to live provoked our decision to leave, and it was this hope that has sustained me throughout my journey as a foreigner in various countries. It was all about rebuilding my shattered life and saving my future. Forced migration should not be reduced to physical and geographic movements only because it also concerns the many lived experiences during the flight. These experiences usually begin as soon as one decides to leave the country; they continue during the journey; and they intensify when one arrives at the border before crossing into the country of asylum. Borders intensify the pain of refugees' lived experiences because they visibly mark the difference between home and elsewhere – thus provoking a confrontation between the asylum seeker and systems. In other words, the artificial geographical borders, like any other boundary, suggest the difference between those who are included and those who are excluded, those who belong and those who do not belong. In this regard, borders amplify the foreigner in me and promote my otherness. In short, borders are akin to building walls rather than bridges, and therefore they are good reminders of separate development, which is against the ethical demands of Ubuntu. Thus when refugees cross the border, they feel relieved. They feel they belong and are included. And they live to tell a story – stories of hope, resilience, and courage.

This chapter pays particular attention to the materials and methods used in a study conducted in five South African cities: Cape Town, Port Elizabeth, Durban, Johannesburg, and Pretoria. The choice of these cities was based on two criteria. First, in South Africa refugees are urban, so they are densely populated in cities rather than rural areas. So one will most likely find refugees in cities than elsewhere. Second, the refugee reception centres were initially located in these five cities, which is why most refugees preferred to live in the cities to be close to where they would go if they wanted to renew their papers. For these reasons, refugees were concentrated in these five South African cities.

The stories of refugees in South Africa are aimed to open up avenues of awareness so we can understand the difficulties and challenges that refugees in Africa face on a daily basis. They are stories of hope because they demonstrate the hope that refugees have despite their challenging experiences. These are stories of courage because they show the hardships refugees have had to face to be where they are, and they are stories of resilience because they explain what refugees go through again and again without giving up. I hope that by reading these refugee stories we will be more compassionate and empathetic in our interventions. Refugee stories can also be a useful tool to educate and inform the public about the state of the refugee crisis.

Materials and Methods

The research was designed and conducted within the frame and following the principles of the case study method because the nature of the research required exploring a specific case, the lived experiences of refugee migrants. The paradigm within which the study was conducted is phenomenology because the research focused on a specific phenomenon, which is the refugee phenomenon. The phenomenon under study required interpretation rather than measurement, which justifies the preference for the interpretive paradigm and the consequent choice of the qualitative approach.

A question guide and a questionnaire were the main instruments of data collection. I used the questionnaire to collect data from the participants who were not refugees. These participants had some form of professional relationship with refugees, and they were drawn from both the local and foreign communities. They were mainly role players who had relevant information concerning refugees and included social workers, healthcare providers, church leaders, and immigration officers. Semi-structured interviews were conducted with refugee participants who were the main and largest group of participants. Existing materials, both textual and audiovisual, were also used not only to review the literature, but also as sources of information. As tools for literature review, they helped with the familiarization of the body of knowledge in the field of forced migration and the theories and principles underlying the phenomenon under study. As sources of information, the content of relevant documents was critically analyzed with the aim of finding and gathering suitable data.

In addition to the semi-structured interviews, data collection was reinforced by a focus group in Cape Town which consisted of conversational interaction with a group of refugee community leaders. The question guide for the interviews, the discussion guide for the focus group, and the questionnaire for the survey were produced in English and translated into French and Kiswahili. I conducted the research in one of these three languages depending on the respondent's choice. At the discretion of the respondent, some interviews consisted of a mixture of French and English, French and Kiswahili, or English and Kiswahili depending on how comfortable the participant was in each language. With the exception of a few participants who requested to have the interviews in their homes, all other interviews, at the suggestion of the interviewees, were conducted at church premises in each of the five cities.

Conducting interviews in the church – an open and public place – put participants at ease. Seventy-five percent of the interviews were taped with the participant's informed consent. The rest were not taped because the participants were not comfortable having them recorded but consented to be interviewed off-record. The main points from these non-taped interviews were recorded manually in a prepared booklet. Each one-on-one interview took around fifteen to twenty minutes, while focus groups were a bit longer and lasted about thirty to forty-five minutes each. The collection of data happened over a span of one year in three phases because the study was designed using the grounded theory method, with follow-up interviews scheduled every six months. The beauty of using the grounded theory method is the ability to systematically obtain and analyze data using the benchmarking method in order to evolve or build "from the ground" a theory within the context in which the phenomenon under study takes place. The observation of participants was done in advance through church services, informal visits with some refugee church members, and most notably, through my active participation in refugee activities. This socialization was made possible particularly because I was part of the refugee community, and I speak most of the languages participants spoke, namely French, English, and Kiswahili.

The sample was selected by triangulating probabilistic and nonprobabilistic methods, particularly simple random, purposive, and snowball. The inclusion criteria were predetermined, which led to the purposive selection of key informants. Refugees were selected using a simple random method, and being a nonprobabilistic approach, it simply meant all potential participants had an equal chance of being selected. Participants who were not refugees were referred by key informants through the snowball method. The sample size was determined using the Raosoft Sample Size Calculator, an online tool, which fixed the sample size at 271 participants across the country, of whom 214 were refugees and 57 were not refugees but important role players. A 5 percent margin of error was accepted which means that I expected and was willing to tolerate no more than 5 percent of participant error in order to make the results more reliable and representative of the target population. For this reason, the confidence level was set at 90 percent to account for any uncertain eventualities during the research process and increase validity.

The coding system was very open because most of the attributes assigned to the different variables had letter values. First, I used well-known codes for the cities that made up the research sites: CTN for Cape Town, PE for Port Elizabeth, DBN for Durban, JHB for Johannesburg, and PTA for Pretoria. I also used a coding system for the participants to make the variables easily recognizable: *Rp* for refugee participants and *n-Rp* for non-refugee participants. To distinguish the variable of men from that of women, for statistical purposes only I prefixed the letters *M* for "male" and *F* for "female" to the codes *Rp* or *n-Rp*. Thus *M-Rp* represents a male refugee participant and *F-Rp* represents a female refugee participant. Likewise, *Mn-Rp* represents a male non-refugee participant and *Fn-Rp* a female non-refugee participant. To indicate the mean of the population, I used the letter *m* for mean as a prefix of *Pop* for population. Thus *mPop* would simply refer to the population average or the mean of the people sampled.

The research was guided by the following dual question: "*What is the role of the church in promoting community transformation and human dignity for refugees, and how does the transformation and the dignity of refugees help them contribute to the socioeconomic development of their host country*?" This chapter reports the results of this transdisciplinary study which sits at the crossroad of forced migration, community development, and practical theology.

Demographic Profiling
General participation rates

The figures and tables below show the demographic representations of both refugees and non-refugee role players in this study.

As seen in Table 6.1, 60.2 percent of the refugees who participated in this study were men, while 39.7 were women; while Table 6.2 indicates that non-refugee participants were comprised of 56.1 percent men and 43.8 percent women. These tables show how strongly represented refugees were (as planned of course) in the research when compared to non-refugees. Table 6.1 further indicates this representation of refugees by gender and how the research was strongly skewed toward male participation. The high representation of men shows that there is a gender disparity in the refugee communities. This disparity is perhaps caused on the one hand by the fact that male refugees outnumber female refugees in the country, and on the other hand by the fact that in most African cultures, men are often the representatives of households and therefore speak on behalf of their families. But also for some reasons, most women did not want to be interviewed. Their refusal to be interviewed may have been influenced by fear as they probably thought that their recorded statements would be attributed to them by the immigration officials.

Table 6.1: Refugee participants by city and gender

City	Men	Women	Total
Cape Town	30	12	42
Port Elizabeth	34	22	56
Durban	34	27	61
Johannesburg	14	11	25
Pretoria	17	13	30
TOTAL	129	85	214
Ratio (%)	60.2	39.7	–

Table 6.2: Non-refugee participants by city and gender

City	Men	Women	Total
Cape Town	2	3	5
Port Elizabeth	7	5	12
Durban	8	6	14
Johannesburg	9	7	16
Pretoria	6	4	10
TOTAL	32	25	57
Ratio (%)	56.1	43.8	–

One of the sources of concern and anger among refugee families is the slowness of the immigration department procedures. Women receive limited information due to these processes that add to the refugee frustration. The absence of women in public places is due to the fact that they are often not at home as they have to look for what the family will eat, or to go to the home affairs department and try to solve the problem of family documentation to avoid a situation where the whole family would be undocumented. This situation results in women not receiving information shared mainly through word of mouth, as most of them are busy with the household affairs according to their needs. So the family responsibilities that women have at home and outside the home prevent them from participating meaningfully in certain activities including interview sessions, which explains why their representation was reduced in these interviews.

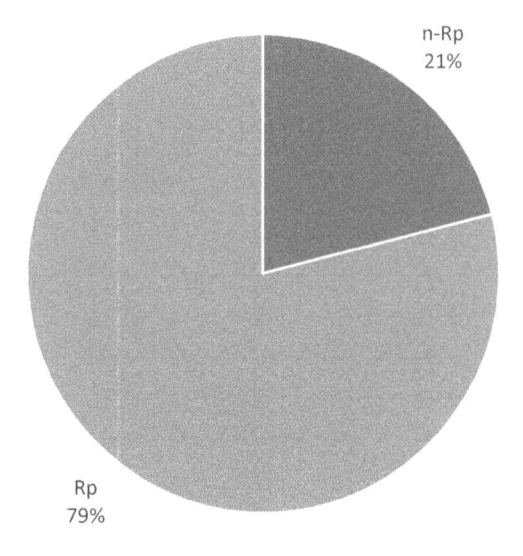

Figure 6.1: Ratio of *Rp* and *n-Rp* representation

Age composition of refugees

The research was concentrated on the "twenty-something" age group of young adults (ages 20–29), as more people in their twenties were available for this study than those of any other age group. The fact that there are many refugees in this age group reveals that refugees in this age group can still achieve their life goals of self-reliance and holistic transformation because age is on their side. Also, these young men and women have potential that can be harnessed positively for the benefit of the community.

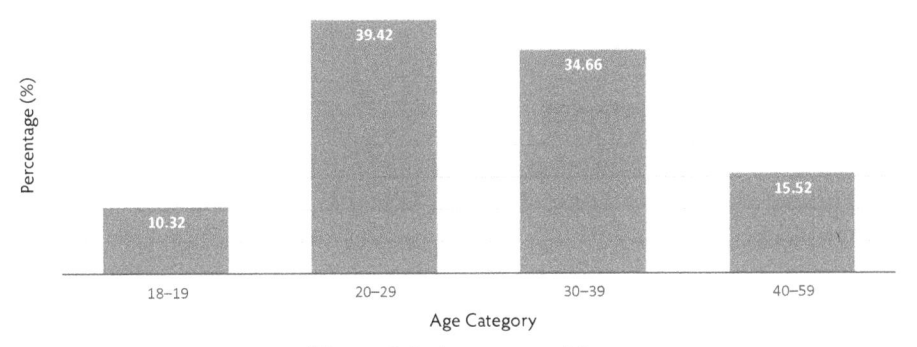

Figure 6.2: Age composition

Place of Origin of Refugees

The survey did not target any specific group within the refugee population. The interviews were conducted with and questionnaires distributed to whoever was willing to be part of the research. The participants included refugees from the Great Lakes region (GLR), the Horn of Africa, and southern Africa. The latter category was dominated by Zimbabweans. The refugee participants in the other category were from countries like Kenya, Uganda, Cameroon, Togo, etc.

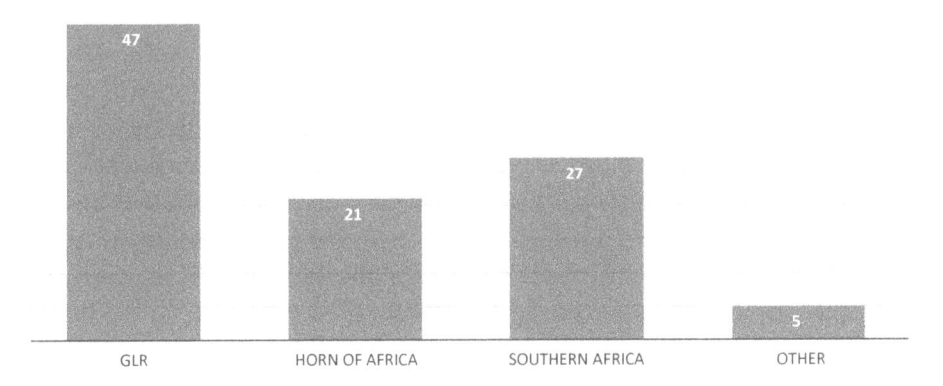

Figure 6.3: Origins of refugees (%)

As Figure 6.3 shows, 47 percent of the participants came from GLR countries including the Democratic Republic of Congo, Rwanda, and Burundi. Refugees from the Horn of Africa made up 21 percent of the participants and came from Somalia, Eritrea, and Ethiopia. Refugee participants from southern African countries, predominantly Zimbabwe, made up 27 percent. Other refugees from various parts of Africa including East Africa and West Africa made up about 6 percent of the participants.

Refugees' Lived Experiences

In my interactions with refugees, it was evident that they are often victims of discriminatory policies. Most of those I talked to felt they were competing with the local population for jobs, the majority of whom also suffer the ordeals of poverty and unemployment. Most of the refugees were actually doing something in the informal sector to pay their rental fees. Security and car guarding are the main areas of work among refugees from the Great Lakes region, while those from the Horn of Africa are more into business such as small shops, and those from southern Africa, in majority Zimbabweans, work in restaurants. In other words, the majority of refugees, regardless of their origin and living conditions, are involved in some money-making activities to survive, and their activities contribute to the economic growth of the country.

Most refugees struggle to adapt to a foreign lifestyle and culture. Many of those who did not come from Anglophone countries indicated that they struggle a lot with the English language, and this is a great obstacle for them because not being fluent in English adds to their frustrations and disappointments. The majority of refugees feel unsafe and helpless at the same time. However, they always stay positive as a strategy for survival. Abdala,[1] a thirty-one-year-old refugee from Eritrea living in Cape Town, told me, "The majority of South Africans don't know what is happening on the continent with their fellow Africans. And the worst thing, no South African thinks there is a white refugee. This will create future problems [and damage] the image of South Africa in other African countries." He further indicated that politicians must ensure unity among all peoples instead of widening the gap between refugees and the local population by encouraging xenophobic tendencies. Doing this is important Abdala insisted, "for the sake of a peaceful and prosperous Africa and the world at large."

Acceptance or rejection of refugees

The majority of refugees felt unloved. According to the survey, 61.5 percent thought they were not accepted by ordinary South Africans, which could indicate that the majority of refugees encounter antipathy from the local

---

1. Names of respondents changed for confidentiality.

population. In other words, the influx and the presence of refugees inhibit the ease and contentment of the local population. Refugees become a pain in the neck to some and to others a threat. As a result, ill-feelings intensify, which increases the degree of xenophobic attitude in the country which may eventually erupt into verbal or physical attacks on the refugees by the locals. Yena, a twenty-nine-year-old woman from DRC, said with sadness and bitterness of heart, "You give up everything you have ever known or had, and come to a foreign country, only to be subjected to all kinds of discrimination and of violence." Yena's situation makes her sad because she feels discriminated against on the basis of the very rights which countries are supposed to protect refugees, but since she is powerless and helpless, there is nothing she can do about it because she is not in her country. Likewise Salma, a thirty-two-year-old Ethiopian refugee, said: "I landed in Kenya and spent six very difficult years in a camp. Inadequate health care when we were sick. The conditions were inhumane. But finally, I arrived here [South Africa]. I like it here even if we are not welcome. My wish is to get my papers sorted then to train myself in something other than hairdressing. Either way, I know my son will have a better future than me."

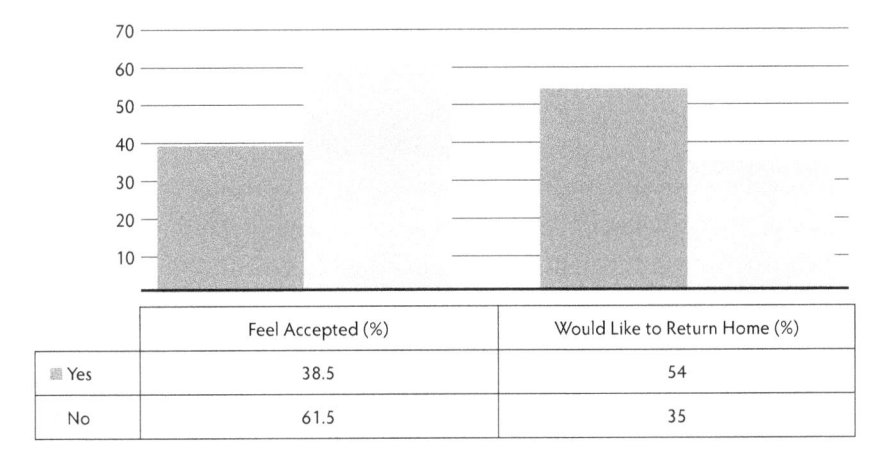

	Feel Accepted (%)	Would Like to Return Home (%)
Yes	38.5	54
No	61.5	35

Figure 6.4: Feelings of acceptance and willingness to go home

Despite this feeling of rejection, refugees have resolved to fight for their survival. In this survey, 41 percent of those I spoke to were self-employed, while the unemployed made up 26 percent of the participants. However in the interviews, most participants indicated that "home is best," and they wanted to return to their respective home countries sooner rather than later. Such decisions to return home are usually strengthened when xenophobic violence erupts.

Xenophobia is definitely a great challenge in Africa, but it is more pronounced in South Africa. Because perpetrators of such violence usually target black people from sub-Saharan Africa, it is only fair to dub them as "Afrophobic" or "negrophobic." As a result, images of refugees from Congo, Burundi, Cameroon, Nigeria, Somalia, Ethiopia, Mozambique, and Zimbabwe who have been brutalized, had their property looted, and even been burnt alive in South Africa shock the world every so often. For some, South Africa has become a no-go zone while, for others it is the better place to be despite the prevalence of xenophobic attacks in the country. A critical analysis of the situation is needed to understand why black South Africans attack and want to get rid of their fellow black Africans from the other parts of the continent.

Several reasons explain these tragic events. While the official position of the government is always against crime, the local authorities, the police department, and most enlightened South Africans talk about criminal elements, spontaneous acts, people taking advantage of the chaos to loot and brutalize sub-Saharan Africans, etc. However, various civil society organizations find these attacks targeting foreigners to be planned. They believe these are acts of xenophobic violence motivated by being fed up with foreigners. This feeling is driven by the belief that South Africans can no longer get jobs because foreigners fill all the positions meant for them. One thing is certain: violence against foreigners in South Africa is directly related to the extreme poverty within which the South African black population is deeply immersed. The increase of poverty in South Africa makes some say that the situation of black people today is worse than it was during the apartheid.

Whose fault is all of this? The ruling party works for the emergence of a black bourgeoisie instead of privileging the common good of the proletariat. As a result, the majority of the black population is less literate and mostly jobless and has become a time bomb. Their misery has made many ready to do anything to satisfy their hatred of life. As long as the South African government continues to deny that acts of violence against foreigners are linked to xenophobia, these acts will continue to recur, and the problem will never be solved. The first step toward a total and effective healing is for patients to recognize that they are sick and need help. To better solve this problem, local authorities and the ruling party must admit that xenophobia is one of the biggest challenges for the country and be proactive rather than reactive about it.

Many refugees recall the incidents of May and June 2008 or the incidents of 2015, among others, which saw thousands of refugees displaced, necklaced, and even murdered across the country. Refugees do not seem to forget these incidents, and they vividly recount their experiences. The fear of the recurrence of xenophobic attacks is evident among refugees and is something they live with. Thus, refugees live in a duality of challenges: endure the effects of xenophobia in the host country or return home to face various forms of persecution and "unfreedom."

Most of the non-refugee participants in this study denied that xenophobia really exists in South Africa: 61.4 percent said South Africans are not xenophobic, while 12.2 percent were of the opinion that they are definitely xenophobic. The remaining 26.3 percent said that not all South Africans are xenophobic, only a section of the population. The majority of non-refugees pointed out that those involved in xenophobic attacks are just criminals, and their actions should be treated simply as criminal acts. Among the refugee participants, 180 (84.1 percent) of the 214 who participated in this survey strongly agreed that South Africa is a xenophobic country. Fourteen (6.5 percent) disagreed with the statement, and twenty (9.3 percent) believed that some South Africans are xenophobic, but not all of them.

As an African Christian, my Christianity is linked to South Africa, just as it is linked to Burundi, DRC, Tanzania, Kenya, etc. My fate is also coherently linked to the fate of this great and majestic continent. Like many others, I have bright hope for the future of this continent while being aware of the many shortcomings and weaknesses we face. However, in particular I have witnessed the emergence and entrenchment of a negrophobic impulse in the consciousness of many black Africans which sporadically results in the hunt for black Africans and their persecution, particularly in South Africa. Of course, not all South Africans are Afrophobic or negrophobic, but these evils are widely shared by a large segment of the population.

Xenophobia is fear or hatred of foreigners or of anything that is foreign. In South Africa, xenophobia is more hatred – rather than fear – of black foreigners from sub-Saharan Africa. This hatred is often but not always accompanied by violent actions, resulting in loss of life and property. The definitional context of xenophobia in South Africa, which targets only blacks from sub-Saharan Africa, makes this xenophobia "afrophobia" because foreign Africans are always the victims, or "negrophobia" because only black foreigners are the targets.[2] So one of the reasons for the xenophobic violence against foreign black Africans

---

2. Reshoketswe B. Mapokgole, "'There Is No Black in the Rainbow (Nation)': A Bikoist and Fanonian Approach to Understanding 'Xenophobic' Violence in South Africa" (Senior Theses, Trinity College, Hartford, CT, 2014), http://digitalrepository.trincoll.edu/theses/425, 36.

in South Africa is the limited resources. It is claimed that in a period of high expectations, especially for black South Africans, services such as housing, education, health care, and employment become insufficient, and this lack is what drives the local population to attack the black foreign population from sub-Saharan Africa. A common belief in South Africa is that every job given to a foreign national is one less job for a South African, which is exacerbated by the currently high unemployment rates; however, no empirical evidence supports these claims.

Socioeconomic conditions of refugees

Due to various circumstances, many refugees end up being their own bosses in that they work for themselves or are self-employed. Skill is essential in the world of business and to acquire it, one needs to be trained and get some experience in entrepreneurship.

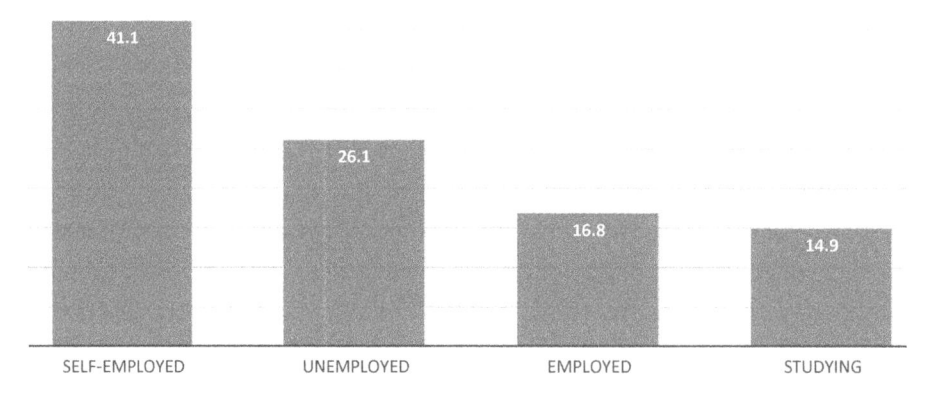

Figure 6.5: Socioeconomic conditions of refugees (%)

Refugees who trade informally on the street or have small shops are often untrained. As a result, they generally do not understand the practicalities of doing business such as the adequacy of production or marketing. Refugees are allowed to work and study, but finding a job in South Africa has become difficult even for the local population, though the government is striving to overcome this challenge. When there is any job opportunity, often it is the local applicant who gets preferential privilege, and at least in part, this situation explains the high rate of unemployment among the refugee participants.

Nevertheless, refugees, like any other human beings, have responsibilities that require financial strength. When salaried employment is not forthcoming, their financial burdens push them to find some form of self-employment. In this study, 41.1 percent of the refugees I spoke to were working for themselves in hair salons, on street vending, parking lot car guarding, especially those from the GLR countries, and Spaza shops, especially those from the Horn of Africa. Those who managed to get "employed" (16.8 percent) mostly worked in security companies as guards. As a result of these work challenges, only a few (14.9 percent) refugees get a chance to pursue their academic dreams of studying at universities or tertiary colleges. The rest (26.1 percent) are unemployed. The self-employment rate among refugee migrants indicates that refugees contribute to South Africa's socioeconomic growth and the growth of the country's employment rate. Figure 6.6 provides a national index of refugee unemployment by city.

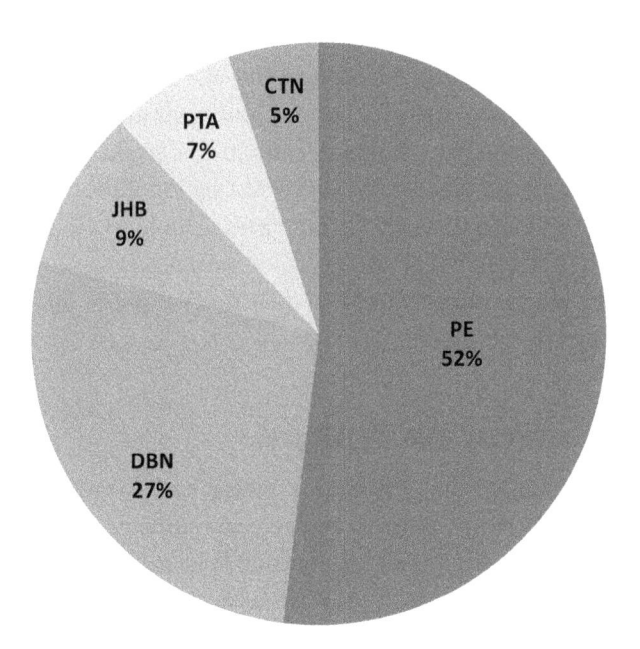

Figure 6.6: Rate of unemployment of refugees by city

Among all migrants, refugees in particular are at risk of unemployment with adverse effects on health and socioeconomic well-being. A series of obstacles prevents employment among refugees in South Africa, but xenophobia and a generally high unemployment rate in the country are the main ones. The lack of formal employment leads most refugees in South Africa to work in the informal sector or to accept any type of employment that comes up. There are several possible explanations for this. One is that the informal sector has the lowest cost in the market, especially in terms of taxes and other financial obligations. Another is that the vast majority of refugee migrants come from African countries with large informal sectors. They therefore see a business opportunity and exploit it to their advantage by innovating what can be economically advantageous to them and at the same time marketable to the public. A final explanation for working in the informal sector is that locals are a priority for employment opportunities. Thus venturing into the informal sector is a survival strategy. Among the few refugees who are formally employed, most are underemployed as the total number of hours worked per week is lower than that of their local counterparts, even if the refugees are ready and available to work more.

Thus refugee migrants work in the informal sector or work in very difficult conditions when they are employed because their willingness to accept any job is often exploited. This is a situation that South African refugees seem to share with most of their peers around the world. In other words, refugee migrants are more likely to work in poor conditions and to occupy positions that locals are unwilling to fill, which explains a certain probability level of employment among refugees in the informal sector, although it is generally self-employment, and in precarious activities. The following deduction can therefore be hypothesized: while migrant refugees are more likely to be employed, they are more likely to be in the informal sector and in precarious jobs where they are exploited.

Treatment and services received by refugees

A number of challenges that refugees face on a daily basis were highlighted in the survey results. Some of those interviewed indicated that they are often turned away when they need medical attention because they do not have proper documents. This does not mean they are undocumented, nor do they have fake documents. It simply means they don't have the green South African I.D. The survey also revealed that refugees from the Great Lakes region of Africa and the Horn of Africa struggle to communicate in proper English, which affects the way they explain to health workers the state of their health. Such misunderstanding often results in wrong or poor diagnosis. At times, health workers would just give refugees "paracetamol" and tell them to go home. Kimba, a twenty-seven-year-old man from the DRC, believes "the worst places [to go] are the hospitals because of nurses' bad attitudes toward refugees whose English is very poor." A Zimbabwean woman from Cape Town had a slightly positive opinion. She said, "I acknowledge getting health care for free at the hospitals. But these days, hospital sisters have become a bit difficult with us though they continue to treat us."

Most refugees do not visit health centres because of the kind of treatment they receive from the nurses. Some refugees thought they were received with an attitude of both apathy and antipathy. For instance, Ronelle, a thirty-nine-year-old woman from Rwanda, said a nurse would not speak to her in English because she is not white. The nurse said, "You must learn isiZulu; why did you start learning English when you came here? Why didn't you learn isiZulu first?" It appears that most medical professionals including nurses demand that refugees speak a South African language instead of English in order to get any attention or help because they are not white, the assumption being that only whites are expected to speak to a black person in English. When faced with this treatment, many refugees may opt to just stay at home and not seek medical attention or may resort to self-medication. Notwithstanding such negative treatment, the majority of refugees in the survey believe hospitals are doing well compared to other institutions; some 59 percent appreciated the services of the hospitals.

The survey indicated that 76 percent of the refugees were not happy with the services offered by the Department of Home Affairs. As for the banks, most refugees complained about the fact that their documents were not recognized. One respondent from Cape Town said the banks are "the most harassing places for refugees here in South Africa" because when he goes there, they make him feel like a criminal and that he is not welcome in this country. This treatment indicates that the services of most institutions needs to be improved especially when dealing with refugees.

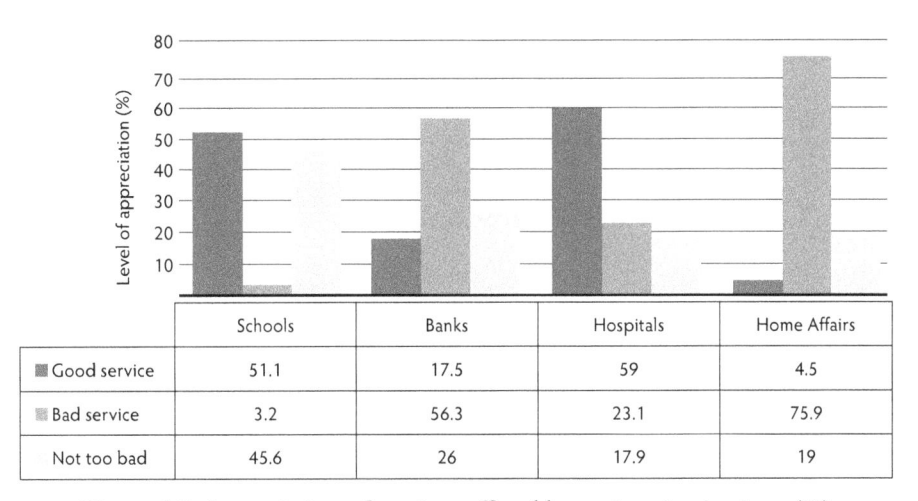

	Schools	Banks	Hospitals	Home Affairs
Good service	51.1	17.5	59	4.5
Bad service	3.2	56.3	23.1	75.9
Not too bad	45.6	26	17.9	19

Figure 6.7: Appreciation of services offered by various institutions (%)

Police Service for Refugees

Refugees do not seem to be fond of the South African police. Most of the participants were either silent or used the "no comment" approach on the question of the South African Police Service (SAPS). As a result, 37 percent of the participants were "neutral" on that matter. Most of them said they didn't want to be in trouble with "those people" (the policemen). However, 35 percent of the participants made it clear that they did not trust the SAPS because the SAPS do not like foreigners. Some accused the SAPS of taking bribes and being the most corrupt officials, while others accuse them of favouring South Africans over refugees when there is clash between members of the two communities. Mahmoud, a Somali trader in Cape Town, said the following concerning the police: "If you tell them your problem, they don't take it normal like someone who have (*sic*) a South African I.D." So, there were mixed feelings concerning the services of SAPS. Still, 28 percent of the participants said they had faith and confidence in the SAPS. Indeed, not all refugees disliked the services of the SAPS. In fact, Bucumi, a thirty-year-old man from Burundi living in Port Elizabeth, mentioned that the SAPS should work hand in hand with foreigners so that foreigners could help them hunt down their fellow foreigners who commit criminal acts. In Bucumi's words, "For the police to be successful, they should get foreigners to their side to get rid of refugee criminals." The graphical representation of the level of trust refugees have in the South African police is indexed in Figure 6.8 by percentage.

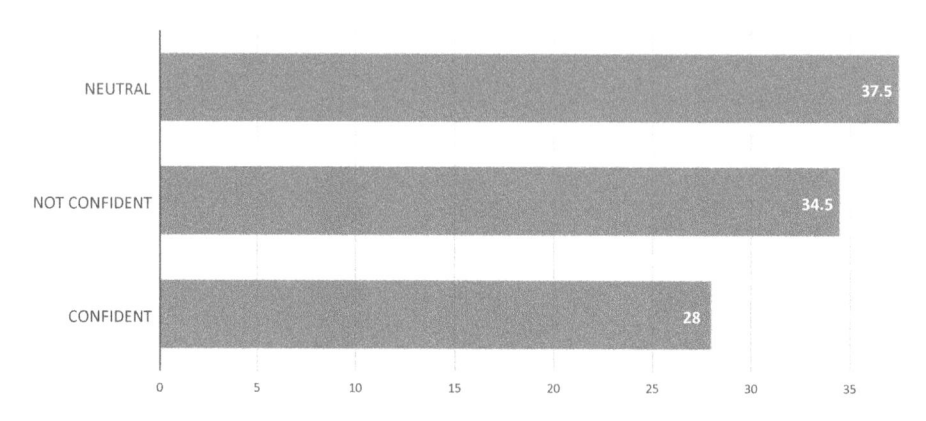

Figure 6.8: Level of confidence with the SAPS (%)

Reasons for Leaving Home

South Africa attracts a large number of refugee migrants. The main reasons for leaving their home countries and fleeing to South Africa include escape from poverty, political violence, and war. But despite the fact that the policies and laws applicable to refugees and asylum seekers in South Africa are largely progressive on paper, law and order is rarely enforced as expected when it comes to refugees. South Africa is one of the most unequal societies in the world, with a growing gap between rich and poor, and refugees from sub-Saharan Africa are caught in the middle of it. They are often targeted in the communities where they live and accused of stealing jobs and resources. The study provided evidence that 56 percent of refugees left their countries due to civil wars, ethnic or religious conflicts, or violations of human rights. This result makes sense because the majority of the participants in this survey were from war-torn countries, and the situation in some of their countries is still unsafe for them. A small number of refugees, however, admitted that they were "pulled" by opportunities in South Africa. They assumed once they were in South Africa, they stood a better chance of finding a better job compared to what they could get in their own country. Figure 6.9 represents the main reasons why refugees leave their countries and flee to South Africa by percentages.

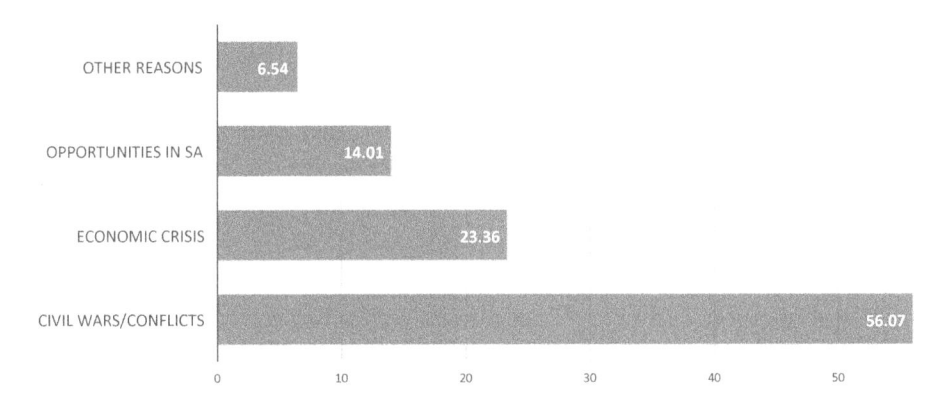

Reason	%
OTHER REASONS	6.54
OPPORTUNITIES IN SA	14.01
ECONOMIC CRISIS	23.36
CIVIL WARS/CONFLICTS	56.07

Figure 6.9: Main reasons refugees left their countries (%)

Arrival in the Host Country

From 1984, with the failure of the Nkomati accords and the escalation of conflict in Mozambique,[3] hundreds of thousands of Mozambican civilians crossed the border to seek refuge in South Africa. The Nkomati accords were concluded in 1984 between South Africa and the Mozambican government. Mozambique was to stop supporting the African National Congress in exchange for a similar disengagement of South Africa from RENAMO, the Mozambican National Resistance or in Portuguese the *Resistência Nacional Moçambicana*. Indeed according to various analysts, the agreements were respected on the Mozambican side, but the South African government continued to clandestinely support RENAMO, which led to the resumption of fighting. The South African government then refused to grant refugee status to asylum seekers from Mozambique. However as Wa Kabwe-Segatti puts it, "the racism of the apartheid regime meant that the authorities, on the other hand, welcomed the ex-Mozambican and Rhodesian settlers with open arms when Mozambique and Zimbabwe gained independence."[4] Without papers, the asylum seekers from Mozambique were considered illegal immigrants. Such a policy prevented international agencies, particularly UNHCR, from providing aid to a population fleeing a conflict for which South Africa was largely responsible.

UNHCR could only intervene in the early 1990s, when the apartheid regime was easing and the conflict in Mozambique was coming to an end. Wa Kabwe-Segatti indicates that the UNHCR and the South African government were to grant a "group refugee" status to Mozambicans who arrived between January 1985 and December 1992.[5] This status is also called "prima facie."[6] It is applied for massive displacements of refugees where case-by-case management is impossible to implement. The provision also concerned Mozambican

---

3. Gerhard Erasmus, "The Accord of Nkomati: Context and Content," The South African Institute of International Affairs (1984), https://media.africaportal.org/documents/The_Accord_Of_Nkomati.pdf, 1–33; see also "What the Nkomati Accord Means for Africa," *The Black Scholar* 15, no. 6 (1984): 15–22. http://www.jstor.org/stable/41067114.

4. Aurelia Wa Kabwe-Segatti, "Du Rapatriement Volontaire au Refoulement Dissimulé: Les Réfugiés Mozambicains en Afrique du Sud," *Politique africaine* 1, no. 1 (2002): 75–92; see also Aurelia Wa Kabwe-Segatti, "Reformulating Immigration Policy in Post-Apartheid South Africa: From the Aliens Control Act of 1991 to the Immigration Act of 2002," IFAS Working Paper Series / Les Cahiers de l' IFAS 8 (2006), 171–85.

5. A. Wa Kabwe-Segatti, "'Clandestins' et 'Makwerekwere' dans l'Afrique du Sud post-apartheid: production de catégories, pratiques administratives et xénophobie," *Social Science Information* 47, no. 4 (2008): 661–80.

6. Bonaventure Rutinwa, "Prima Facie Status and Refugee Protection," *New Issues in Refugee Research* 69 (2002).

contract workers who had become refugees following the deterioration of the situation in their country of origin. In the texts, of course, nothing obliged the refugees to return to Mozambique by their own means or within the framework of the voluntary repatriation programme (VRP). However, the status they held offered them no assurance that they would be able to integrate permanently into the South African society, if that were their final choice. From its development, the VRP thus revealed its limits by not guaranteeing the protection of Mozambicans who had preferred to remain in South Africa.

It is indeed striking that at the time of the VRP, tens of thousands of Mozambicans were forcibly evicted by the South African army and police.[7] These expulsions were part of the Aliens Control Act of 1937 and the Aliens Control Act of 1991.[8] Under apartheid, South Africa practiced an immigration policy which was based on an openly racist legislation known as the "Two-Gate policy."[9] In 1986, an amendment to the Aliens Control Act first removed the term "European" from section 4 (3) (b) which required all immigrants to be "assimilated" to the white population. This was conceived in such a way as to favour an immigration of "white" and qualified populations.[10] The South African government continued to recruit inexpensive, low-skilled, "black" labour from neighbouring countries on a temporary status. Mozambique, in particular, provided a major part of those cheap labourers, who went to work in the mines of the Transvaal or on the plantations of the present provinces of North West and Mpumalanga. As part of bilateral agreements, the recruiting office of the major South African mining companies, the WNLA (Witwatersrand Native Labour Association), had thus obtained exemptions which officially allowed them to bypass the usual immigration procedures of the Aliens Control Act.[11] It is therefore hardly surprising that Mozambicans now constitute the majority of those expelled from South Africa. What Mozambicans have suffered in previous years in South Africa, the majority of refugees now in South Africa continue to suffer.

---

7. Tshidiso Maloka, "Mines and Labour Migrants in Southern Africa," *Journal of Historical Sociology* 10, no. 2 (1997): 213–24.

8. Wa Kabwe-Segatti, "Reformulating Immigration Policy," 179.

9. Jonathan Crush and David A. McDonald, "Introduction to Special Issue: Evaluating South African Immigration Policy after Apartheid," *Africa Today* 48, no. 3 (2001): 1–13. See also Maloka, "Mines and Labour Migrants."

10. Wa Kabwe-Segatti, "Du Rapatriement Volontaire," 85.

11. Maloka, "Mines and Labour," 219. See also Wa Kabwe-Segatti, "Du Rapatriement Volontaire," 78–81.

The study revealed that most of the refugees came to South Africa during the 2000–2010 decade, prior to which only a few were in South Africa. Some participants from the Great Lakes region arrived in South Africa in mid-1990s immediately after the ethnic conflicts of Burundi, Rwanda, and DRC. However, among the refugees from the Horn of Africa, especially Somali, were those who have been around since early 1990s.

As soon as they arrive in South Africa, asylum seekers are expected to go to the nearest refugee reception centre (RRC) to apply for asylum. There were initially five RRCs in South Africa located in the five major cities from which the participants of this study were drawn. However, some of these reception centres have recently been shut down. The decision to close these offices was the result of a court ruling after complaints by some business owners that the centres were becoming a nuisance in the areas. For example, the North-End refugee office in Port Elizabeth was closed in November 2011; the Crown Mines refugee office in Johannesburg was closed in May 2011; and the Maitland refugee office in Cape Town was closed in June 2012. This left only two fully operational RRCs in South Africa: the Umbilo office in Durban and the Marabastad office in Pretoria. Until recently, refugees all over South Africa travelled to either Durban or Pretoria to renew their papers or get any other form of documentation. Today even the Marabastad RRC in Pretoria has been closed, and refugees now have to travel to Durban or return to the entry point in Musina if they want to regularize their stay or apply for another document such as the refugee identity card or a travel document.

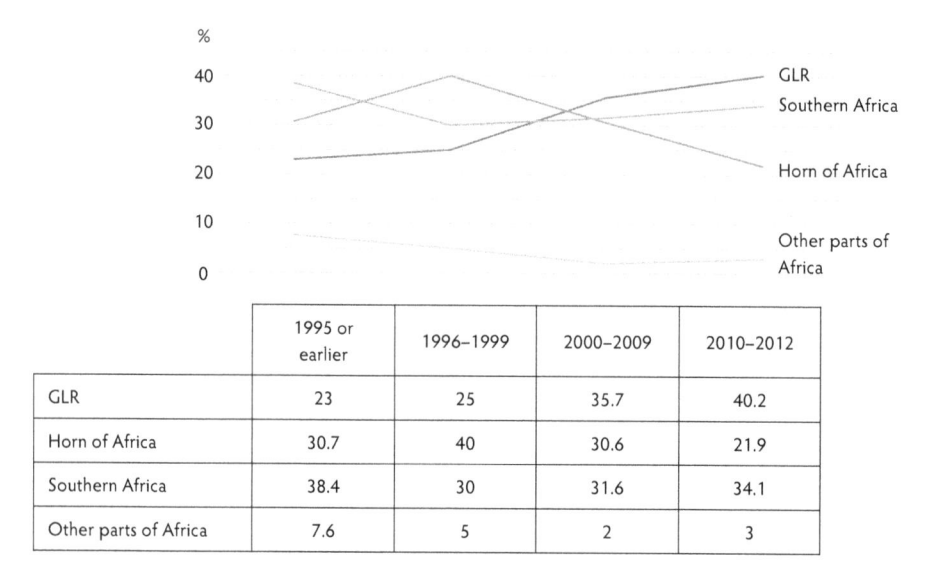

	1995 or earlier	1996–1999	2000–2009	2010–2012
GLR	23	25	35.7	40.2
Horn of Africa	30.7	40	30.6	21.9
Southern Africa	38.4	30	31.6	34.1
Other parts of Africa	7.6	5	2	3

Figure 6.10: Arrival of refugees in South Africa by country of origin (%)

The question of documentation

Refugees need proper documents that will give them access to specific services in the host country. Indeed, with the right documents they have various rights including the right for employment, the right for education, and the right for freedom of movement among others, although most of these rights often remain inaccessible. In South Africa when asylum seekers arrive at the RRC, their fingerprints are taken and their personal records filled out on a form. Among the questions asked on that form are the country of origin and the reasons for coming to South Africa. This visit is often considered as the first interview. Then refugees are given a temporary permit, an asylum seekers' permit or Section 22, the duration of which varies from anything from one week to recently six months. This permit allows refugees to have a second interview to obtain a refugee status or Section 24 permit, which is renewable every four years. However, refugees nowadays complain that even this Section 24 permit is no longer granted for four years. They can go to the home affairs office to have their refugee status renewed and be granted six months, a year, or any other unconventional period depending on the mood of the immigration officer. This makes the validity of the Section 24 permit more or less the same as that of the Section 22 permit.

Most surveyed refugees had an aversion to the whole process of documentation. They indicated that they had to return to the RRC several times before their application for refugee status was approved. The survey also revealed that most applications were rejected, eventually, and the victim had approximately three weeks to appeal. In such cases, lawyers for human rights have to intervene to get these rejections reconsidered or overturned. Asylum seekers also have to wait for a very long time to become refugees after having been given a Section 22 temporary permit. This state of affairs illustrates the many challenges relating to the documentation of refugees in South Africa. Bilombele, a forty-two-year-old Congolese refugee in Port Elizabeth, had this to say with regard to his documentation: "There is poor [system of] documentation, and that creates chaos. As a refugee I can't open a bank account. I'm forced to keep my money in my pocket. When robbers know this, they target us to steal. The bank refuses to accept my refugee status as a legal document due to the reason that Home Affairs couldn't give the necessary information with regard to my refugee status."

In a similar vein, Rudo, a twenty-nine-year-old lady from Zimbabwe trading in Cape Town, reported the following: "This affects me in a negative way. Because with this A4 size permit they give us, we get no job; even with the status or I.D.; no job. That is why I do not do my professional job." This situation was more sensitive for Tshibala, a thirty-eight-year-old man from the DRC who had lived in South Africa for twelve years. He said, "I have been trying to get an I.D. since 2005, but they never responded, and didn't tell me why."

From these respondents, it is obvious that refugees struggle to access certain services due to the lack of communication between the Home Affairs Department and most service providers, especially on the validity of refugees' documents. Thus refugees face professional discrimination because they receive documents from the government that are deemed legal on paper but which are not accepted by the same issuing government or public institutions. In other words, whether someone is still an asylum seeker or is already recognized as a refugee in the country does not matter because, quite frankly, having refugee status does not make a difference in terms of services received from various government institutions. Besides most South Africans, even professionals, do not know the difference between an asylum seeker and a recognized refugee, and this lack of knowledge on something that basic dictates the way they view and treat refugees.

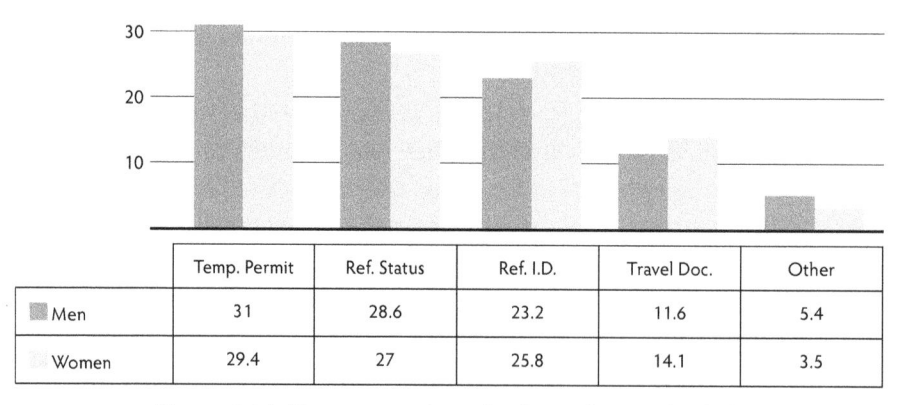

	Temp. Permit	Ref. Status	Ref. I.D.	Travel Doc.	Other
Men	31	28.6	23.2	11.6	5.4
Women	29.4	27	25.8	14.1	3.5

Figure 6.11: Documentation of refugees by gender (%)

Figure 6.11 illustrates the documentation state of the refugees surveyed in South Africa. As can be observed, at the time of this study, many refugees had only the temporary permit, which means they had to go regularly to the nearest RRC for an extension of this document because they were still asylum seekers, and their application for the refugee status was still under review.

The role of the church

It is important to note that the refugee participants were from different faith communities, mainly Christians and Muslims but none atheist, which is indicative of the fact that refugees in South Africa are generally religious. Though religious affiliation was not included in this survey, I asked respondents to tell in general what they thought of the church in South Africa. Even members of non-Christian communities such as Somalis took their time to answer this question. As the table below indicates, refugees were overwhelmingly comfortable with the role that the church played in ensuring their stay in the country was comfortable.

Table 6.3: Feelings of refugees toward the church (%)

	Happy	Not happy
Men (ratio)	105 (81.3%)	24 (18.6%)
Women (ratio)	70 (82.3%)	15 (17.6%)

To show her excitement about what the church did (and still does), Bethlehem, a thirty-five-year-old woman from Ethiopia living in Cape Town, had this to say: "Wow! If it wasn't for the church, it would have been very difficult for me. They fill my hope and make me go far. They energize me in everything." Bethlehem's statement justifies the degree of happiness with the church as shown in Table 6.3.

A church that welcomes strangers is, in any case, a sign of contradiction in that it is a place where joy and pain, tears and peace are mixed. This welcome becomes especially visible in societies that are hostile to those who are not welcomed, such as South Africa. In this study, many refugees appreciated the role of the church saying that it was their only place of refuge when xenophobic attacks erupt and they had nowhere else to flee. During the recent xenophobic violence in South Africa, churches around the country opened their doors to welcome refugees, and they lived in these churches for months even as locals and business owners nearby continued to demand their eviction. Alberto, a forty-seven-year-old Mozambican who has lived in South Africa for about twenty-four years but who does not have citizenship or even permanent residence, said with agony –

> I didn't feel safe in Gugulethu [a township in Cape Town] where I lived for many years; more than ten years. I arrived in South Africa in 1992, still very young, just after Mandela came from prison. If the system in this country was good and friendly to us, black

Africans, I was going to have South African ID by now. But I'm still an asylum seeker, and my children who were all born here are still asylum seekers, too. Why? Now I live here in this small house with my wife and the little ones; the big ones live with their friends now. I got afraid to go back to my house in Gugulethu after staying inside the Methodist church for like four months because we were safe there with my family.

Like Alberto and his family, most of the refugees had vowed not to leave the church premises until they were resettled outside South Africa. UNHCR does not practice collective resettlement; all requests are considered individually on a case-by-case basis. The refugees who ran to the church for shelter may have been tired of waiting because UNHCR did not appear to be meeting their resettlement expectations. It was then that they decided to reintegrate into the local communities, but Alberto and his family were traumatized by the xenophobic violence and were not ready to face the people who nearly killed them in Gugulethu. Resettlement applies to cases where voluntary repatriation cannot be considered and where integration into the local community is impossible for security reasons. In addition, UNHCR only resettles those who have already been recognized as refugees. Asylum seekers do not benefit from the resettlement programme. In the case of Alberto and his family, they are still asylum seekers despite Alberto himself having lived in South Africa for almost a quarter of a century. His family cannot be resettled to a third country. This situation shows that there are obvious shortcomings in the entire South African immigration system.

The church plays an important role in the spiritual, social, and economic life of refugees. Despite being traumatized by the xenophobic violence Alberto has survived on numerous occasions, he said that the church has shaped and continues to shape his motivation to integrate and his quest to belong, especially since resettlement does not seem to be happening anytime soon. Thus refugees tend to integrate into the local community even if the local government does not facilitate the process. Cultural and linguistic issues are often a challenge and an obstacle to refugees' attempts to integrate into the local community, so are important issues that must be considered when policies for the integration of refugees into the local community are being established. It appears that refugees who have developed religious attributes and are affiliated with a local church are more likely to cope with the trauma related to their lived experiences, including xenophobia, because the church provides the opportunity to make sense of it.

Three durable solutions to the protracted refugee situation are often suggested; namely, repatriation to the country of origin, resettlement in a third country, or local integration in the country in which the refugee lives.[12] However, the complexity of integration makes the concept confusing in practice. Many debates focus on the meaning of integration, what it implies in terms of entitlements and rights, and its effects on both refugees and the host community. As the church tries to help refugees integrate, local authorities should design integration policies so that host and refugee communities can coexist and share available resources without conflict. Integration must therefore allow refugees to retain their own identity and, at the same time, adapt psychologically to their new situation.

One of the roles of the local church is to love and welcome strangers (cf. Lev 19:34; Matt 25:34–36; Deut 10:19). Refugees are among the most vulnerable people in the world, which is why God calls us to seek their protection and well-being. In Durban, Mkhize, a fifty-five-year-old pastor of a local Baptist church where a good number of refugees attend, said that the first thing local church leaders can do is educate their members about forced displacement in the world today so they can be better informed about the phenomenon themselves. In his words, "Encourage your church community to be informed, because from the deportation of Adam and Eve from the garden of Eden to the exile of John on the island of Patmos, the biblical account is filled with stories of forced displacement. So, church leaders, we need to educate our members about the context of forced displacement in the Bible." Indeed, it is important for Christ's followers to see the pattern of God at work amid forced displacement in the Scriptures so that they anticipate his power at work in today's refugee crises. Pastor Mkhize continued, "As you develop an informed understanding of the realities of refugees with a deep biblical perspective of forced displacement in the Bible, be intentional in incorporating this into your teaching." He insists that leaders of local churches should encourage their members to pray for refugees in their own city because, "They are now part of our life. We must therefore be intentional and keep our eyes open; look for them at work, school, and church. Look for them in your community. Pray for opportunities to love them."

In this study, one of the questions I frequently asked refugee participants was, "What are your biggest challenges as a refugee?" The answers were varied. A thirty-six-year-old Angolan said, "It is very difficult to find affordable

---

12. K. Wright and R. Black, "Poverty, Migration and Human Well-being: Towards a Post-crisis Research and Policy Agenda," *Journal of International Development* 23, no. 4 (2011): 551.

housing." A twenty-four-year-old woman from Zimbabwe said, "It is very difficult to find a good job to pay bills." A twenty-nine-year-old Somali woman said, "It is difficult to learn English." A thirty-one-year-old Zimbabwean woman said, "It is difficult to know how to access and navigate the social welfare system." A thirty-four-year-old man from DRC said, "It is difficult to understand the school system and help children with their homework." A forty-three-year-old Ethiopian woman said, "It is difficult to learn to navigate public transport system." A forty-nine-year-old from South Sudan said, "I don't know yet where the main services and shops are." And a fifty-five-year-old Eritrean said, "It is difficult to understand this new culture." Of course, asylum seekers and newly arrived refugees often need help with various things including temporary shelter and a safe living space, basic food items, clothes and shoes, local transport, and communication with loved ones back home. These are some of the needs that local congregations are to help refugees with.

My interaction with refugees showed that they are generally happy with the little the church is doing to make sure they are settled. Although a local church cannot directly meet all of the needs of refugees, we can often refer refugees to services that can help them. Refugees also face challenges related to deep personal needs such as coping with loss, regaining hope, making new friendships, finding and integrating into a local community, etc. In my case, having lived as a refugee for so many years, I have visited refugees and displaced people in a few countries. Listening to their stories and witnessing their daily struggle in their country of asylum or during their flight, and through my own lived experiences, I have come to understand that for the vast majority of refugees, there is nothing as powerful as their faith that helps them cope with fear, loss, grief, and misery. Faith is so essential to the hope and resilience of refugees.

The history of the early church reveals how finding the solution to conflicts and the acceptance of the cultures of others constitute two of the first salient features of church mission. The early Christians practiced church mission through welcoming the stranger with *philoxenia* – a Greek word meaning love and hospitality toward a stranger – the opposite of xenophobia. Indeed, welcoming and hospitality are fundamental characteristics of church mission, including ministry among asylum seekers, refugees, and internally displaced persons. Providing hospitality stems from a commitment to be faithful to God and to listen to his voice in the Holy Scriptures. Thanks to hospitality, the stranger is welcomed into the local church and into the local community, which should be a place of safety where they can find comfort, respect, and acceptance.

The church is key to enabling refugees to overcome their trauma, make sense of their loss, and rebuild their lives from scratch. As the church we should help refugees reconfirm their identity as individuals and as members of a community. We should also provide personal and collective support to refugees which is crucial for their ability to recover from conflict and all its related ordeals. The church can contribute far more than many realize to the protection and well-being of refugees and, ultimately, to the quest for durable solutions. It is clear that refugees face a wide variety of difficult challenges, and as the church we may not be able to meet them all, but we clearly have much to offer. It is not surprising to see how the needs of foreigners such as refugees and asylum seekers are mentioned by Jesus in Matthew 25:35–36, "I was hungry and you gave me food, I was thirsty and you gave me something to drink, I was a stranger and you welcomed me, I was naked and you gave me clothing, I was sick and you took care of me, I was in prison and you visited me."

In this chapter, the voices of refugees are heard through their personal stories. They are voices of hope, resilience, and courage despite the challenges confronting them. We saw that although most of the respondents felt rejected and their socioeconomic conditions were inadequate due to unemployment and other life challenges related to their condition as refugees, and although they felt mistreated by the police, refugees find comfort in the church and appreciate what the church is doing for them. Local authorities and public institutions should consider partnering with the church so that they can combine their efforts to deal with the refugee phenomenon. These combined efforts can lead to transformational development structures and measures that can benefit both the local community and the refugee community. The next chapter looks at the principles of transformational development and proposes a framework that can be used to help vulnerable communities such as refugees achieve holistic change.

Discussion Questions

1. Why is it important to listen to the stories of refugees, and what attitude should we display before refugees so they do not feel rejected?
2. How can we as individual Christian believers show hospitality to refugees?
3. What steps can we as a local church take to "speak up" on behalf of refugees?

4. Our upbringing can prevent us from having relationships with certain groups of people – for example those of a different age, gender, ethnicity, or tribe, or those who are poor.
   - How can we overcome these feelings and help our children grow up and relate to people of all kinds, including refugees?
   - What are you doing to meet the needs of people in general and refugees in particular within your community?
5. Read Genesis 23:2–4 and Hebrews 11:8–10.
   - In what way was Abraham a foreigner?
   - What did God want to teach Abraham through this experience?
6. Read Hebrews 11:13–16.
   - What helped Abraham and the other people listed in Hebrews 11 to live as foreigners and strangers on this earth?

7

Principles of Transformational Community Development

When refugees arrive in a host country, they show great relief. Some express it by letting their tears flow, while others do so by remaining silent. They feel relieved to have gone through the anxieties and fears, but also to have arrived in a space where they are no longer confronted with fear, persecution, and death as was the case in their country, or in the countries they have gone through. In my case, no border of any kind whatsoever would have stopped my determination, which was mixed with both despair and hope. This determination characterized my will to move forward, never to stop, until a place of protection was reached. I was of course aware of the risks facing me, and the dangers ahead of me, but that only boosted my confidence to weigh my chances and negotiate how best I could move forward. There was no choice but to keep going, and even fenced or guarded borders could not thwart my resolve to keep going and reach a place of safety. I had hope that my life has a future. My lived experiences are proof that hope knows no borders.

There is no more important quality for community transformation than hope. Change begins with individuals, and then it grows as we work together with the hope for a better and more fruitful future. Such a perspective requires a participatory approach applied at every stage of a community transformation plan, and it is crucial to achieving the level of participation needed for lasting change. So, there is a need to strengthen church mission by proposing principles that will guide a praxical framework of transformational community development. These principles specify our role as the church in fostering human flourishing. The principles will guide any Christian actively involved in development practice in becoming a catalyst for community transformation. It should be noted that refugees are the objects of many writings and the subject of countless theorizations within the development spectrum. Yet there seems to be few or no results on the refugee phenomenon due to the lack of reflection and action. A theory must be converted into concrete actions to serve as praxis. Therefore, we must be committed as the church to assisting those refugees in need while fostering self-sufficiency. We must be committed to offering access to available opportunities while promoting awareness of unity in diversity for the benefit of the community we serve. In other words, we need to do more work as the church when we are involved in the process of community transformation. Ann Morisy emphasizes that the new approach to mission is community ministry.[1]

> The full expression of community ministry involves a process which has a number of features or stages. The most obvious aspect is that of responding to an issue of local concern. Such issues might include a growing level of debt in a neighbourhood, the need to provide additional support for people with mental health problems, or the need to provide support for single parents.[2]

Morisy's statement is a call to transformational community development which indicates that we need to be actively involved in community ministry "as a method of sharing the faith."[3] This assertion is indeed true because faith as a pillar of the Christian life is demonstrated not only in words but also in deeds – that is, not only through *kerygma* but also through *diakonia*. The "kerygmatic" aspect of the gospel is the proclamation of the good news through words, like a herald. The diaconal aspect of the gospel is the proclamation of the good news through acts of service. Therefore, it is diaconal for us the church to be of service to refugees. For us the church to be effective in our ministry of *diaconia* to refugees, we need to have a structure of transformational community development to guide our interventions. The PRAISE framework below highlights some fundamental principles that define community development work. These principles are strongly interdependent and can be used in any community development activities. Depending on the activity, some principles may be more important, but the other principles can always be taken into account when determining the optimal approach.

---

1. Morisy, *Beyond the Good Samaritan*.
2. Morisy, 5.
3. Morisy, 7.

PRAISE: A Framework for Transformational Community Development

Transformation is change, and change has always been difficult, which is why most people do not want change because it disrupts the status quo. Change is necessary. However, to be successful in implementing change in a community, we need to have the right framework. This is where the six principles of PRAISE come in. They describe how to consistently and effectively implement transformational change in a community. The six principles of PRAISE are not a linear process of the "step by step" type but rather a circular framework whose implementation process depends on the identified needs of the community. The PRAISE framework is a set of principles against which a transformational development plan can be measured. The principles respond to God's concern for the poor. They encourage capacity building by getting us actively involved in the real issues of the community. The PRAISE principles help us to turn community challenges into opportunities for hope. In brief, the six PRAISE principles assist us to alleviate the impact of poverty, and in so doing, we become more relevant in the community as the church. The sequence of the framework is decided by the user.

Figure 7.1: The PRAISE framework[4]

---

4. Figure conceived and drawn by the author.

Promoting human dignity

Christian social thought is based on a vision that recognizes the incomparable and inalienable dignity of a human being made in the living image of God. Thus, the principle of human dignity comes from God. As the church we are therefore expected to endorse the ethical demands of human dignity because, in essence, a human being has transcendent worth from God. When we promote the values of human dignity for the poor, we will be equipped with a guideline for action and reflection, while the poor will be equipped with a tool for conscience formation. Conscience is linked to morality, which is inherent in all humans and to God. The formation of conscience is therefore the activity of moral self-transcendence, the conscious and critical determination of that which constitutes who we are and frames our knowledge of the world. So when as the church we promote and defend the dignity of those who are pushed to the margins of society, we are contributing to their formation of conscience as they begin to be more and more aware of who they are. Their conscience is restored as if it had never been damaged by the state of indignity to which they were subjected. A conscience that is shaped by and aware of facts, evidence, etc. enables us to know ourselves and our world and act accordingly.

Indeed, the dignity of a human person is attested to by the fact that human beings are not as other living beings – their uniqueness is marked by divine originality and likeness. Promoting human dignity is basic for community transformation since dignity is not dependent on any human quality or individual merit. The chief end of transformational community development is to positively impact every aspect of an individual person in a sustainable way. The change in question is holistic. A holistic approach means that the transformation agent provides support that impacts the person as a whole, not just one aspect of their needs. The support should positively consider and therefore have an impact on all aspects of their being by taking into account their physical, emotional, social and spiritual well-being. Bragg finds that "true transformation depends on the establishment of all people's dignity and self-worth [because] people need self-esteem to be fully human."[5] We are well positioned as the church to help those in vulnerable situations – such as refugees – to restore their dignity.

Our role as the church is to pursue our own salvific end by not only communicating the way of eternal life to humanity but also by spreading, in a certain way, over the whole world the light that the divine life radiates. We

---

5. W. G. Bragg, "From Development to Transformation," in *The Church in Response to Human Need*, ed. V. Samuel and C. Sugden (Grand Rapids: Eerdmans, 1987), 42.

share this light in particular by defending and promoting the dignity of the human person, by strengthening social cohesion, and by providing our daily activities with a penetratingly deeper meaning. This work is not a secondary role that we would like to play in addition to our salvific mission; rather, it is a central function in our missional task. Indeed, the gospel message has an imperative social impact, which is why we are all meant to make it a factor of social progress. As members of human society, Christians have the divine mandate to participate in activities of community transformation according to the plan of God. Human beings are social beings by nature, and it is in this very nature of being social that human beings find the foundation of their relations to others. Thus, our commitment to promote human dignity appears to be a natural duty; but above all, it is a divine duty since we bear the image of God. In other words, the fact of being human gives us the responsibility to work for the flourishing of communities in general and for the well-being of every human person in particular. Because of the social character of the person, there is thus a link – an interdependence – between the dignity of the person and the sustainable transformation of the entire community.

To promote human dignity is to announce the salvation found in Christ and to help men and women enter into this divine perspective because salvation in God presupposes integral well-being here and now. So transformational community development is a call to us to take an active part in the salvific mission of promoting human dignity in all its perspectives by reaffirming that the joys and hopes, the sorrows and anxieties of the poor, the downtrodden, and the marginalized are also our joys and hopes, sorrows and anxieties. This identification is truly an interpellation to commit ourselves to the cause of humanity, especially the poorest, as a sign of close solidarity with the whole human family of which we are members. Social commitment to the promotion and respect of human dignity is an imperative requirement of the Christian faith if we are to holistically and sustainably transform the lives of people in a given community.

We are in a world that judges us on the basis of our actions, our functions, and our capacities more than on our being. Nevertheless, human beings in essence have value, regardless of their social rank, their race, or their ethnicity, and independently of any other criterion of judgment or distinction. This natural dignity was conferred on human beings by God, meaning my dignity resides in my divine nature (Gen 1:27–28). Therefore, what makes refugees sacred is their bearing of the divine mark. To affirm their primacy over, for instance, the economic, political, or industrial structures; the inviolability or sanctity of their dignity; and their right to life from conception to their natural end is a Christian's duty. Making dignity the *sine qua non* of transformational community development is a constant of church mission. The church that promotes the dignity of a human person thus engages effectively in the community transformation process. Nowadays human dignity is not always valued, and the person of a human being is often reduced to a machine of production or pleasure. The living and working conditions and the wages and hours of work of some employees, violence against women around the world, and exploitation and abuse of vulnerable people are all proof of this instrumentalization and commodification of the human person. Therefore, we have a pressing mandate to challenge the systems and structures that reduce human dignity to nothingness. Indeed, we do not have a magic formula to solve social problems; however, by our commitment to promoting the dignity of a human person, we also aim to improve the well-being of all people.

Non-respect of human dignity hinders human flourishing. Thus, we must eradicate poverty as an evil if we are to foster human flourishing and attain community transformation. We as the church exist to work for the protection of the dignity of every person including those millions of people who find themselves in the unenviable situation of forced displacement. All of human beings without distinction are created in the image and likeness of God (Gen 1:26–27) and therefore bear the divine mark of dignity. It would be all too easy to objectify refugees by simply considering them as elements of a "phenomenon" or a "crisis," forgetting that they have been faced with the painful situation of forced displacement that pushed them to leave their countries. Nevertheless, refugees can find solace and assurance in the belief that we do not have a city here that lasts forever, and that is why we seek that which is to come (cf. Heb 13:14). However, passivity has no place in the Christian life. If we are aware of the suffering of others, it is our duty as the church to act.

A church that is concerned about human dignity is God-honouring, Christ-centred, Spirit-led, faith-grounded, and people-focused. This is not, however, a question of Christian humanism, which stresses the life of Jesus vis-à-vis individual freedom and dignity without believing in the existence of God. The PRAISE principle of promoting human dignity makes an individual believer not only a doer of routine liturgies but someone who is committed to transforming the life of an individual other in a holistic way, which is also an act of worship that honours God. The promotion of human dignity helps individuals to discover the potential hidden within them and to develop this capacity to obtain better and lasting results. In other words, promoting human dignity suggests that we look beyond human characteristics and focus only on the humanity of people. To do this, we must stop stereotyping and focus only on the *imago Dei*. When we promote human dignity, we put in place strategies and structures in response to human needs.

Responding to human needs

The humanitarian needs of the current refugee crisis in Africa are immense, and we are called upon, always and again, to respond to and provide for the needs of the poor and the disadvantaged. Globalization leaves people "powerless to resist its momentum."[6] Most refugees live in situations of poverty, powerlessness, and constant struggle. Such a state of affairs warrants that we champion the implementation of integrated programmes for holistic transformation and ensure there is coherence between *missio Dei* and *diakonia*. In this way, we contribute to alleviating poverty and suffering.

When we respond to the needs of refugees in community, we simply confirm that there is a place for the poor and the powerless in God's purpose. Meeting the basic needs of refugees becomes a process that leads to strengthening their humanity and restoring their dignity. Much in a successful community transformation process is about meeting people's needs. According to Abraham Maslow, human needs can be structured into five stages that are ordered by hierarchy because the lower needs in the pyramid must be satisfied before those positioned on the top of the pyramid.[7] However, this hierarchy does not mean that a need cannot be satisfied if the previous one is not completely satisfied. It is our task as the church to respond to the needs of those whom the global system leaves behind.

Basic requirements: These are survival needs that uphold every other need on the pyramid. These basic requirements are essential because they are all that human bodies need to survive. If these needs are not met, the human body cannot function optimally. Maslow considers these needs to be the most important, as all other needs become secondary until these are met. To be involved in the process of community transformation, we need to first identify these needs and respond to them accordingly. They include the need for food, water, shelter, sanitation, and clothing. So these needs are basic, and they must be met in order to survive. People who are desperate to feed their families are a perfect representation of people at this level. Such people are willing to give

---

6. Morisy, *Beyond the Good Samaritan*, 125.
7. Corporate Finance Institute, "Maslow's Hierarchy of Needs," CFI (2021), https://corporatefinanceinstitute.com/resources/knowledge/other/maslows-hierarchy-of-needs/.

up their dreams, safety, and freedom (including committing criminal acts) in order to obtain food. When we meet these needs as the church, we restore the dignity of the people concerned.

```
                    Self-
                 actualization
                Personal needs
                 Social needs
              Safety and security
              Basic requirements
```

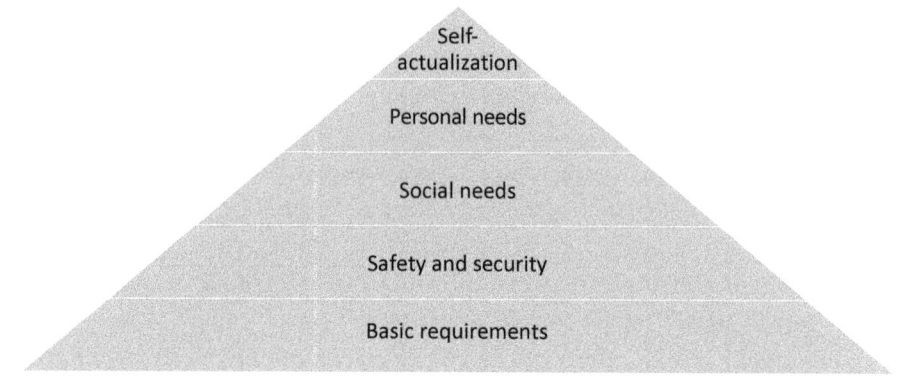

Figure 7.2: The human needs pyramid (adapted from Maslow's hierarchy of needs)

Safety and security needs: These are the second most basic needs. Safety and security needs are classified into three categories: physical security, financial security, and emotional security. *Physical security* is linked to the external security of our body. If people do not feel physically secure, their insecurity and stress levels increase, which affects their ability to concentrate and think, and their overall quality of life. *Financial security* refers to financial independence, the ability to pay the necessary bills and bear other unavoidable financial burdens. The third category is *emotional security*. People can feel emotionally safe if the other people in their surroundings are trustworthy, friendly, and cooperative and if they are in an open environment where they can share thoughts, ideas, and feelings. These needs are basically about protecting someone from harm and comprise the need for "inner peace," sleep, job security, health, and a safe environment.

Social needs: When a person feels safe, he or she will feel the need to be loved and accepted by others. So the social needs mainly relate to the need for love and belonging. It is said that the degree to which one enjoys life is represented by the strength of one's social relationships. Being part of a social group gives one a feeling of comfort. The social can be placed in two different categories: *sexual needs* and *non-sexual needs*. People who feel rejected by their friends or who are unhappy in intimate love represent this category of needs. When we as the church assist them to meet these needs for love and belonging, the affected people flourish and become much more motivated. We are called to respond to the social needs of the people in the community we serve and beyond. Meeting these needs includes responding to the need for socialization, for a loving family, for a community of faith, and for intimate friendship.

Personal needs: Each person has a unique set of personal needs above basic survival needs that must be met for them to be at their best. These include confidence and self-esteem. Meeting these needs are essential for people to prosper. In this stage, we begin to view people as individuals in order to take note of and respond to their personal needs. People seek to meet the needs of self-respect and self-confidence because these needs are most focused on the inner life, especially the needs for strength, self-control, and self-respect. It is essential to feel respected and recognized, and we as the church have the obligation to bring out the feelings of self-worth in people by meeting their personal needs.

Self-actualization needs: Self-actualization is the desire that leads to the realization of one's full potential. These needs include the need to be informed, to be educated, and to be creative. To meet the needs for self-actualization is to help people become all that they are capable of becoming. There are two levels of self-actualization, namely lower self-actualization and upper self-actualization. Lower self-actualization is associated with the need to gain the respect of others. It is about a need for attention, a desire for recognition, and an attraction to prestige. Upper self-actualization is self-respect, self-esteem, and self-worth. These inner qualities are essential because they prompt us to strive to be confident, independent, and free while having an aptitude that allows us to take charge of our own destiny. The two levels of self-actualization are intimately linked. As the church, it is our responsibility to equip those in positions of vulnerability with knowledge and skills so that they are able to participate in for example large-scale projects or be part of important missions to fill the need for self-actualization. Thus when as the church we are called to respond to the human needs of the most vulnerable and in particular refugees, we must ascertain the level of need to be filled. However, we must keep in mind that the needs vary depending on the personal circumstances of individuals. Therefore, we need to regularly reassess at which level of Maslow's pyramid the people in need are.

As the church we are required to do theology socially by caring for those in need. As Hughes and Bennet put it, "A human life that begins to flow from the heart of God will not be content with the injustices in the world that keep people in poverty."[8] We should not only tell those in need that Jesus came to set the oppressed free, to open the eyes of the blind, and to declare the year of God's favour (cf. Luke 4:18–19) but to also be practical by actually responding to their various needs as much as possible. The famous statement by Lao Tzu, the great Chinese philosopher and writer, gives us perspective: "Go to the people. Live with them. Learn from them. Love them. Start with what they know. Build with what they have . . . when the work is done, the task accomplished, the people will say: 'we did it ourselves'"![9]

People are more likely to fully accept a development activity aimed at community transformation when they are actively involved in the process. When they see their own ideas and fingerprints on the work that aims at responding to their needs, they will have a sense of ownership that feels real and authentic. Thus, responding to human needs calls for concrete actions with the full participation of the community in need of transformation. We are to be responsive to the needs of those in need in ways that show holistic care and love because the refugee phenomenon "is not only about the reasons and mechanics of the move to another place; [but also] about life in that new setting."[10]

Advocating for peace and justice

According to the dictionary, the word "advocacy" refers to the act of pleading, interceding for someone, speaking in favour of a person, or lobbying for an idea. Advocacy is one of the strategies to promote just and sustainable alternatives to structures that perpetuate the impoverishment of people. In other words, it is through advocacy that we can speak out against systems and policies that negatively affect the community and come up with just and sustainable alternatives. We should not be silent or discreet like the "underground church." Some of the advocacy activities that we can do to ensure a successful transformation of the community include education and mobilization of the population, engaging in direct dialogue with officials, taking an official position, and circulating petitions. Advocating for peace and justice is an indication that we have taken our rightful position as a peacemaking Christian community. We can make peacemaking in the community an everyday reality. Peace is not

---

8. Hughes and Bennett, *God of the Poor*, 154.
9. Cited in August, *Quest for Being Public Church*, iv.
10. Carroll, *Christians at the Border*, 71.

the signing of agreements between two antagonistic elites; it is rather a mutual understanding between ordinary members of the community. Therefore, we need to establish bonds of trust and interdependence between communities as a way of advancing lasting peace. When peace reigns, everyone will be provided with opportunities to pursue livelihoods and improve their well-being. Put differently, without peace human lives are vulnerable, and the prospects for sustainable development weaken.

Where there is no peace, the processes of transformational community development and capacity building are all affected. This is why we are to take initiative in peacemaking, peacebuilding, and peacekeeping as the church. Advocating for peace involves building a culture of justice and reconciliation by educating the community, because living at peace is much deeper than just the absence of conflict. Building this culture of peace and reconciliation entails proactivity promoting an ethos that refuses violent behaviours and that values defusing injustices. Advocacy is critical for the well-being of refugees and for church mission. It facilitates our work by tackling the root causes of some serious problems facing our society such as poverty and unemployment. Through advocacy, we contribute for instance to the protection of children, the promotion of justice, and the awareness of human rights. That is to say, advocacy is a significant tool in finding solutions to the ills of the society.

As the church we must foster peacebuilding initiatives that act on the root causes of the conflict, promote mediation, encourage local participation, value traditional practices, and introduce ways to ease tensions peacefully. Advocacy for justice includes both climate justice and environmental justice, and targets the economic, political, social, environmental, and spiritual well-being of every human being, including refugees. Therefore, as the church we must support the implementation of policies and practices that allow us to live together in harmony with the earth and that consider the responsibilities of decision makers.

In the context of the refugee phenomenon, we are called to empower the refugee community in all aspects at the local, national, and international levels through advocacy. We can take the voices of refugees to decision makers with the intention of changing prejudiced policies and practices. As the church, we are a peacemaking and just community, and are therefore expected to advance affirmative actions by fostering a sustainable process of transformational community development. This advocacy step may involve writing letters to concerned people or calling relevant offices and pleading with them to make decisions and policies that benefit the vulnerable such as refugees. Our voice as the church is a catalyst for community transformation. In brief, our advocacy is about lobbying for policies that favour all – refugees included. It is our mandate to listen to the concerns of the people we represent.

As the church, we are called to commit ourselves to the justice, peace, and integrity of all creation. This commitment also consists in feeding the hungry who need bread and helping the exploited who need justice, the victims of discrimination who need to be able to claim their human dignity, and the masses who seek the meaning of life. Everyone needs to make peace with this wicked world and live according to the justice of God. We must therefore focus on the strategies and necessary tools to support actions for the consolidation of peace and justice, which is one of the means of dealing with the refugee phenomenon.

Identifying areas of need

The community has an important role to play when it comes to community change. One of the first steps is to involve the community and help them see the need for change. The key to successful change is a mixture of will, collaboration, useful information, access to material resources, and strategic organization. The more community members know about their conditions, the more they will be aware of the impact of their conditions on their well-being. It is from this awareness that we can see members of a community organizing, planning, and sharing tasks with agents of community transformation.

One of the strategic plans that we must undertake as the church is community assessment to identify areas of need. Developing a plan to identify areas of need can help changemakers understand how to satisfy these community needs in a sustainable and effective manner. This assessment can then allow agents of change within the church to implement a plan aimed at evaluating the resources available. Thus, areas of need are the gap between what is and what should be. Identifying areas of need will help us better understand the community, as each community has its own needs and strengths as well as its own culture and social structure that defines it. A community assessment discovers not only the needs and resources, but also the culture and the underlying social structure that will help us understand how to respond to identified needs and use available community resources.

The word "need" basically means the gap between what exists and what is desired. Identifying needs involves gathering information to learn about the wants and short- and medium-term solutions of community members. Identifying the needs of a community allows us to pass judgment on the well-being of the community. It also allows us to discover and understand the individual and collective needs, and to portray the strengths and weaknesses of the community. Although this principle creeps into the middle of the PRAISE framework, it is of course the first step in planning a project using a community approach, and a guarantee of success if carried out carefully. Identification of needs is basically an analysis of needs. So this identification is necessarily analytical and structured, but it can be easily adapted to different community contexts. We the church know our community best and are in the best position to determine the method we will employ to properly identify and analyze the needs of our community. The results of our needs analysis will be included in the action plan.

Identifying areas of need will help us prioritize programmes to be undertaken. It is obviously imprudent to try to solve the problems of any given community without fully understanding what they are. In the same way, not taking advantage of community resources means not only tackling a problem without using all the tools at our disposal to solve it, but also missing an opportunity to increase the community's capacity to solve their own problems. Identifying needs and resources before launching a community transformation initiative means that we know from the start what we are dealing with and are less likely to be blinded later by something we did not expect.

It is really important to identify the needs of a community before starting a project or activity. The important reasons for identifying needs include

1. The information obtained makes it possible to adapt the project to the priority needs expressed by community actors;
2. The identification of needs makes it possible to determine the services that will meet these needs and to take into account the proposed solutions;
3. Identifying needs provides evidence and confirms the existence of needs that stakeholders may assume;
4. Carrying out a needs analysis increases the credibility of a program in the eyes of users and partners and facilitates the search for resources;
5. The needs analysis implies taking into consideration the opinion of community members who are potential users of new services because the more people are involved in a project, the more they will use the services and gain from them.

Identifying and analyzing needs is essentially a four-step process. The first step in needs analysis is to plan. We need to ask ourselves and answer the following questions: What kind of information are we looking for? Who are the key people to collect this information? What human, financial, and material resources do we need to carry out our analysis?

Once the type of information to collect is specified, it is important that we take the time to plan the activities that will allow us to raise awareness and inform the key people we have identified. We should also think of activities or events that will allow us to start consulting with target people and gathering information. The projects set up according to a community development approach require the population to regain power in order to change their situation. As the church it is our responsibility as agents of transformation to mobilize the community and involve them from the planning stages of the project. The community must be able to express their needs and propose solutions. The mobilization of and consultation with members of our community will allow us to set up services that meet their needs and are adapted to our culture and values.

The second step is to determine the types of data needed to achieve a fair picture of the community and its needs. To achieve a general portrait of a community's needs, those who will provide services and those who will be partners in the project must meet. Data collection should aim to collect the opinions of parents, adolescents, and adults; school, social, and health workers; seniors; partners; and community leaders. The people to be met should be chosen on the basis of their experience and knowledge of the community. At this stage, some of the data we need to collect includes (i) Sociodemographic data such as population, location of the community, history of the community, housing, employment, etc. (ii) Available resources such as health care and social services offered inside and outside the community, human and financial resources, community organizations, etc. (iii) Local dynamics, values within the community, strengths and weaknesses of the community, consultation and mobilization within the community, the training needs of stakeholders, and needs in terms of care, services, resources, and infrastructure. Different methods can be used to collect this data.

The third step in the process is to determine which method will be used. There exist four scientific methods which are often used in research or evaluations that may inspire us as church development agents. In the case of needs identification and analysis carried out with a local approach, it is possible to adapt these methods to our needs and our resources. As we do so, we should not hesitate to use what is right for us as a church and let go of what is not right for us. However, using several of these methods can allow church development agents to paint an even more accurate picture of the community and its needs.

Individual Interviews: The first method is basically the individual interview. This method consists of a conversational discussion, face to face or by telephone, during which an interviewer asks questions for an interviewee to answer in order to know his or her experience and opinion on a subject. If desired, these interviews can be taped. As part of an identification and analysis of needs, a semi-structured interview is recommended. Some questions are planned, but the interviewers can adjust their interview guide during the discussion. The interview takes place in three stages: (i) *Opening*: During the first few minutes, the interview has to break the ice by starting with general questions. This is when the relationship of trust is created between the church development agent and the community member. At this stage, as development agents we must remember to ask the participant's permission to record the meeting. (ii) *Interview*: Using an interview guide that includes the questions or topics you want to cover can serve as a reminder. Open-ended questions are preferable because they are not answered with yes or no, but allow us to know more in depth the opinion of the participant. In addition, questions should be simple, short, and to the point. (iii) *Closing*: When the interview ends, we must summarize the important points the participant has mentioned to make sure we understood correctly. We should remember to thank participants and tell them what the information they have shared will be used for. It is important to set a minimum number of interviews in advance. However, we should stop doing interviews when we believe beyond reasonable doubt we have all the information to understand the needs of the community, and that we will no longer get essential new information.

Focus Groups: The second method is the focus group or discussion group, which is an interview technique that ideally brings together six to twelve people. However, focus groups can be conducted with a smaller number of people and still obtain interesting information. It is preferable that the participants of a focus group have similar characteristics such as age, gender, socioeconomic status, and language which will make it easier for participants to express themselves. A discussion guide with specific and orderly questions should be used. This guide allows a facilitator to discuss all the topics that have been planned with the participants. However, the facilitator who is a development agent must not stop the spontaneity of the participants but must explore any interesting subject, even if unplanned. The facilitation of the focus group is at the heart of the meeting. The facilitator must demonstrate a desire to understand, listen, be open, and be neutral. It is better for the facilitator to guide the participants rather than adopting an authoritarian and domineering style. Facilitators must also ensure that each participant has the chance to speak and that the time is respected.

Surveys: The third method of data collection is the survey. This method consists of the use of a questionnaire. A survey can be used to reach individuals who cannot be reached through an interview or a focus group. Just as the instrument for an individual interview is the interview guide and the instrument for a focus group is the discussion guide, so the instrument for a survey is the questionnaire. A questionnaire is a tool that collects facts, opinions, beliefs, or attitudes and can be administered by postal mail, hand-to-hand, telephone, or email. These ways of administering the survey have advantages and disadvantages. As church development agents we have to choose the one that will collect the most quality information at the lowest cost in time and money, and which will encourage a large number of people to respond. Since it is not possible to reach all members of a community, it is advisable to obtain a sample that represents the members of the community as much as possible.

A questionnaire should be developed in three steps: (i) Preparation of a preliminary version: Here we develop clear and simple questions. The explanations at the start of the questionnaire must also be simple and precise. The questionnaire layout should make it easy to read. (ii) Testing: Here we distribute the questionnaire to a few people to make sure that the questions are easy to understand and that the vocabulary used is correct. (iii) The final version: The final version of the questionnaire must be prepared according to the comments received during the testing.

Documentary Research: The fourth method is documentary research. This method allows us to gather information about the community by consulting documents that already exist. These documents can be summaries of meetings, grant applications, summaries of popular consultations, a history of the community, pamphlets, fact sheets, newspaper articles, audiovisual archives, etc. The information collected from these documents can be used, along with the other methods, to draw a portrait of the community including the population, age, employment, housing, etc. The documents can also give us clues about programmes that have already been put in place in the community and needs that had already been expressed by members of the community.

There are, of course, alternative methods of finding information. For example, a community can form a discussion group on social networks; organize a dinner discussion, a general assembly, or a community forum; or even use a suggestion box left in a frequented place. The important thing is to find the best methods for the community and combine them to get the opinions of as many people as possible.

The results obtained from the needs analysis should be presented and used to build an action plan. Indeed, the information provided by the identification and analysis of needs will allow us as the church to identify objectives to be achieved and to target the clientele to whom new services should be offered. Several sections of the analysis report that we have drafted can be directly inserted into the action plan. In closing, we must not forget that this is just a framework and that it is up to us to identify the method or methods that are best suited to identifying and analyzing the needs of our community according to the time and resources we have.

We need to make great effort as the church to identify the needs that people have and specific conditions of vulnerability among them. This identification of needs enables us to set priorities and reach out to the community with much care. Identifying community needs is best done through joint efforts – and this is where partnership comes in. We need partnership because the local church cannot meet needs all alone. Partnership is meant for mutual cooperation to identify problems and find solutions to the problems together. When we are in partnership with other congregations, denominations, or organizations, our programmes for capacity building are often a success because there is a network of support. In partnership there is sharing and an exchange of resources and ideas, as well as mutual cooperation. A partnership is to be a permanent venture to make the joint effort stable. In a partnership, all the players assist each other in identifying the areas of need in a given community and dealing with common challenges that are beyond the ability of one local church or change agent. So partnership is important in assessing the situation of the community and gathering all the possible information.

Partnership building is a process that treasures solidarity between members and fosters readiness to act in response to identified community needs. With partnership and commitment, we can easily tackle the causes of the problems in the community. Thus, partnership among churches within the context of community transformation is our practical responsibility to respond to the real needs that people have in the community. When as a local church we are in partnership with other churches or Christian development organizations, we build bridges rather than walls. Partnership, therefore, is about building bridges whereas resistance to partnership indicates congregational centredness, which is synonymous with building walls. So we need to involve relevant people in the community as much as possible in identifying needs, and thus allow them to participate in the programme. As the church our goal is for community members to see themselves as co-responsible for the dynamics of change and to implement these dynamics in their living environment and ensure their long-term results. When we involve community members in identifying their own needs and help them respond to those needs themselves, they become their own agents of transformation.

Supporting the most vulnerable

Traditionally, certain groups are considered vulnerable participants including minors, pregnant women, detainees, and people with disabilities. In recent years, other categories of vulnerable people have been added including illiterate or poorly educated people, those with limited economic resources, women in some places, and the elderly. It is necessary to help less able people to obtain basic needs. To accomplish this, we need a plan to support vulnerable populations. This support plan is the main tool for planning and implementing interventions in response to the needs of the community, and it is a main frame of reference for all our interventions. It is the action plan of activities and interventions that have been determined on the basis of the available information that was gathered during the identification of needs. The preparation of a community action plan helps community members to become realistically and concretely involved in the planning and execution of their own development activities. By making the whole community reflect on the resources and possible involvement of each member, everyone will become aware of their capacities and the resources already available. We therefore start from possible avenues of development in order to concentrate on the resources necessary for their implementation, on the groups to be involved, and on the moment when the activities could start.

For example, a possible intervention for a livestock health problem in a community might be building a pond in which the livestock can be immersed. The construction of this pond would be a main development activity for the community members. This example shows the importance of involving the local community in the development of a support plan for the most vulnerable in the community, which helps to avoid the situation where the agent of transformation suggests an intervention of which the community is not necessarily in need. Community groups to be involved in developing a support plan are the council of community elders and the youth representatives who have been identified.

As the church, we have many ways to support those in need – from assisting them with material things to orienting them on what and how to do things.

As refugees are among the most vulnerable human beings in the world, they deserve the same type of treatment as other vulnerable communities. The kind of support we can offer them as the church varies from food, housing, and employment to counselling to help them make the transition to self-sufficiency. Supporting vulnerable refugees in the community does not only mean assisting them financially, as they may only need moral support. Refugees can be in need of the support that only we can offer as the church, which might be simply helping them adapt to life in the new country. Our whole purpose in supporting the vulnerable is to deal with the sociopolitical injustices and consider the needs of those in the community we serve. However, supporting the vulnerable is about introducing circumstances that allow people to participate in the process of their own transformation.

Supporting vulnerable people is a path to socioeconomic liberation, which is why the whole story of salvation is one of redemptive liberation. The liberation brought by our support of the most vulnerable is the liberation from everything that can deprive us of our creative and innovative potential, including oppression by others, oppression by systems, and oppression by circumstances which upset the community as a unit of transformational development. The implication is that transformational community development must be authentic, holistic, sustainable, redemptive, and liberating. So, the basis for supporting the most vulnerable is a permanent concern for the poor, the marginalized, the excluded, and the downtrodden. The Bible has many passages that emphasize concern for people in situations of vulnerability. For instance, Deuteronomy 15:1–6 indicates that the Israelites had to forgive the debts of the poor every seventh year if poverty was to be eradicated in the Jewish society and an economically ideal society created. The prophet Amos was harsh with those who deviated from this purpose by exploiting the poor (Amos 2:6–8; 5:11–13). We can gather much insight from the prophet Amos on how God feels about economic injustice.

Supporting vulnerable people can be done in different ways: financially on a regular basis, anonymously through donations, or in many other ways as explained. However, the most important thing is to make it a ministry. Supporting vulnerable people is essential for us as a missional church. We do not just have to support refugees; we can make it a ministry to invite refugees over for lunch or dinner at our homes or even visit them at their homes. Opening our houses for those in need such as refugees is transformational. In brief, as the church we must support the most vulnerable so they can have the knowledge and develop the skills needed for self-reliance.

Working with the most vulnerable and supporting their proposed solutions to meet identified needs increases the effectiveness of our initiatives by ensuring that our interventions are adapted to the local context and needs. For example, adapting agricultural production to climate change involves helping farmers find appropriate local solutions that allow each farmer to increase productivity using less water. This kind of help ensures that the solutions meet the needs of farmers. And that logic should extend to the children and youth who have the most at stake. Involving them will help internalize actions, which means less investment will be required in engaging with them as adults. Supporting locally designed solutions is also a practical approach as it will improve buy-in to actions, which means solutions are more likely to last.

Empowering for self-reliance

Involving the community in the transformation process means equipping the members with self-reliance skills so that they assume more responsibilities and ensure the success of their own actions. This equipping of self-reliance skills is called the "empowerment" of the community. Self-reliance is the social and economic capacity of an individual, household, or community to meet basic needs – including protection, food, water, shelter, personal security, health, and education – sustainably and with dignity. Self-reliance as a development approach aims to provide and strengthen sustainable livelihoods for people while reducing their vulnerability and long-term dependency. The climax of transformational community development is self-reliance, which prevents the situation where support leads to perpetual dependency. Self-reliance results from a process of empowerment but does not involve merely stopping support as doing so could aggravate misery and suffering in the community. When we put in place an empowerment strategy that promotes self-reliance in a given community, the community will develop the skills and capacity to produce. Members of such a community will generate income and contribute in socioeconomic growth of the country. In the context of the refugee phenomenon, the refugee community will be a self-sustained community that provides opportunities to all. To empower communities and encourage self-reliance in community members is to promote coexistence.

An empowerment programme aimed at self-reliance is integrated. It focuses on agendas that benefit all members of the community. These self-reliance programmes are apparent in the opportunities or training offered by the church. The integrated nature of transformational community development contributes in changing the common social view and political stance vis-à-vis those in need. In encouraging self-reliance by means of integrated programmes of development, we contribute to the promotion of dignity for all and the empowerment of the entire community.

To involve the community, it will first be necessary to do community mobilization, which is a process that enables the community to make the decisions they need to be able to plan for transformational change and implement related strategies. Three main determinants for effective mobilization are (i) Meaning – community intervention should be meaningful work for those involved. They need to understand what they are doing and know why they are doing it. (ii) Consideration – which is the respectful attitude, trust, and recognition of the work to be done. (iii) Responsibility and accountability – the ability of community members to contribute to the successful process of transformation to their satisfaction and take responsibility for results.

Creating an environment conducive to participation is important in the process of community empowerment. A supportive environment for participation encourages creativity, values local initiatives, and broadens the resource base on which our interventions can rely. To maximize community participation and bring the transformation agenda as close as possible to the community, it will be necessary to develop skills within the community. As the community becomes more involved in the implementation of the programme, community members will need new skills to perform their functions. We must therefore be able to provide them with different types of support so that they can play a more important role, train other volunteers, or help them monitor certain field activities and the progress of the programme.

Resources will also need to be found within the community to encourage and support their participation. For example, an incentive system that encourages participation is an important motivator. In addition, it will be necessary to mobilize external resources to launch activities. Even if the community mobilizes some of its own resources, we as the church still sometimes have to tap into external resources. Finally, we must ensure the survival of our programme. Now that our programme is operational and starting to show tangible results, we must start thinking about ways to increase and diversify its funding. In fact each time a single source of funding is used, it creates a dependency that goes against the sustainability of the programme.

In Africa, we tend to value something that has been accomplished as a result of collective efforts rather than something that has been accomplished individually. Doing something together in a strong throng brings a kind of pride to a typical African, albeit inherently. So, in my culture whenever one calls for *esale*, rarely will people decline the invitation – unless they are really unable. Empowerment is best illustrated in the Babembe tradition of *esale*, which is a practice where you invite people such as neighbours, friends, relatives, acquaintances, and even passers-by to help you make bricks or build a house or do some kind of work – anything – at home, in the plantation field, or anywhere else. *Esale* is considered by the Babembe as an act of solidarity and collective empowerment. Of course, when *esale* is called, lunch is on the person inviting others. When you are unable to do something alone, you call others to come and "lift you up" by giving you the support you need. And when all is done, you would proudly say, "I did it."

It is through *esale* that I managed to build my brick house in Nyarugusu. I was tired of sleeping in a tent due to the cold, and we had no beds or mattresses. So, when I decided to build a house of mud bricks, the only way I could do it was through *esale*. I invited friends, family members, and acquaintances, and as expected, they responded. We used locally available resources to build this house such as trees and bamboo. The roof of the house was straw, which was also an available resource in the camp. This is a practical illustration of community-led empowerment which we can adopt at church level as a participatory approach for transformational development. The tradition of *esale* as practiced by the Babembe community is actually taken from the biblical narrative of Nehemiah. When Nehemiah rebuilt the walls of Jerusalem, he adopted a participatory approach for community empowerment. He made sure he involved a range of people in the project: rich and poor, men and women, local residents, and people living further afield. Each family built the part of the wall directly in front of their houses, giving people a sense of identity and uniqueness in repairing the walls (Neh 1:1–7:73). Here, we can see that a commitment to empowerment and participatory action are important elements if people are to live life to the full (cf. John 10:10). As the church we should encourage the participation of all community members in order to help them own and control the process of their transformation.

Transformational community development is not about giving people what they want so that they can survive; rather it is about giving people what they need so that they can live. It is about providing people with what is required so they have what they need. It is about equipping people with the skills, the knowledge, and the expertise that will enable them to provide for themselves what they need. This enabling does not completely rule out the provision of material stuff. For instance, to equip people with the skill to plough, it suffices to offer adequate tools for farming to begin with. To equip people with the skills of livestock raising, it would be prudent to give them what is necessary for animal husbandry. This provision should be done without forgetting that the goal of community empowerment is self-reliance. Self-reliance requires that we allow people to participate in the activities of community transformation. Bragg finds that when someone participates "in the process of their own transformation it becomes meaningful, effective and lasting."[11] Adopting a participatory approach to transformational community development recognizes the dignity, value, skills, knowledge, and experience of all and models a new transformed way of life that sees broken relationships restored.

The famous statement by Chester "evangelism and social action are inseparable"[12] means that a human life which begins to flow from the heart of God will not be content with the injustice in the world which keeps people in poverty.[13] Such injustices perpetuate poverty, forcing people to leave their homelands in search of better living conditions as refugees. Therefore, as the church we do not only tell refugees about God's love without minding their well-being, we put that love into action. Put differently, Langmead says, "Refugees and asylum seekers are the most powerless, marginalized and dislocated people in the world, clearly a high priority for those who follow Jesus. Christian ministry to refugees stands or falls on its response of hospitality to such groups."[14] So durable solutions cannot be achieved if refugees are deprived of the most basic rights and remain passive recipients of assistance or if they remain dependent on humanitarian aid. Situations in which refugees are unable to achieve self-reliance risk fuelling resentment and providing breeding grounds for further conflict. Self-reliant refugees are more empowered and likely to find durable solutions to their plight.

For the love of God to be understood by those who live in dire situations, such as refugees and asylum seekers, we need to demonstrate it. The central thrust of biblical teaching on economic activity is that everyone should enjoy the benefits that accrue from it.[15] The love and care that we provide to refugees today is necessary and good, but it is not enough to transform the community in furtherance of God's kingdom. We are meant to integrate our social responsibility and our active involvement for service in community. We do so in ways that protect and care for those in need. The promotion of the self-reliance of displaced people must be an integral part of the church if we are

---

11. Bragg, "From Development to Transformation," 44.
12. Tim Chester, *Good News to the Poor: Sharing the Gospel through Social Involvement* (Nottingham: Inter-Varsity, 2009), 65.
13. Hughes and Bennett, *God of the Poor*, 154.
14. Langmead, "Refugees as Guests and Hosts," 1.
15. Hughes and Bennett, *God of the Poor*, 157.

to find lasting solutions to the refugee phenomenon. The assistance we provide to refugees and other displaced persons can only be effective if such material assistance is focused on strengthening their self-reliance and empowerment. This is why the transformational development approach involves communities in decision-making and planning and sees refugees not as passive recipients of aid but as partners playing an active role in development activities and community interventions. The PRAISE framework provides us with a strategic paradigm for *missio Dei* and equips individual believers with spiritual tools to restore the *imago Dei*.

When empowerment occurs, we will need to step back; but before stepping back, we will need to do a final assessment. We are supposed to carry out an evaluation at the end of the programme, but sometimes also midterm. During the evaluation we analyze the changes that our work has made and their likelihood for sustainability. In other words, the evaluation answers the question, "What difference did we make?" The final or midterm evaluation is done well if there has been constant monitoring throughout the programme cycle. Monitoring is the continuous process that allows us to identify any issues much earlier, which gives us the opportunity to make any necessary changes to our tools or overall process. Monitoring also shows us how far we are moving towards or away from our goals. In other words, monitoring answers the question, "How are we doing?"

When we do an evaluation at the end of our programme cycle, we should study the community practice, intervention, or initiative to determine whether it has met its objectives. In other words, evaluation helps us determine what works and what could be improved. Evaluation in a community development programme should always be community based. A community-based evaluation focuses on community members and all that concerns them, and should be conducted in partnership with those same community members. This partnership between us and the community during the execution of the programme and its evaluation process should give us a good picture of the impact that the programme has had in the community. Also, the report of this evaluation will not be contested by community members since they were involved in the whole process.

Expected results of the PRAISE framework

Community intervention does not happen overnight. It takes months, sometimes even years, before any real results can be achieved. Community transformation is a process that invites people to become active members of their community. It takes time, energy, and strong faith, but it is worth it. Some of the expected outcomes of using the PRAISE framework during the community transformation process include the following:

Basic needs met – When we use the PRAISE framework in a community transformation programme, we expect the satisfaction of basic needs such as for food, water, sanitation, health, shelter, education, and information.

Good stewardship of resources – The PRAISE model allows for the sustainable and compassionate use and distribution of resources, ensuring that everyone's material needs are met now and in the future.

Evangelism – As we are involved in the process of community transformation using the PRAISE framework, people will give their lives to Christ as their Lord and Saviour following the demonstration of our faith through practical action and care.

Values change – The PRAISE framework allows people to recognize their true worth as made in the image of God and challenges or transforms their values and worldview.

Commitment to service – Using the framework encourages Christian communities in their commitment to Jesus Christ through worship, prayer, and service to the poor and refugees.

Opportunities to explore the Christian faith – The PRAISE framework provides us with opportunities to meet, recognize, and follow the Lordship of Jesus Christ.

Christians in leadership – The PRAISE framework leads to Christians serving their communities and taking positions of leadership and responsibility even outside the church.

Transformational community development is defined as change that benefits the community as a whole. Examples of transformational community development can be very simple, for example encouraging more people to vote or donating to charity, or very complex such as reducing domestic violence, reducing school dropout rates of children, or promoting the inclusion of refugees in national service delivery programmes. The transformation can happen slowly as a result of a cultural, behavioural, or mindset change, or it can happen quickly as a result of an intervention led in response to a natural disaster or a change in public policy. As the church, we can play a role in influencing cultural, behavioural, or mental change and public policy, and even intervene through social actions to help reduce poverty in the community.

In this chapter we have seen that for transformational development to happen in a community, we need a well-structured framework. I propose the PRAISE framework which has six circular principles namely, the promotion of human dignity, the response to human needs, advocacy, identification of needs, support for vulnerable people, and empowerment for self-reliance. In the chapter we further indicate that the foundation of our social actions as the church is the inherent dignity of the human person, created in the image and likeness of God. Therefore as the church, we are called to a holistic transformational development that embraces the well-being of everyone in all of their dimensions. In this regard, we emphasize the necessity to collaborate with other organizations to meet the needs of refugees in our communities. As the church, we have a duty to empower refugees by supporting the most vulnerable among them and responding to the needs that make them so vulnerable. The next chapter brings this book to a conclusion by expressing some closing remarks to recap everything we have discussed.

Discussion Questions

1. How does PRAISE as a transformational development framework facilitate church praxis in community?
2. How can we put the PRAISE framework into practice to meet the needs of refugees in our community?
3. Why is Maslow's pyramid of needs important in responding to the general needs of refugees?
4. Read Nehemiah chapter 3.
   - What does this chapter teach us about participatory action and team work?
   - How should we respond to community members who do not want to participate in transformation activities organized by the local church in our community?
5. What are the expected results of PRAISE when used as a framework for holistic transformation in our community?

8

Conclusion

Teaching development at university requires a commitment to practice as well. I have been fortunate over the past few years to devote myself to teaching development and practicing it in various communities across Africa with several community organizations. One of the programmes I would like to mention is RAMSHA – *Rafiki Mshauri* – a peer-educator programme on reproductive health for young people ages fourteen to twenty-four, which I helped found in 2000 in the Nyarugusu refugee camp. The RAMSHA programme released my love for community development from within me, and my involvement in mobilizing young people on issues important to us was the highlight of my time in RAMSHA. This humble start was strong enough to stimulate my desire, love, and passion for community development, and I ended up majoring in community development in my postgraduate studies.

Even as a student, I was involved in various community development activities mainly for refugees. So for me as a trained community development theorist and practitioner, the questions to ask are what is our role as the church in the process of community transformation? What is our contribution? What are our possibilities and our limitations? Many of us have started working with communities because we believe that we are part of a larger struggle against injustice, against inequality and its many forms, and against the systems that produce them, such as capitalism. As the rhetoric of social justice resonates across the wide variety of Christian community organizations, we need to contextualize our interventions so they become service oriented, people-driven, and church-led.

Here we learned that transformational community development is a process by which the community members identify the barriers – weaknesses and threats – that continue to push them into poverty, and the resources – strengths and opportunities – that might help them overcome those barriers so they can flourish according to John 10:10. God is concerned for the welfare of those who have been pushed to the margins of society from the centre, which is why on several occasions he instructed the Israelites to remember the refugees among them and to treat them with love, compassion, and justice and never to mistreat them (Exod 22:21) or take advantage of them (Deut 24:14). These commands are God's attempt to disturb the centre and include the excluded. As the church, our mission is to also care for refugees (cf. Lev 19:9–10); to treat them as citizens (cf. Lev 19:34), and to give them a share of our tithes (cf. Deut 14:28–29). In the New Testament, Jesus began his life on earth as a refugee and therefore can identify with those who are in a similar situation as he experienced (Matt 2:13–23). In other words, God is concerned and cares for helpless and vulnerable people including refugees among us, and we the church have the responsibility to join God in his mission.

We also emphasized that the Bible is about a people on the move. Starting from the book of Genesis, we see Adam and Eve being displaced from their original home (Gen 3:22–24). Throughout the rest of the Bible, the story of migration – forced or voluntary – is ever present. We even see the Bible ending with a narrative of the apostle John being forcibly exiled to the strange island of Patmos where his freedom was thoroughly restricted (Rev 1:9). Most of the heroes of the Old Testament were migrants: in Genesis 12:1, Abraham receives the call to go to an unknown place. In Genesis 19, Lot takes his family and flees the land of Sodom. In Genesis 23, Abraham is a stranger and an alien in the land of Canaan. In Genesis 46:1–7, Jacob migrates with his family to Egypt to escape famine. In Exodus 1:15–2:10, Moses was born as a refugee. Pharaoh orders that all Hebrew babies be killed, but Moses is hidden and is saved by Pharaoh's daughter.

We indicated that in the first pages of the New Testament narrative, Jesus was not in Nazareth where his family was from but in displacement in Bethlehem where he was born (Luke 2:1–4, 39). This story could have been different with Jesus born in Nazareth, more comfortably, because moving let's not forget is usually a constraint. But this birth happened "elsewhere," and not at the family home. Shortly after Jesus was born, he and his family experienced exile – a forced displacement. The massacre of children by Herod in Bethlehem forced the child, Joseph, and Mary to flee to Egypt (Matt 2:13–15). They were likely welcomed by other displaced Jews and treated well there by the Egyptians despite their foreignness. In the Bible, the triune God is also functionally ever on the move. The entire Bible is basically a book that narrates stories of migration in various forms.

We saw that in Deuteronomy, God defined the relationship between himself and his chosen people. The book is filled with instructions and laws meant to guide both the individual and communal life of God's people (Deut 1:16; 10:17–19; 24:14, 17–18; 27:19). Also in Deuteronomy we find numerous passages in which God instructs his people to care for refugees. For example, in Deuteronomy 6:10–13, God tells the people of Israel that the land he gave them is a gift from him so they can remember that they were once refugees. In Deuteronomy 14:28–29 and 26:12–13, God instructs them to give refugees who had obtained their status for permanent residence a portion of tithe. The idea is that God's people should have solidarity with the displaced, those who are away from their home, land, customs, and language. In brief, we are to care for those who are away from what is familiar. Migration is a global phenomenon that is inescapable because of the dimensions it takes and the effects it has on the countries of departure as well as on the host countries.

The history of Israel gives a special place to migratory movements. The Bible was written by refugees and for refugees, as Joan Maruskin points out, which is why the Bible gives directions for responding to sisters and brothers around the world who come to a land seeking safety, sanctuary, and sustenance.[1] Maruskin further makes the following assertion: "The Bible begins with the migration of God's Spirit and ends with John in exile [and] between those two events, the uprooted people of God seek safety, sanctuary, and refuge, and the living God gives [them] directions for welcoming the stranger."[2]

Throughout, we made it clear that the biblical story is a story of migration as most of the biblical figures in the Old Testament were refugees or foreigners at some point in their lives. Also, the New Testament message is centred on the person of Jesus who was also a refugee and migrant at some points in his life. Therefore, most narratives in the Bible relate to the refugee phenomenon. A few cases exemplify this more. For instance, because of sin, Adam and Eve were forced to depart from their original home where they had enjoyed a glorious relationship with God and harmonious living with both the flora and the fauna. They were displaced from their original home (Gen 3). Due to a family feud between two brothers, Cain, the big brother and farmer, and Abel, the younger brother and shepherd, Cain murdered Abel and then fled to a faraway land where no one could find him. He became a refugee in a distant land, far away from his parents (Gen 4). While Noah expected imminent changes in weather

---

1. J. M. Maruskin, *Immigration and the Bible: A Guide for Radical Welcome* (Washington: United Methodist Women, 2012).

2. Maruskin, 1.

patterns that would cause a catastrophic natural disaster, he built a very large ark in which he would escape the heavy rains. Abandoning all, he left his home with a few of his family members aboard the ark he had built himself, and only "returned" home when it was safe to do so (Gen 6:16–18; 7:1–8:22).

Obeying God's command, Abraham left his own people and home in Ur of the Chaldeans. He became "stateless" for the rest of his life, trusting in God's promise of provision of a land for his descendants (Gen 12). In Genesis 23:4, Abraham calls himself "a stranger and an alien." These terms are akin to "refugee" and "asylum seeker" in the modern context of forced human migration. Joseph was a victim of human trafficking having been sold by his own siblings to some foreign businessmen, the Ishmaelites, who took him to Egypt where they also sold him. In Egypt, Joseph worked as a slave for a local rich man, Potiphar, and while on duty, Joseph experienced sexual harassment. He was sent to jail despite being the victim. However, after his release from jail, Joseph was very useful for Egypt, his host country, and contributed greatly to its socioeconomic development and to the welfare of the entire population (cf. Gen 37, 39–41). The story of Joseph is a concrete reminder that during the ancient biblical days, human migration was used as a way to overcome the challenge of poverty or food shortage. Food shortage caused Jacob to migrate with his entire household to Egypt where his son Joseph had permanent residence and sociopolitical influence, despite having been a refugee. The Israelites lived in Egypt as refugees for a very long time before going back to Canaan. In fact, none of those who went to Egypt returned to Canaan (Gen 42:1–5; 45:9–11; 46:26–27).

As indicated, Jesus was also a refugee at a certain point in his life. He was displaced with his parents from Israel to Egypt for "fear of persecution." They left their home due to Herod's search for Jesus and murder of infants in the country and went to seek asylum in Egypt (cf. Matt 2:13–15). In 1 Peter 2:11, the apostle refers to Christian believers – those who have been chosen and given a new birth in Christ – as "aliens and exiles." Peter was telling the believers scattered in Pontus, Galatia, and Cappadocia that their stay or existence here on earth was not permanent. Likewise, Paul told the church at Philippi that "our citizenship is in heaven" (Phil 3:20) – which also denotes the foreignness of Christians under the sun. These and many other biblical passages attest to the fact that the Bible is a book about forced migration from Genesis to Revelation. The Bible refers to Christian believers as alien people in the world because their original and eternal home is not here on earth but in heaven. In other words, we are in the world but are not of this world (John 15:19; 17:14; Phil 3:20). Similarly, migration is not only about the reasons and mechanics of moving from one place to another; it is also about life in the new setting.[3] The migratory movements recorded in the Bible are today's version of the refugee phenomenon.

God kept reminding the Israelites that they were once foreigners, and for that reason, they were to treat the foreigners among them with dignity and respect (cf. Lev 19:33; Deut 24:17–18). In this global generation we are called to evangelize the world with all its uncertainties, imperfections, weaknesses, and violence. It is in this context that we can speak of the issues facing Christianity today. We must witness about Christ to refugees in today's perspectives of the refugee phenomenon. The foundations of our ministry must be solidly grounded in biblical theology because refugees are people who have been caught up in the trials and tribulations of life.[4] The basis of church theology on the question of refugees is to be constant in every context in order to proclaim the centrality of Christ with relevance.

The people of Israel in the days of Jacob were economic refugees who had fled famine in the land of Canaan and ended up living generation after generation as refugees for four centuries. God had migrated with his people. He had been their guide and fed them. He protects the vulnerable. The Lord is impartial. Not only did he establish justice for the poor, but also for the strangers who lived among the people of Israel. And not only does he establish justice, but he "loves the strangers, providing them food and clothing" (Deut 10:18). When we read the Old Testament, we sometimes have the impression that God wanted the people of Israel to be a totally separate people, without contact with others. That was not the case. God did not want his people to be influenced by the bad customs of other peoples, but if strangers came to their land, they were to treat them well as God was their protector. The Master of the Universe is particularly concerned about vulnerable people, including foreigners.

In the ancient Near East, life depended on belonging to a home, to a community. Those outside this home, without a father or a husband or without family ties, would have been in danger of death because they would not have had the means to get food or clothing. In the same way that God had offered his love and support to us, we should offer our love and support to refugees. His command is: "You shall also love the stranger [refugee], for you were strangers [refugees] in the land of Egypt" (Deut 10:19). If we are friends with someone, we will be much less tempted to oppress and be unfair to them. In

---

3. Carroll, *Christians at the Border*, 71.
4. Carroll, 87.

the book of Leviticus, God explains further: "When an alien [refugee] resides with you in your land, you shall not oppress the alien. The alien who resides with you shall be to you as the citizen among you; you shall love the alien as yourself, for you were aliens in the land of Egypt: I am the LORD your God" (Lev 19:33–34). Israelite obedience to this instruction was so empowering for the refugees that 1 Chronicles 22:1–2 describes how they played a very important role in building the temple, and in 2 Chronicles 2:17–18 describes how Solomon identified all the refugees in the land and gave them jobs.

God desires a people who love as he himself loves: to love those who come from without, who have no home. The liberation of the people of Israel from Egypt was a foreshadowing of the liberation of sin offered to us in Jesus. As the apostle Peter points out, the believer in Jesus is a migrant on this earth, a stranger and a traveller (1 Pet 2:11–12). We are fully present on this earth that God has entrusted to humanity, but we are aliens to the sinful systems of humanity. We are waiting for resettlement to a better place where suffering, evil, and sin will no longer exist. Through the mercy of Jesus Christ, the members of every people group in the world can be linked together to form a new people: God's children, a people who manifest to the whole world the love they have received from God. May God who is Father, Son, and Holy Spirit help us to live this love every day, even though we often do not know how to do it! The world is alerted to unprecedented migrations from a variety of crises in Africa, but seeking asylum is absolutely not new in the Christian sphere.

As nations, networks, and organizations strive to find solutions to the prevailing situation in countries shaken by war, upheaval, and instability, as well as the resulting refugee crisis, it is important that as Christians we fully recognize what the Bible calls us to do and what our place is in the midst of such a crisis. Central to our faith, the incarnation of our Lord Jesus Christ is the most powerful demonstration of what it means to provide for the needs of refugees, far from their legitimate home country. Between two fixed points, that of the departure which they have lost sight of and that of the arrival which they do not see yet, migrants are wandering, often lost on the way. They are where most biblical heroes were: Adam and Eve, who were forced to leave the garden; Cain who had to flee far from his comfort zone; Abraham who received the order to leave everything and go without knowing where he was headed; Hagar who was chased with her son away from the tribe; Joseph who was a victim of human trafficking; Jacob who emigrated for economic reasons; and Ruth who chose to leave her home and migrate to the country of her mother-in-law! And finally, the whole people of Israel who were deported as exiles to Babylon. Nowadays, migrants discover in their wandering that God does not stay in their country of origin, but that he travels with them, crosses the borders with them, and reveals himself to them in the fragility of their refugee condition.

It cannot be overemphasized that God is himself a migrant. He does not hold up and stay. He moves. He moves with men and women who move. The moving of God alongside his people explains why transformational development in the light of forced migration and integration invites us to rethink the world from this angle. It is our responsibility to invent a more equitable, more responsible, and more welcoming world for those whose hope is in short supply. The social teaching of the church has a body of doctrine (*orthodoxia*) and practice (*orthopraxia*) that is articulated as we interpret events in the course of history.

Christianity is generally understood as "correct belief" in the Scriptures and "correct conduct" or practice consistent with the Scriptures, which is respectively orthodoxy and orthopraxy – in Greek, *orthodoxia* and *orthopraxia*. One side of the Christian divide often emphasizes the first – "correct" beliefs – but tends to overlook the second because salvation is by faith and not by works (Rom 3:28; 5:1; 11:5–6; Eph 2:8–9;). The other side of the divide places more emphasis on "correct" practices to the detriment of the former because "faith without works is dead" (Jas 2:26; see also Eph 2:10). Here I must emphasize that James teaches believers that genuine faith in Christ produces a transformed life and good works (Jas 2:20–26). He is not saying that salvation is by works, but rather that people who are truly saved by faith (*orthodoxia*) will have good works (*orthopraxia*) to show as a result of their saved life. But if people claim to be Christian believers and do not have an orthopraxy to show as a result of their orthodoxy, then James says that such believers most likely do not have genuine faith in Christ. This explanation of James is also made explicit by Paul when he exhorts the church in Ephesus that we were created to do good works (Eph 2:10). In other words, Paul also expected a completely changed life from which good works flow as a result of salvation by faith in Jesus Christ.

Orthodoxy is therefore believing with sincerity the teaching of the Bible, while orthopraxy is practicing with rectitude the teaching of the Bible. The teaching and actions of Jesus in the New Testament show that both *orthodoxia* and *orthopraxia* are important. So good theology requires that both orthodoxy and orthopraxy guide our reflections and actions since they are two sides of the same Christian coin. In other words, true Christianity is a good balance between orthodoxy and orthopraxy. It is about believing and living the gospel, thus translating what we believe into action. While salvation is by faith alone, our faith is nonetheless nonexistent if it is not put into action. Here the premise is that correct beliefs require correct actions, and incorrect actions result from incorrect beliefs.

Transformational development is a theological attempt to stimulate the desire and love for correct social actions that are rooted in correct Christian beliefs. Transformational community development articulates the holistic approach according to which mission encompasses all of the tasks for which we as the church are sent into the world. That being said, there are specific aspects that need to be highlighted. The main themes of a theology of transformational development include migration and integration, social justice and solidarity, ownership and distribution of property, and rights and duties of human beings starting with the right to life, the economy, and culture. By constituting a true theology of transformational development, our sole purpose as the church is *orthopraxia* – to help people live the gospel through the daily realities of our lives following the teaching of the Bible in order to create social conditions that are valuable. Our purpose is not to create a humanly perfect society, but to enable human persons, created in the image and likeness of God, to live the gospel and to have great intimacy with God in the depths of their soul. Therefore, the theology of transformational development invites us to enter into the logic of the love of God in our daily life. Living according to the principles of theology of transformational development is a human response to the greater love that God constantly shows humanity.

We should also see that the refugee phenomenon is particularly present in Old Testament ethics. These ethical obligations insist on the protection of refugees by the law and encourage the practice of generosity toward them. These obligations can be understood as a commandment to love refugees placed next to the commandment to love our neighbours: "When an alien resides with you in your land, you shall not oppress the alien. The alien who resides with you shall be to you as the citizen among you; you shall love the alien as yourself, for you were aliens in the land of Egypt: I am the LORD your God" (Lev 19:33–34). This passage shows that we are to treat foreigners or refugees as citizens and with love. It is God himself who protects refugees (cf. Ps 146:9) and who loves them by giving them bread and a mantle (cf. Deut 10:18). In other words, the commandment of love towards refugees has its foundation in the love of God himself. The biblical texts bring us a testimony for today that God presents himself to us in the form of the stranger, and he is particularly close to people who are in a situation of foreignness. The closeness of God is concretized for us in our way of acting, as the body of Christ, toward refugees.

We have seen how God insists that refugees should not be oppressed: "You shall not oppress a resident alien; you know the heart of an alien, for you were aliens in the land of Egypt" (Exod 23:9). This instruction and many other similar ones ensure the integration of refugees into the local community (Exod 22:21; Deut 27:19; Ps 146:9; Jer 22:3; Zech 7:9–10). The instructions include provisions for refugees to be treated equally and to be included in community activities and celebrations. Cities of refuge were to be availed in the event of accidental murder (Num 35:15). Refugees were to be included in the feasts and celebrations of the Jewish community (Deut 16:14; 26:11). Part of the tithe collected by the priests was to be used not only to feed them and their families, but also to help provide food for refugees, widows, and orphans (Deut 14:28–29). Moreover, the farmers were instructed to leave the gleanings of their fields for the poor and the refugees (Lev 23:22), and all Israelites were to treat the refugee as one did with the poor among the Israelites (Lev 25:35).

It should be noted that the last two points concerned the satisfaction of the basic needs of refugees, particularly food. The truth even today is that people come to live in our countries for various reasons and often without any resources. As believers we must show hospitality to them. This hospitality is the reason why the author of the Epistle to the Hebrews urges us to continue loving one another as brothers and sisters and to never forget showing hospitality to foreigners because in doing so, some were hospitable to angels unknowingly (Heb 13:1–2). In this and a few other passages hospitality is presented as a mark of those who follow Jesus (see Rom 12:13; 1 Pet 4:9; 3 John 1:5–8). We Christians must support each other, including the foreigners who come to worship with us. Every day we the church must be a welcoming community.

Transformational community development gives us benchmarks for living the gospel daily. The set of principles and values of this theology are here to help us live our faith, our hope, and our love. This theological triad can remain a dead letter if we do not try to live it out in our relations with others. In our daily life, good will is not enough because it is not those who say "Lord, Lord" who will be able to see the Lord at the end of our earthly pilgrimage, but those who do his will in seeking to love and serve the least, that is the undeserving, the marginalized, the hopeless, the helpless, and the refugee (cf. Matt 7:21). In brief, transformational community development exists to be discovered, to be studied, and to be put into practice. Often we observe a certain silence on the social problems of our time. It should be noted, however, that when we practice a transformational theology of development for the purpose of community empowerment, we accomplish an integral part of our teaching on the holism of human life. In particular, lay people must assimilate the principles of theology of transformational development so that they become capable of working for its expansion and of applying it correctly. As Tim Chester puts it,

> Integral mission or holistic transformation is the proclamation and demonstration of the gospel. It is not simply that evangelism and social involvement are done alongside each other. Rather, in integral mission our proclamation has social consequences . . . And our social involvement has evangelistic consequences as we bear witness to the transforming grace of Jesus Christ. If we ignore the world, we betray the word of God which sends us out to serve in the world. If we ignore the word of God, we have nothing to bring to the world. Justice and justification by faith, worship and political action, spiritual and material, personal change and structural change, belong together.[5]

This concept of transformational development brings nothing new under the sun because it is perfectly in continuity with Jesus himself who has demonstrated the intrinsic link between being, saying and doing. Jesus is the best missionary of God, or "the missionary par excellence," and therefore the model to follow. This is a recurrent point in the discourse of the theology of transformational development: the person and the ministry of Jesus Christ are not only the content of the gospel, but also the example to be followed. This is the Christological model of a theology of transformational development. If Christ is at the centre of the gospel and missionary activity, his way of being the missionary of God also becomes a model for our life and mission.

By listening to and observing the Lord, we who are his witnesses will find a kind of "road map." In his life of service and sacrifice, Jesus Christ is the model for every Christian disciple. In his life and by his death, Jesus gave us a model of identification with the poor and to include the excluded. At the cross, God shows how seriously he takes justice: he reconciles to himself both the rich and the poor by fulfilling the demands of his own justice. We serve the poor through the power of the risen Christ, with the help of the Spirit in our walk. We are living in the time of a humanity on the move. By the ease of transport and the speed of communication, the migratory movement characterizes the contemporary era. Men, women, and children on the move are found everywhere crammed into small boats on African lakes and rivers or stepping into the dusty streets of countries far from their own countries of origin, and these movements continue to characterize migration in Africa. All of these migratory movements are accompanied by hopes and fears, generating

---

5. Tim Chester, *Justice, Mercy and Humility: Integral Mission and the Poor* (London: Paternoster, 2002), 9.

a feeling or experience of exclusion and fear, or even inclusion and opportunity. We find our hope in knowing that everything will be subject to Christ, and that evil will finally be defeated. We confess that all too often we have not lived a life worthy of the gospel. We who receive an undeserved love must show kindness, generosity, and openness to others. The grace of God is the heartbeat of the theology of transformational development. Grace requires us to help the most disadvantaged.

Policy makers often misunderstand our potential on account of the traditional misconceptions of our role as the church and the belief that we have nothing concrete to offer in terms of socioeconomic development. Such misconceptions are often nurtured by the idea that our technical capabilities are often limited. However, when local governments promote collaborative relationships with the church and engage church leaders in their development agenda, our ability to provide services becomes more and more evident. In the same way, as the church we must seek a better understanding of the government political processes to facilitate dialogue and help establish a closer partnership as the local church is often at the heart of our immediate community, defending not only our Christian belief, cultural values, and social tradition, but also being a force for positive change, community transformation, and sustainable development. Because of our central position in the community as the church, we are well positioned to play vital roles, for example, to ensure and maintain improved hygiene and sanitation. We are also well positioned and equipped to play the role of a messenger since, for example, we are expected to preach messages that will encourage the community to improve their sanitation and hygiene. We are further expected to play the role of an implementer by helping communities improve living conditions through technical, spiritual, and even material support. Finally, we are to do advocacy by reaching out to decision makers on behalf of local communities. To ensure that transformational community development is integrated into the development agenda of the church, we need to engage with other stakeholders, including civil society, to identify and synergize with communities and organizations that have similar social goals. Christian development organizations and community-based organizations need to consider the local church as a partner that can build their capacity. As for us, the church, we will have to overcome confessional and sectarian differences which often hinder collaboration of this magnitude. This collaboration will help us identify the poor living conditions of community members that contribute to poverty in the community.

Payne states that refugees are "the most in need of compassion, assistance, and good news" of all the displaced persons or migrants in a host country.[6] This statement is echoed by Langmead who observes that "the global phenomenon of vulnerable people becoming refugees is the major humanitarian challenge."[7] On the one hand, the challenge brings together various actors in order to find practical ways to respond successfully to this global phenomenon, and on the other hand, it offers us a great opportunity for mission. We must consider the refugee phenomenon as an opportunity for the Great Commission because, although the migratory movements of refugees can be tragic, they facilitate evangelism of the nations.[8] Thus, the refugee phenomenon should be seen as God's plan for kingdom expansion.

Transformational community development is a constant improvement of the well-being of communities. A human person is therefore the heart of any activity meant to result in transformational development. To achieve sustainable development in our communities, development activities must be transformational and must focus on improving the well-being of people. This focus on the improvement of well-being leads to agency and explains why Tamas defines transformational development as "a process in which people become more active agents in improving their circumstances."[9] A human person is both an active participant and a beneficiary of transformational development activities; therefore, development that is not aimed at improving the well-being of a human person is not transformational development and cannot be sustainable.

Christians should respond to the global refugee crisis with *compassion*. To have true compassion for the needy, as demonstrated by Jesus (Mark 8:2), means that we are aware of their needs, that we care about the people involved, and that we are ready to act on their behalf. To have compassion for the needy is the proof of God's love in us (1 John 3:17). We honour God when we are kind to the needy (Prov 14:31). In addition, Christians should respond to the global refugee crisis by *taking action*. That is, Christians should do everything in our power to alleviate the suffering caused by the global phenomenon of refugees. Like Tabitha, we should always do good and help the poor as well as the deprived (Acts 9:36). However, compassion and action are not enough.

---

6. J. D. Payne, *Strangers Next Door: Immigration, Migration and Mission* (Downers Grove, IL: InterVarsity, 2012), 107.

7. Langmead, "Refugees as Guests and Hosts."

8. Payne, *Strangers Next Door*, 68.

9. A. Tamas, "Spirituality and Development: Concepts and Categories," *CIDA* (1999): 7.

Christians should also respond to the global refugee crisis with *hope*. Believers can act on behalf of refugees with the certainty that they help God's work in the world. Believers work with the hope that Jesus will return with justice and make decisions for the poor of the earth (Isa 11:4).

Unlike the internally displaced people who flee the adverse circumstances but find themselves as refugees inside their own country, refugees have to leave their country of origin and find themselves in a foreign territory, sometimes in a refugee camp. The fear that prompts refugees to leave their country puts their very lives at stake, either through direct threats or through the physical or psychological attacks they have witnessed. Leaving is a matter of life or death and stems from a desire for life, even survival. More often than not, refugees left in a hurry, bringing with them only what they could carry with them. Being a refugee does not constitute an additional identity label; being a refugee deeply determines concrete existence and identity. Regardless of the challenges that refugees experience on a daily basis and in different ways, theirs is a narrative that expresses hope against all hopes. They put their hope into action as a livelihood strategy by seizing every available opportunity to build up renewed hope. In their quest for a better tomorrow, they often rise above the dependence on relief and handouts from charitable organizations, and instead engage in various trades, however insignificant, for their self-sustenance.

In spite of the fact that the life of a refugee is often characterized by unprecedented suffering, the apostle Paul indicates that suffering and pain are not an excuse for despair (cf. Rom 5:3–5) and are not to thwart our rejoicing in hope. Those who hope have much to celebrate despite the circumstantial challenges they encounter on a daily basis. In other words, hope breaks the boundaries of impossibility and makes rejoicing in suffering a real possibility. This is why those who hope for a better tomorrow have the ability to rejoice unashamedly in the suffering of a "worse" today. Hence, refugees have resilient hope and are not ashamed of their painful past or even their current suffering. Amidst all the conflicts and bloodshed on the African continent – and behind the living conditions of those affected by such violence – are narratives of courage, resilience, and hope.

Whether traumatized or resilient, refugees often live in expectant hope. Their situation can be resolved in four ways: return to the country of origin when conditions are conducive to do so, which is called voluntary repatriation; local integration where the law allows; relocation to a third country, which is called resettlement; or attempting to gain access by one's own means – and at one's own risk – to a third country. In my case, the last option applied. For refugees who choose repatriation or resettlement, the expectation of an unlikely future can be long, numbering in years and sometimes even decades. The neighbouring countries where refugees are hosted often do not have sufficient resources – or the desire – to integrate them. This expectation animates refugees' desire and hope, while at the same wears them down due to its length. For the minority of refugees who find a home in a country where they can settle, the wait will then take the form of official recognition of status, possible naturalization, or even family reunification. In this situation, a peaceful resolution of the wait allows a new life.

Forced migration reveals to us an experience of an itinerant God. In a postmodern world marked by mobility, it echoes the human condition and informs a renewed relationship with God. God meets us at the heart of our movement. Refugees are moved by a quest, a desire to live and to thrive in another space, a space which is not theirs. The path between the departure and the destination is the place without a place but where God himself accompanies the refugee. In this sense, a refugee and a pilgrim embody the foundational experience of the wayfaring of Abraham, father of believers, who set out to know God (Gen 12). Abraham entered into an experience of God only by agreeing to move. Here, the knowledge of God is coextensive with the self-knowledge of the wayfarer. God reveals himself in the tension of movement.

The refugee experience brings to light the personality of a God on the move, a God in the image and likeness of whom we are created (Gen 1:26) and who has become flesh (John 1:14). Inhabiting body and space along the migratory route, a refugee reflects the image of an incarnate God who, in Jesus Christ, espouses the experience of human finitude. A God who, in Jesus Christ, experiences exile, from a birth outside the family home (Luke 2:4–7) and exile in Egypt, passing through the temporary condition of being a refugee (Matt 2:13–23), to dying outside the city walls. Through the suffering that may arise in violence or effort, the refugee bears witness to a God who also suffers, even to death on the cross. Crossed by unspeakable suffering, God nevertheless transcends it in resurrection. By their resilience, by their indomitable desire for life, refugees point in the direction of a living God who is faithful and not discouraged. The migration experience is a walk with God, a step that leads to a new living space.

We have seen that transformational community development is Ubuntu put into action. One of the central goals of transformational community development is to bring people together to hear the gospel, in fellowship, in prayer, and in the breaking of bread. The whole community of early church believers was so deeply united in heart and soul that they ceased to claim private ownership of their property (Acts 4:32). Instead, they had everything in common. To live in such a fraternal communion or *koinonia* means to be of one heart, mind, and soul; it is establishing fellowship from all points of view and synchronizing it with the human, spiritual, and material aspects of people to meet their holistic needs. Indeed, a true Christian community is also committed to distributing earthly goods and to carrying out social actions, *diakonia*, so that no one is in need and all can receive the goods they need (Acts 2:45; 4:35). The early communities, made up of joyful and generous hearts, were open and missionary, which is why they enjoyed the favour of all the people (Acts 2:46–47). Even before intervention activity, transformational community development means witnessing or *marturia*, which is a way of life that shines to others.

In closing, I am reminded of Psalm 84. This is one of the Hebrew songs composed by a wayfaring pilgrim. The scene is set in the glory days of Israel when every year crowds would migrate to Jerusalem for the Feast of Tabernacles. Indeed, pilgrimages to the temple were a grand feature of the Jewish life. The Jews would make the journey from all over Israel to the Holy City to worship at the temple. Families journeyed together, making music which grew at each stopping place. They camped in sunny glades, sang in unison along the roads, sweated together over the hills and laboured through the mire. As they went along, they stored up happy memories that would never be forgotten. Their homes might have been far away from the temple, but they journeyed nevertheless. Psalm 84 expresses the heartbeat of one unnamed pilgrim, a wayfaring stranger, as he journeyed to Jerusalem. This wayfarer recounts his experiences of the journey towards the temple and indicates that it was a journey of both tears and joy. It was a journey of tears or suffering because pilgrims had to pass through "the valley of Baca" (v. 6) to get to the temple. It was a journey of joy because the pilgrims were, nevertheless, happy to be in the presence of God in the end.

When I was a refugee, there were times when I felt life was unfair due to the many challenges that we faced as a result of our status. These challenges are similar to the challenges referred to in Psalm 84:6 when this wayfarer talks about passing through "the valley of Baca," which is Hebrew for "weeping" or "tears." It was an arid, dry, and waterless place filled with thorns, wild animals, pitfalls, snakes, and all sorts of danger. Pilgrims passed through this waterless valley on their way to Jerusalem to worship, but it was nearly impossible to go through it without facing extreme hardship and suffering. It was almost impossible to get to the temple in Jerusalem without shedding tears or experiencing all sorts of adversities. This was no fun place. It was a place of utter suffering. Before enjoying the presence of the Lord in the temple, wayfarers had to pass through this valley. Today, refugees pass through difficult times and dry moments during their emigration process. Their journey often involves going through times of weeping and of wanting to give up. However, such situations can become a source of blessing because according to Psalm 84, the pilgrims make the valley of Baca "a place of springs" and find that "the early rain also covers it with pools" (Ps 84:6). So, this dry and arid place, this place of weeping and of tears and suffering can actually become a place of refreshment and personal blessing for wayfarers.

Many refugees face terrible trials such as sickness in the family or in their own body, watching a loved one as their body deteriorates and the quality of life fails, troubles in relationships with families being destroyed, etc. Many refugees experience times when their faith is tempted, times when their love for God is tested, times when they have no idea what God is up to, times of weeping. Such are times when only hope keeps them going. Theirs is a journey of hope. When I look back on my life as an individual, I can testify that there were times when only hope kept me going. I would not trade those times of weeping, as hard as they were, for anything. God showed up and provided me with hope in full supply. He gave me strength, refreshment, and blessing in my valley of Baca. I would have never known how great God's faithfulness is had I not walked through my valley of Baca as a refugee in various African countries. A refugee can indeed experience God's empowerment in dry times. Those who receive strength from God are those "whose hearts are set on pilgrimage" (Ps 84:5 NIV). In other words, God can turn one's valley of Baca into "a place of springs" (v. 6) when they set their heart on the journey. God can turn our bitter, salty tears into pools that will refresh our exhausted selves while taking us from strength to strength and from glory to glory.

In Psalm 84:9–12, we find that the journey to the temple did not end in tears and sorrow; it rather ended in joy. In my case, my life as a refugee may have had many challenges; however, the Lord lifted me up in ways I could never have imagined. I can justifiably identify with David when he asked, "Who am I, O Lord GOD, and what is my house, that you have brought me thus far?" (2 Sam 7:18). Throughout my life as a refugee, there were times of weeping and times of suffering, but God turned my valley of Baca into a spring of fresh water. When we have tasted the excellences of heavenly goodness, we will never again settle for any of the mediocrities of this earthly vessel because in the presence of God, there is every imaginable and unimaginable good and satisfaction. Hence, "a day in your courts is better than a thousand elsewhere" (Ps 84:10), says the wayfarer. I would not trade a day in God's presence for anything on earth. Once one tastes what the Lord gives, nothing else satisfies.

The final joy of our destination makes our current struggle worth it. We are all strangers and pilgrims in a dry and thirsty land. This world is not the home of those who love the Lord. We are travelling to our final destination. We are wayfaring strangers. It is for this reason that Paul urges us to always "Rejoice in hope, be patient in suffering, persevere in prayer" (Rom 12:12). That is the only way we can finish the journey as wayfarers.

Discussion Questions

1. Why do we say the Bible is a migration manual?
2. How can the biblical tradition help us to better understand the experiences of displaced migrants?
3. What do we mean by the terms "orthodoxy" and "orthopraxy," and how do we relate them to the refugee phenomenon?
4. In what practical ways can we show our love to forced migrants with the resources we already have?
5. Most of us have different perceptions of people from elsewhere.
   - Before reading this book, what was your perception of refugees?
   - How has this book helped to change those perceptions?

Let us pray:

Eternal God, in Exodus 22 you tell us to never brutalize refugees or oppress them, and in Leviticus 19 you say if refugees live with us, they will be for us as fellow citizens, and we must love them as we love ourselves. Help us to keep your word, lest we make mistakes. Help us to be doers of your word, lest we deceive ourselves. We pray to you, King of kings, for only you can change our hearts of stone and our selfish desires and give us hearts of flesh and hospitality so that we know how to welcome refugees in our midst according to your word.

Help us, Divine Master, to use our resources to be a blessing to refugees in our communities. We want to be your instruments for the holistic transformation of refugees so that we can all have life in its fullness according to John 10:10. We also pray for the countries where refugees come from and the countries to which they have fled. Grant their hosts your peace, Lord, and your wisdom to be hospitable to them and respond to their needs with justice, mercy, and love.

May refugees be blessed with abundance, and may they find peace and security. May they benefit from the social actions and transformational interventions of your church so that we can all lead dignified lives that honour your holy name. We pray for the families of all refugees who died on the road while fleeing their country and those who died in their country of asylum as a result of inhumane treatments such as xenophobia. Please forgive us Lord for all that we do wrong to the refugees who live among us, who are also created in your image.

Prince of Peace, we pray that we humble ourselves and learn from the talents, knowledge, and skills you have blessed our refugee brothers and sisters with. Above all, may we see Jesus Christ through the life and behaviour of the refugees in our community.

Eternal Father, we remember refugees who do not know Jesus Christ as Lord and Saviour, and pray that you meet them, dear Lord, at your appointed time so they can also experience the joy of your salvation. Give us the wisdom to be able to accept our differences and the courage to mortify our fears so we can share with refugees the resources you have blessed us with. We pray all this with thanksgiving, believing and trusting in the mighty name of Jesus Christ our Lord and Saviour, in whom we live, and move and have our being. Amen!

Bibliography

Adams, R. H., and J. Page. "Do International Migration and Remittances Reduce Poverty in Developing Countries?" *World Development* 33, no. 10 (2005): 1645–69.

ADET. "O.N.G.: Amis des Etrangers au TOGO, UN Refugees and Migrants" (2013). https://refugeesmigrants.un.org/sites/default/files/amis_des_etrangers_au_togo-ts5.pdf.

Alvarez, J., E. Avarientos, and T. H. McAlpine. "Our Experience with the Bible and Transformational Development." In *Working with the Poor: New Insights and Learnings from Development Practitioners*, edited by Bryant L. Myers, 56–77. Monrovia: World Vision, 1999.

Amit, R. "Security Rhetoric and Detention in South Africa." *Forced Migration Review* 44 (2013): 32–33.

Amit, R., D. Vigneswaran, T. Monson, and G. M. Wachira. *National Survey of the Refugee Reception and Status Determination System in South Africa*. Forced Migration Studies Programme. Johannesburg: Wits University, 2009.

Anders, G. "Being without Time: On Beckett's Play 'Waiting for Godot.'" In *Samuel Beckett: A Collection of Critical Essays*, edited by M. Esslin, 140–51. Englewood Cliffs: Prentice-Hall, 1965.

Anderson, L. *You and Your Refugee Neighbor*. Pasadena: William Carey Library, 1980.

August, K. T. *Equipping the Saints: God's Measure for Development*. Bellville: Print Man, 2010.

———. *The Quest for Being Public Church: The South African Challenge to the Moravian Church in Context (1737–2004)*. Bellville: Print Man, 2009.

Babbie, E. R. *Practice of Social Research*. Cape Town: Oxford University Press, 2001.

Baker, T. L. *Doing Social Research*. 2nd ed. Los Angeles: McGraw-Hill, 1994.

Bakewell, O. "'Keeping Them in Their Place': The ambivalent relationship between development and migration in Africa." *Third World Quarterly* 29, no. 7 (2008): 1341–58.

Barbour, R. *Introducing Qualitative Research: A Student's Guide to the Craft of Doing Qualitative Research*. London: SAGE, 2008.

Barry, K. "Home and away: The construction of citizenship in an emigration context." *New York University Law Review* 81, no. 1 (2006): 11–59.

BBC News Africa. "Burundi Country Profile." Accessed 2012. http://www.bbc.co.uk/news/world-africa-13085064.

———. "DC Congo Country Profile." Accessed 2012. http://www.bbc.co.uk/news/world-africa-13283212.

———. "Q&A: Sudan's Darfur Conflict." 23 February 2010. http://news.bbc.co.uk/2/hi/africa/3496731.stm.

---. "Rwanda Country Profile." Accessed 2012. http://www.bbc.co.uk/news/world-africa-14093238.

---. "South Africa Country Profile." Accessed 2012. http://www.bbc.co.uk/news/world-africa-14094760.

---. "Sudan Country Profile." Accessed 2012. http://www.bbc.co.uk/news/world-africa-14094995.

Beale, G. K., D. J. Brendsel, and W. A. Ross. *An Interpretive Lexicon of New Testament Greek*. Grand Rapids: Zondervan, 2014.

Beauchemin, C. "Des villes aux villages: L'essor de l'émigration urbaine en Côte d'Ivoire." *Annales de Géographie* 111, no. 624 (2002): 157–78. doi:10.3406/geo.2002.1663.

Beauchemin, C., and B. Schoumaker. "Migration to Cities in Burkina Faso: Does the Level of Development in Sending Areas Matter?" *World Development* 33, no. 7 (2005): 1129–52. doi:10.1016/j.worlddev.2005.04.007.

Beckett, S. *Waiting for Godot*. 2nd ed. Kent: Whitstable Litho, 1965.

Beek, K. A. "Spirituality: A Development Taboo." *Development in Practice* 10, no. 1 (2000): 31–43. doi:10.1080/09614520052484.

Belvedere, M. F. "Insiders but Outsiders: The Struggle for the Inclusion of Asylum Seekers and Refugees in South Africa." *Refuge: Canada's Periodical on Refugees* 24, no. 1 (2007): 57–70. doi:10.25071/1920-7336.21368.

Bevans, S. B., and R. P. Schroeder. *Constants in Context: A Theology of Mission for Today*. New York: Orbis, 2004.

Bielawski, M. "Thinking about Church with Hope: The Example of Waclaw Hryniewicz." In *The Challenge of Our Hope*, edited by W. Hryniewicz, 269–85. Washington, DC: RVP, 2007.

Black, R., S. Ammassari, L. M. Hilker, S. Mouillesseaux, C. Pooley, and R. Rajkotia. "Migration and Pro-Poor Policies in Sub-Saharan Africa." Department for International Development, London. 2004. https://www.researchgate.net/publication/242611209_Migration_and_Pro-Poor_Policy_in_Africa.

Black, R., S. R. G. Bennett, S. M. Thomas, and J. R. Beddington. "Climate Change: Migration as Adaptation." *Nature* 478 (2011): 477–79.

Black, R., M. Collyer, R. Skeldon, and C. Waddington. "Routes to Illegal Residence: A Case Study of Immigration Detainees in the United Kingdom." *Geoforum* 37, no. 4 (2006): 552–64.

Black, R., C. Natali, and J. Skinner. "Migration and Inequality." Washington, DC: World Bank, 2005. http://www.rrojasdatabank.info/wir2006/black.pdf.

Blavo, E. Q. *The Problem of Refugees in Africa: Boundaries and Borders*. London: Ashgate, 1999.

Blaxter, L., C. Hughes, and M. Tight. *How to Research*. Buckingham: Open University Press, 2000.

Blokhin, Andriy. "The 5 Countries That Produce the Most Carbon Dioxide (CO2)." *Investopedia* (27 October 2020). https://www.investopedia.com/articles/investing/092915/5-countries-produce-most-carbon-dioxide-co2.asp.

Boeije, H. *Analysis in Qualitative Research*. London: SAGE, 2010.
Bonhoeffer, Dietrich. *Sanctorum Communio: A Dogmatic Research on the Sociology of the Church*. London: Collins, 1963.
Bosch, D. *Transforming Mission: Paradigm Shifts in Theology of Missions*. Maryknoll, NY: Orbis, 1991.
Botman, R. H. "Hope as the Coming Reign of God." In *Hope for the World*, edited by W. Brueggemann, 69–81. London: Westminster John Knox, 2001.
Bourdeau, M. "Auguste Comte." *The Stanford Encyclopedia of Philosophy*, edited by E. N. Zalta. Stanford, CA: Center for the Study of Language and Information (CSLI) (8 May 2018). https://plato.stanford.edu/entries/comte/.
Bowers-du Toit, N. "'Rise Up and Walk': Tracing the Trajectory of the Carnegie Discourse and Plotting a Way Forward." *NGTT* 55, no. 3–4 (2015): 511–31. doi:10.5952/55-3-4-651.
Bragg, W. G. "From Development to Transformation." In *The Church in Response to Human Need*, edited by V. Samuel and C. Sugden, 21–47. Grand Rapids: Eerdmans, 1987.
Brown, C., and U. Falkenroth. "Patience, Steadfastness, Endurance." In *The New International Dictionary of New Testament Theology*, edited by C. Brown, 764–65. London: Paternoster, 1976.
Brown, O. *Migration and Climate Change*. International Organization for Migration (IOM), Research Series 31. Geneva: IOM, 2008. doi:10.18356/26de4416-en.
Brueggemann, W. "Communities of Hope Midst Engines for Despair." In *Hope for the World*, edited by W. Brueggemann, 150–57. London: Westminster John Knox, 2001.
———. "Hope." In *Reverberations of Faith: A Theological Handbook of Old Testament Themes*, edited by W. Brueggemann, 100–102. London: Westminster John Knox, 2002.
Bruwer, E. *Beggars Can Be Choosers: In Search of a Better Way Out of Poverty and Dependence*. Pretoria: University of Pretoria, 1994.
Burkey, S. *People First: A Guide to Self-Reliant Participatory Rural Development*. London: Zed Books, 1996.
Buscher, D. "New Approaches to Urban Refugee Livelihoods." *Refuge: Canada's Periodical on Refugees* 28, no. 2 (2011): 17–29.
Butler, R. A. "The Congo Rainforest." Mongabay (1 August 2020). https://rainforests.mongabay.com/congo/.
Cambrezy, L. "Un aspect méconnu de la crise rwandaise: Les réfugiés de Nairobi." *Politique Africaine (Paris, France)* no. 68 (1997): 134–41.
———. "Territoire et dimension géopolitique de l'accueil des réfugiés. Les colonies agricoles des exilés du Soudan en Ouganda." *Nature Sciences Sociétés* 14, no. 4 (Oct. 2006): 365–75. doi:10.1051/nss:2007004.
Cambrezy, L., and S. Laacher. *L'asile au Sud: Afrique, Méditerranée, La Chronique*, no. 53, 1–4. Paris: Ceped, 2007.

Carbonnier, G. *Religion and Development: Reconsidering Secularism as the Norm.* London: Palgrave Macmillan, 2012.

Carling, J. "Gender Dimensions of International Migration." Geneva: Global Commission on International Migration, 2005.

Carroll R., and M. Daniel. *Christians at the Border: Immigration, the Church, and the Bible.* Grand Rapids: Baker Academic, 2008.

Castles, S. "Environmental Change and Forced Migration: Making Sense of the Debate." Working Paper 70. Geneva: UNHCR, 2002.

Cavanaugh, W. T. *Migrations of the Holy: God, State, and the Political Meaning of the Church.* Grand Rapids: Eerdmans, 2011.

Charman, A., and L. Piper. "Xenophobia, Criminality and Violent Entrepreneurship: Violence Against Somali Shopkeepers in Delft South, Cape Town, South Africa." *South African Review of Sociology* 43, no. 3 (2012): 81–105.

Chester, T. *Good News to the Poor: Sharing the Gospel through Social Involvement.* Nottingham: Inter-Varsity, 2009.

———. *Justice, Mercy and Humility: Integral Mission and the Poor.* London: Paternoster, 2002.

CIA. "Congo, Democratic Republic of the." World Fact Book (9 March 2021). https://www.cia.gov/the-world-factbook/countries/congo-democratic-republic-of-the/.

Cilliers, J. H. *In Search of Meaning between Ubuntu and Into: Perspectives on Preaching in Post-Apartheid South Africa.* Copenhagen: Societas Homiletica, 2008.

Cohen, L., L. Manion, and K. Morrisson. *Research Methods in Education.* 5th ed. London: Routledge Falmer, 2000.

Corporate Finance Institute. "Maslow's Hierarchy of Needs," CFI (2021). https://corporatefinanceinstitute.com/resources/knowledge/other/maslows-hierarchy-of-needs/.

Couture, P. "Human Dignity, Injustice and Ubuntu: Living the Metaphor of *Bwino/Bumuntu*/White lime in the Democratic Republic of Congo." In *Practicing Ubuntu: Practical Theological Perspectives on Injustice, Personhood and Human Dignity*, edited by J. S. Dreyer, Y. Dreyer, E. Foley, and M. Nel, 9–21. Pretoria: LitVerlag, 2017.

Crush, J., and V. Williams. *Transnationalism and New African Immigration to South Africa.* Toronto: Canadian Association of African Studies, 2002. https://scholars.wlu.ca/cgi/viewcontent.cgi?article=1066&context=samp.

Crush, J., and D. A. McDonald. "Introduction to Special Issue: Evaluating South African Immigration Policy after Apartheid." *Africa Today* 48, no. 3 (2001): 1–13.

Crush, J., and V. Williams. *International Migration and Development: Dynamics and Challenges in South and Southern Africa.* United Nations Expert Group Meeting on International Migration and Development. New York: United Nations, 2005.

Dadosky, John Daniel. "Ecclesia De Trinitate: Ecclesial Foundations from Above." *New Blackfriars* 94, no. 1049 (2013): 64–78. https://loneranresource.com/pdf/contributors/LC2001-07_Dadosky-Ecclesia_De_Trinitate.pdf.

Dadush, U., and M. Niebuhr. "The Economic Impact of Forced Migration." Washington, DC: Carnegie Endowment for International Peace, 2016.

Dear, J. *Our God Is Non-Violent – Witnesses in the Struggle for Peace and Justice*. New York: Pilgrim, 1990.

De Gruchy, S. "A Christian Engagement with the Sustainable Livelihoods Framework." *Missionalia* 33, no. 1 (1 April 2005): 56–72. https://hdl.handle.net/10520/AJA02569507_375.

Department of Home Affairs (DHA). "Refugee Status and Asylum." Department of Home Affairs, Republic of South Africa (2021). http://www.dha.gov.za/index.php/immigration-services/refugee-status-asylum.

Dryden-Petersen, S., and W. Gilles. "Introduction: Higher Education for Refugees." *Refuge: Canada's Periodical on Refugees* 27, no. 2 (2010).

Duchrow, U. *Alternatives to Global Capitalism*. The Hague: International Books, 1995.

Elsner, B. "Does Emigration Increase the Wages of Non-emigrants in Sending Countries?" (n.d.). https://wol.iza.org/articles/does-emigration-increase-wages-of-non-emigrants-in-sending-countries/long.

Erasmus, G. "The Accord of Nkomati: Context and Content." The South African Institute of International Affairs (October 1984): 1–33. https://media.africaportal.org/documents/The_Accord_Of_Nkomati.pdf.

Farrant, M., A. McDonald, and D. Sriskandarajah. *Migration and Development: Opportunities and Challenges for Policymakers*. IOM Migration Research Series 22. 2006. doi:10.18356/843e659c-en.

Ferris, E. G. *Beyond Borders: Refugees, Migrants and Human Rights in the Post-Cold War Era*. Geneva: World Council of Churches, 1993.

Flick, U. *Designing Qualitative Research*. London: SAGE, 2007. doi:10.4135/9781849208826.

———. *Managing Quality in Qualitative Research*. London: SAGE, 2007. doi:10.4135/9781849209441.

Forbes-Martin, S. *Refugee Women*. Maryland: Lexington Books, 2004.

Fourchard, L., and A. Wa Kabwe-Segatti. "Introduction of Xenophobia and Citizenship: The Everyday Politics of Exclusion and Inclusion in Africa." *Africa: The Journal of the International African Institute* 85 (2015): 2–12.

Fyodorov, N. "Philosophy of the Common Cause." In *History of Russian Philosophy*, edited by V. Zenkovskij, 968. London: Routledge, 2003.

Gagnon, A. J., L. Merry, and C. Robinson. "A Systematic Review of Refugee Women's Reproductive Health." *Refuge* 21, no. 1 (2002): 6–17.

Getui, M. N., and P. Kanyandago, eds. *From Violence to Peace: A Challenge for African Christianity*. Nairobi: Acton, 1999.

Ghosh, B. "Migrants' Remittances and Development: Myths, Rhetoric, and Realities." IOM International Organization for Migration (2006). https://publications.iom.int/system/files/pdf/migrants_remittances.pdf.

Gifford, P. *African Christianity: Its Public Role*. Bloomington: Indiana University Press, 1998.

Goldewijk, B. K., and B. G. Fortman. *Where Needs Meet Rights: Economic, Social and Cultural Rights in a New Perspective*. Geneva: WCC Publications, 1999.

Gonin, Patrick, and Véronique Lassailly-Jacob. "Les réfugiés de l'environnement. Une nouvelle catégorie de migrants forcés?" *Revue Européenne des Migrations Internationales* 18, no. 2 (2002): 139–60. doi:10.4000/remi.1654.

Greider, W. *One World, Ready or Not: The Manic Logic of Global Capitalism*. New York: Simon & Schuster, 1997.

Groody, D. G. "Crossing the Divide: Foundations of a Theology of Migration and Refugees." *Theological Studies* 70 (2009): 638–67.

Gutierrez, G. "Option for the Poor: Assessment and Challenges." *Theological* 1, no. 2 (1993): 121–34.

Hailey, J. *Ubuntu: A Literature Review*. London: Desmond Tutu Foundation, 2008.

Hall, D. J. *The Steward*. Eugene: Wipf & Stock, 1990.

Harrell-Bond, B. E. "Can Humanitarian Work with Refugees Be Humane?" *Human Rights Quarterly* 24, no. 1 (2002): 51–85. doi:10.1353/hrq.2002.0011.

Harzig, C., D. Hoerder, and D. Gabaccia. *What Is Migration History?* Cambridge: Polity, 2009.

Hassim, S., T. Kupe, and E. Worby, eds. *Go Home or Die Here*. Johannesburg: Wits University Press, 2008.

Haut-Commissariat des Nations Unis pour les Refugiés. *Les réfugiés dans le monde. Cinquante ans d'action humanitaire*. Paris: Éditions Autrement, 2000.

———. *Réfugiés: Tendances mondiales en 2005*. Genève: UNHCR, 2005.

Henning, E., W. Rensburg, and B. Smit. *Finding Your Way in Qualitative Research*. Pretoria: Van Schaik, 2004.

Hryniewicz, W. *The Challenge of Our Hope: Christian Faith in Dialogue*. Washington, DC: Council for Research in Values and Philosophy, 2007.

Hughes, D. *Power and Poverty: Divine and Human Rule in a World of Need*. Nottingham: InterVarsity, 2008.

Hughes, D., and M. Bennett. *God of the Poor: A Biblical Vision of God's Present Rule*. Carlisle: OM Publishing, 1998.

Hugon, P. *Public Ethical Economics: Global Public Goods and Common Heritage*. Paris: UNESCO, 2003.

Hutchinson, Mary, and Pat Dorsett. "What Does the Literature Say about Resilience in the Refugee People? Implications for Practice." *Journal of Social Inclusion* 3, no. 2 (2012): 55–78. doi:10.36251/josi.55.

Jacobsen, D. A. *Doing Justice: Congregations and Community Organizing*. Minneapolis: Augsburg Fortress, 2001.

Jacobsen, K. *Refugee Livelihoods in Urban Areas: Identifying Program Opportunities*. Boston: Feinstein International Center, Tufts University, 2012.

Kane, M. C., and S. F. Kane. "A Last Resort in Cases of Wrongful Detention and Deportation in Africa." *Forced Migration Review* 44 (2013): 36.
Keely, C., and S. S. Russell. "Responses of Industrial Countries to Asylum Seekers." *Journal of International Affairs* 47, no. 2 (1994): 400–417.
Keifert, P. R. *Welcoming the Stranger: A Public Theology of Worship and Evangelism*. Minneapolis: Fortress, 1992.
Keller, T. J. *Ministries of Mercy: The Call of the Jericho Road*. New Jersey: P&R, 1997.
Kerwin, D. M. "The Faltering U.S. Refugee Protection System: Legal and Policy Responses to Refugees, Asylum Seekers, and Others in Need of Protection." Washington, DC: Migration Policy Institute, 2011. https://www.researchgate.net/publication/285626911_The_Faltering_US_Refugee_Protection_System_Legal_and_Policy_Responses_to_Refugees_Asylum-Seekers_and_Others_in_Need_of_Protection.
Keshgegian, F. A. *Time for Hope: Practices for Living in Today's World*. London: Continuum, 2006.
Khoza, R. *Ubuntu: African Humanism*. Johannesburg: HSRC, 1994.
Kiama, L., and D. Likule. "Detention in Kenya: Risks for Refugees and Asylum Seekers." *Forced Migration Review* 44 (2013): 34–35.
Kiely, R., and P. Marfleet. *Globalisation and the Third World*. New York: Routledge, 2000.
Klaasen, J. "The Interplay Between Theology and Development: How Theology Can Be Related to Development in Post-modern Society." *Missionalia* 41, no. 2 (2013): 182–94.
Kniveton, D. R., C. D. Smith, and R. Black. "Emerging Migration Flows in a Changing Climate in Dryland Africa." *Nature Climate Change* 2, no. 6 (2012): 444–47.
Koenane, M. L. J. "*Ubuntu* and Philoxenia: *Ubuntu* and Christian Worldviews as Responses to Xenophobia." *HTS Teologiese Studies/Theological Studies* 74, no. 1 (10 April 2018): 46–68. https://hts.org.za/index.php/hts/article/view/4668/11090.
Kossé, K. "Unity of Believers." In *Africa Bible Commentary*, edited by T. Adeyemo, 1288. Nairobi: WordAlive, 2006.
Kretzschmar, L., W. Bentley, and A. Van Niekerk. *What Is a Good Life? An Introduction to Christian Ethics in the 21st Century*. Kempton Park: AcadSA, 2009.
Laliberté, D. "Crises Humanitaires, Santé des Réfugiés et des Déplacés: Un Cadre Analytique." Revue Européenne des Migrations Internationales 23, no. 3 (2007). http://journals.openedition.org/remi/4207.
Landau, L. B. "Attacks on Foreigners in South Africa: More Than Just Xenophobia?" *The Strategic Review for Southern Africa* 30 (2008): 1.
———. *Forced Migrants in the New Johannesburg: Towards a Local Government Response*. Johannesburg: University of the Witwatersrand, 2004.
———. *The Humanitarian Hangover: Displacement, Aid and Transformation in Western Tanzania*. Johannesburg: Wits University Press, 2008.
Langmead, Ross. "Refugees as Guests and Hosts: Towards a Theology of Mission among Refugees and Asylum Seekers." In *Religion, Migration and Identity: Methodological*

and Theological Explorations, edited by Martha Frederiks and Dorottya Nagy, 171–88. Boston: Brill, 2016. http://www.jstor.org/stable/10.1163/j.ctt1w8h267.13.

The Lausanne Covenant, The Lausanne Movement (1974), https://www.lausanne.org/content/covenant/lausanne-covenant#cov.

Ledwith, M. *Community Development: A Critical Approach*. Bristol: Policy, 2011.

Lee, E. S. "A Theory of Migration." *Demography* 3, no. 1 (1966): 47–57. https://doi.org/10.2307/2060063.

Lewis, B. "Forging an Understanding of Black Humanity through Relationship: An Ubuntu Perspective." *Black Theology: An International Journal* 8 (1 April 2010): 69–85.

Lotter, H. *Injustice, Violence, and Peace: The Case of South Africa*. Amsterdam: Rodopi, 1997.

———. *When I Needed a Neighbor Were You There?* Epping, Western Cape: Creda Communications, 2008.

Louw, D. J. "Theory of Science within Theology: Scientific Research as a Theological Problem." Unpublished Study Guide. Stellenbosch: University of Stellenbosch, 1998.

Magesa, L. *Christian Ethics in Africa*. Nairobi: Acton, 2002.

Maloka, T. "Mines and Labour Migrants in Southern Africa." *Journal of Historical Sociology* 10, no. 2 (1997): 213–24.

Maluwa, T. "The Refugee Problem and the Quest for Peace and Security in Southern Africa." *International Refugee Law Journal*. University of Cape Town, 1995.

Mapitsa, C. "Local Politics of Xenophobia." *Journal of Asian and African Studies* (2016): 1–17.

Mapokgole, Reshoketswe B. "'There Is No Black in the Rainbow (Nation)': A Bikoist and Fanonian Approach to Understanding 'Xenophobic' Violence in South Africa." Senior Theses, Trinity College, Hartford, CT, 2014. http://digitalrepository.trincoll.edu/theses/425.

Marshall, J.-P. "The Economic Ethics of the Bible." *Political Economy* 3, no. 27 (2005): 66–81.

———. "To the Bible's Origins of the Normative Economy." *Ecology And Politics* 2, no. 29 (2004): 215–26.

Marshall, K. "Development and Religion: A Different Lens on Development Debates." *Peabody Journal of Education* 76, no. 3–4 (2001): 339–75.

Maruskin, J. M. *Immigration and the Bible: A Guide for Radical Welcome*. Washington: United Methodist Women, 2012.

Mason, J. *Qualitative Researching*. London: SAGE, 2002.

Mbeki, T. "Africa – War and Peace." Public lecture, Tshwane University of Technology, 16 September 2010. Pretoria: Tshwane University of Technology, 2010. https://www.polity.org.za/article/sa-mbeki-public-lecture-by-the-former-president-of-south-africa-on-africa-war-and-peace-pretoria-16092010-2010-09-16.

Mbiti, J. S. *African Religions and Philosophy*. London: Heinemann, 1969.

Mercy Corps, "The Facts: The Humanitarian Crisis in the Democratic Republic of Congo." Mercy Corps (17 July 2019). https://www.mercycorps.org/articles/dr-congo/quick-facts-humanitarian-crisis-drc.

Metz, T. "Ubuntu as a Moral Theory: Reply to Four Critics." *South African Journal of Philosophy* 26, no. 4 (2007): 369–87.

Miles, M. B., and A. M. Huberman. *Qualitative Data Analysis*. London: SAGE, 1994.

Misago, J. P. "Politics by Other Means? The Political Economy of Xenophobic Violence in Post-Apartheid South Africa." *The Black Scholar: Journal of Black Studies and Research* 47, no. 2 (2017): 40–53.

———. "Responding to Xenophobic Violence in Post-Apartheid South Africa: Barking Up the Wrong Tree?" *African Human Mobility Review* 2 (2016): 443–67.

Moltmann, J. *God for a Secular Society: The Public Relevance of Theology*. Minneapolis: Fortress Press, 1999.

———. *Hope and Planning*. London: SCM Press, 1971.

———. *Theology of Hope*. London: SCM Press, 1967.

Mooneyham, W. S. *What Do You Say to a Hungry World?* Waco: Word Books, 1975.

Morisy, A. *Beyond the Good Samaritan: Community Ministry and Mission*. London: Continuum, 1997.

Mouton, J. *How to Succeed in Your Master's and Doctoral Studies*. Pretoria: Van Schaik Publishers, 2001.

Mpetsheni, L. "Ubuntu – A Soteriological Ethic for an Effaced *Umntu* in a Post-1994 South Africa: A Black Theology of Liberation Perspective." Unpublished PhD Thesis, University of Pretoria, 2019. https://repository.up.ac.za/handle/2263/75269?show=full.

Msabah, B. A. "Empowerment by Hope: A Phenomenological Study on the Health and Wellbeing of African Refugees." Unpublished Doctoral Dissertation, University of Stellenbosch, 2016. http://scholar.sun.ac.za/handle/10019.1/98666.

———. "'And the Greatest of These Is Hope': Reframing the Global Refugee Crisis." *Transformation* 35, no. 2 (2018): 1–7. doi:10.1177/0265378818783590.

———. "Horizons in Transformational Development and Transnational Migration: Does Hope Matter?" *Scriptura* 117, no. 1 (2018): 1–14. http://www.scielo.org.za/pdf/scriptur/v117/03.pdf.

———. "Refugee Migrants as Agents of Change: Strategies for Improved Livelihoods and Self-Reliance." *Verbum et Ecclesia* 40, no. 1 (2019): a1851. doi:10.4102/ve.v40i1.1851.

———. "Situating the Global Refugee Crisis within the Context of Ecclesial Diaconia and Praxis: The Case of Cape Town, South Africa." In *Diaconia in Dialogue: The Challenges of Diversifying Contexts*, edited by P. Launonen and M. Valtonen, 166–188. Helsinki: The International Society for the Research and Study of Diaconia and Christian Social Practice, 2017. https://www.theseus.fi/bitstream/handle/10024/136186/DIAK_tyoelama_12_verkko.pdf?sequence=1.

Msabah, B. A., and N. B. du Toit. "The Impact of Gentrification on the Refugee Community: Interfacing Practical Theology and Human Geography." *Stellenbosch Theological Journal* 5, no. 3 (2019): 473–94. http://www.scielo.org.za/pdf/stj/v5n3/23.pdf.

———. "'We Live, and Move, and Have Our Being': Refugees' Vulnerability and the Ecclesial Challenge for Diaconal Praxis." *Diaconia* 8, no. 2 (2017): 188–200. doi:10.13109/diac.2017.8.2.188.

Mummert, J. R., and J. Bach. *Refugee Ministry in Local Congregation*. Harrisonburg: Herald, 1992.

Murithi, T. "Practical Peacemaking Wisdom from Africa: Reflections on Ubuntu." *Journal of Pan African Studies* 1, no. 4 (June 2006): 25–34.

Mususa, P., and F. Nyamnjoh. "Migration and Xenophobia in Southern Africa." In *Building Peace in Southern Africa*, edited by D. Hanar and C. Saunders. Cape Town: Centre for Conflict Resolution, 2010.

Myers, B. L. *Walking with the Poor*. New York: Orbis, 2003.

Nel, M. "Practical Theology and the One Body of Christ: Toward a Missional-Ecumenical Model." *Missionalia: Southern African Journal of Mission Studies* 36, no. 1 (2008): 153–54.

Neville, C. *The Complete Guide to Referencing and Avoiding Plagiarism*. Berkshire: McGraw-Hill, 2010.

Newland, K. *Seeking Protection: Women in Asylum and Refugee Resettlement Processes*. United Nations Division for the Advancement of Women – Consultative Meeting on "Migration and Mobility and How This Movement Affects Women," 2–4 December 2003. Malmö, Sweden: United Nations, 2004. https://www.un.org/womenwatch/daw/meetings/consult/CM-Dec03-EP8.pdf.

Ngewa, S. "What Is the Church?" In *Africa Bible Commentary*, edited by T. Adeyemo, 1431. Nairobi: WordAlive, 2006.

Niebuhr, H. R. *The Responsible Self: An Essay in Christian Moral Philosophy*. London: Harper & Row, 1963.

Ntibagirirwa, S. *Philosophical Premises for African Economic Development*. Geneva: Globethnics, 2014.

Nussbaum, M. C. *Capabilities: How to Create the Conditions for a Fairer World?* Paris: New Horizons, 2012.

O'Donovan, W. *Biblical Christianity in African Perspective*. Carlisle, UK: Paternoster, 2000.

"Organisation of African Unity." Addis Ababa: Convention Governing the Specific Aspects of Refugee Problems in Africa, 1969. https://au.int/sites/default/files/treaties/36400-treaty-0005_-_oau_convention_governing_the_specific_aspects_of_refugee_problems_in_africa_e.pdf.

Osmer, R. R. *Practical Theology: An Introduction*. Grand Rapids: Eerdmans, 2008.

Payne, J. D. *Strangers Next Door: Immigration, Migration and Mission*. Downers Grove, IL: InterVarsity, 2012.

Perkins, J. M. *Beyond Charity – The Call to Christian Community Development*. Grand Rapids: Baker Books, 1993.

Piguet, E. "Climate Change and Forced Migration." Research Paper 153. Geneva: UNHCR, 2008.

Plemon, J. "The Parable of the Good Samaritan: 5 Lessons Learned." Crosswalk.com. (6 January 2019). https://www.crosswalk.com/family/career/the-parable-of-the-good-samaritan-5-lessons-learned.html.

Potts, Deborah. "Making a Livelihood In (and beyond) the African City: The Experience of Zimbabwe." *Africa* 81, no. 4 (2011): 588–605. doi:10.1017/S0001972011000489.

ReliefWeb. "North West Tanzania: Nyarugusu Refugee Camp Profile." UNHRC (2018). https://reliefweb.int/sites/reliefweb.int/files/resources/65654.pdf.

Renaud, F., J. J. Bogardi, O. Dun, and K. Warner. "Control, Adapt or Flee: How to Face Environmental Migration?" Bonn: United Nations University – Institute for Environment and Human Security (2007): 1–48. http://collections.unu.edu/eserv/UNU:1859/pdf3973.pdf.

Richmond, A. H. *Global Apartheid. Refugees, Racism, and the New World Order*. Oxford: Oxford University Press, 1994.

Roberts, K. "Understanding the Causes of Poverty in the DRC." *Borgen Magazine* (6 September 2018). https://www.borgenmagazine.com/poverty-in-the-drc/.

Robinson, J., D. Turton, G. Mohan, and H. Yanacopulos. *Development and Displacement*. Oxford: Oxford University Press, 2002.

Robinson, S. "The Deadliest War in the World." *Time Magazine*, 28 May 2006. http://content.time.com/time/subscriber/article/0,33009,1198921,00.html.

Rodier, C. "La construction d'une politique européenne de l'asile entre discours et pratiques." *Hommes et Migrations*, no. 1240 (2002): 81–93.

Rosen, A. "The Origins of War in the DRC: How the Region Became Overrun by Warlords and Lacking Any Kind of Functional Government." *The Atlantic* (26 June 2013). https://www.theatlantic.com/international/archive/2013/06/the-origins-of-war-in-the-drc/277131/.

Rosenkranz, E. "Those People: Political Construction of Refugees and Asylum Seekers in South Africa." Thesis from Lund University, Sweden, 2013. https://www.semanticscholar.org/paper/%22Those-people%22-Political-Construction-of-Refugees-Rosenkranz/5d62113ae420a69c57934977b3d6791fb0eb20c3#references.

Ross, C. "Creating Space: Hospitality as a Metaphor for Mission," ANVIL 25 (2008): 167–76.

Roux, N. "Migration and Urbanization: Towards a 10-Year Review of the Population Implementation in South Africa (1998–2008)." Pretoria: Department of Social Development, 2009.

Rutinwa, B. "Prima Facie Status and Refugee Protection." *New Issues in Refugee Research* 69 (2002): 1–27. https://www.unhcr.org/research/working/3db9636c4/prima-facie-status-refugee-protection-bonaventure-rutinwa.html.

Sapsford, R., and V. Jupp. *Data Collection and Analysis*. London: SAGE, 2006.

Sawyer, Ida. "Présentation sur la crise politique en RD Congo et ses répercussions en matière humanitaire, de droits humains et de sécurité." Human Rights Watch (9 April 2018). https://www.hrw.org/fr/news/2018/04/09/presentation-sur-la-crise-politique-en-rd-congo-et-ses-repercussions-en-matiere.

Schmidtz, D., and R. E. Goodin. *Social Welfare and Individual Responsibility*. Cambridge: Cambridge University Press, 1998.

Sen, Amartya. *Development as Freedom*. Oxford: Oxford University Press, 1999.

———. *Inequality Re-examined*. Cambridge: Harvard University Press, 1992.

Silverman, D. *Interpreting Qualitative Data*. 3rd ed. London: SAGE, 2006.

Simon, D. "The Climate Change Challenges for Regional Integration in Southern Africa." *South African Geographical Journal* 92, no. 2 (2010): 96–104. https://www.tandfonline.com/doi/pdf/10.1080/03736245.2010.523527.

Sine, T. "Development: Its Secular Past and Its Uncertain Future." In *The Church in Response to Human Need*, edited by V. Samuel and C. Sugden. Grand Rapids: Eerdmans, 1987.

Sol, J. *Refugees: A Challenge to South African Churches*. Pietermaritzburg: South African Council of Churches, 1982.

Soulen, R. K., and L. Woodhead. *God and Human Dignity*. Grand Rapids: Eerdmans, 2006.

Speckman, M. *A Biblical Vision for Africa's Development*. Pietermaritzburg: Cluster, 2007.

Spencer, N. *Asylum and Immigration: A Christian Perspective on a Polarised Debate*. London: Paternoster, 2004.

Spohn, W. C. *What Are They Saying about Scriptures and Ethics?* New York: Paulist, 1984.

Stemmett, J. "A Biblical Theology of Ministry to Refugees for Baptist Churches in South Africa." Master of Theology Thesis, University of Fort Hare, 2008.

Strong, J. *Strong's Exhaustive Concordance of the Bible*. Peabody: Hendrickson, 2009.

Sutton, R., D. Vigneswaran, and H. Wels. "Waiting in Liminal Space: Migrants' Queuing for Home Affairs in South Africa." *Anthropology Southern Africa* 34, no. 1–2 (2011): 30–37.

Swanepoel, H., and F. de Beer. *Community Development: Breaking the Cycle of Poverty*. 4th ed. Lansdowne, South Africa: Juta, 2006.

Swindal, J. "Faith and Reason." *Internet Encyclopedia of Philosophy*, 2001. Accessed 17 October 2013. http://Www.Iep.Utm.Edu/Faith-Re/.

Swinton, J., and H. Mowat. *Practical Theology and Qualitative Research*. London: SCM, 2006.

Tamas, A. "Spirituality and Development: Concepts and Categories." *Canadian International Development Agency* (1999): 1–24. http://www.tamas.com/sites/default/files/2019-06/spirit_devt.pdf.

Tasker, R. V. "Hope." In *The New Bible Dictionary*, edited by J. D. Douglas, 535–36. Leicester: Inter-Varsity, 1962.

Thomas, D. R. *A General Inductive Approach for Qualitative Data Analysis*. Auckland: School of Population Health, 2003.
Tinder, G. *The Fabric of Hope: An Essay*. Emory University Studies in Law and Religion. Grand Rapids: Eerdmans, 1999.
Trochim, W. M. "The Research Methods Knowledge Base." 2nd ed., accessed 2006. http://www.socialresearchmethods.net/kb/.
Tutu, D. M. *No Future Without Forgiveness*. New York: Doubleday, 1999.
Tyndale, W. "Poverty and Development: Has Religion a Contribution to Make?" *Commentary: International Movement for a Just World* 1, no. 2 (2001): 1–5.
UNFPA. *Libérer le potentiel de la croissance urbaine. État de la population mondiale 2007*. New York, 2008.
United Nations General Assembly. "Assistance to Refugees, Returnees, and Displaced Persons in Africa (covering the period 1 January 2007–15 June 2008)." Report of the Secretary General. 63rd Session. A/63/321. United Nations (2008). https://reliefweb.int/sites/reliefweb.int/files/resources/A8EC3D90D252F76D492576640006F24D-Full_Report.pdf.
———. "Note on International Protection." Report of the High Commissioner. 60th Session. A/Ac.96/1066 (26 June 2009). Geneva: Executive Committee, 2009. https://www.unhcr.org/excom/excomrep/4a78441b9/note-international-protection-june-2009.html.
United Nations High Commissioner for Refugees. "2020 Statistical Yearbook." https://unstats.un.org/unsd/publications/statistical-yearbook/files/syb63/syb63.pdf.
———. "Convention and Protocol Relating to the Status of Refugees," including the "1951 Convention Relating to the Status of Refugees" and "1967 Protocol Relating to the Status of Refugees." Geneva: UNHRC (2010). http://www.unhcr.org/3b66c2aa10.html.
———. "Global Trends: Forced Displacements in 2019." Copenhagen: Statistics and Demographics Section (2020). https://www.unhcr.org/5ee200e37.pdf.
———. "Livelihood Programming in UNHCR: Operational Guidelines." Geneva: UNHCR (2012). https://www.unhcr.org/publications/operations/4fbdf17c9/livelihood-programming-unhcr-operational-guidelines.html.
———. "Promoting Livelihoods and Self-Reliance: Operational Guidance on Refugee Protection and Solutions in Urban Areas." UNHCR (2011). https://www.unhcr.org/publications/operations/4eeb19f49/promoting-livelihoods-self-reliance-operational-guidance-refugee-protection.html.
———. "OAU Convention Governing the Specific Aspects of Refugee Problems in Africa." UNHCR, Addis-Ababa (10 September 1969). https://www.unhcr.org/about-us/background/45dc1a682/oau-convention-governing-specific-aspects-refugee-problems-africa-adopted.html.
———. "Refugee Data Finder." Geneva: Refugee Statistics (8 December 2020). https://www.unhcr.org/refugee-statistics/.

Vearey, J. "Learning from HIV: Exploring migration and health in South Africa," *Global Public Health* 7, no. 1 (2012): 58–70.

Vearey, J., and G. Snyman. "Stop Spreading Dangerous Lies: Foreign Migrants Are Not Root Cause of SA's Problems." *City Press* (24 September 2019). https://www.news24.com/citypress/Voices/stop-spreading-dangerous-lies-foreign-migrants-are-not-root-cause-of-sas-problems-20190924.

Wa Kabwe-Segatti, A. "'Clandestins' et 'Makwerekwere' dans l'Afrique du Sud post-apartheid: Production de catégories, pratiques administratives et xénophobie." *Social Science Information* 47, no. 4 (2008): 661–80.

———. "Du Rapatriement Volontaire au Refoulement Dissimulé: Les Réfugiés Mozambicains en Afrique du Sud." *Politique africaine* 1, no. 1 (2002): 75–92.

———. "Reformulating Immigration Policy in Post-Apartheid South Africa: From the Aliens Control Act of 1991 to the Immigration Act of 2002." IFAS Working Paper Series / Les Cahiers de l'IFAS 8 (2006): 171–85.

Warner, K. "Human Migration and Displacement in the Context of Adaptation to Climate Change: The Cancun Adaptation Framework and Potential for Future Action." Environment and Planning C: Government and Policy 30, no. 6 (2012): 1061–77.

Watuna, Benjamin Babunga. "*Et Si Nous Parlions d'Histoire?*" Facebook (26 October 2019). https://www.facebook.com/groups/528706633982349/?multi_permalinks=1265851536934518&notif_id=1572090676267850&notif_t=group_activity&ref=notif&__m_async_page__=1&_rdc=1&_rdr. Used by permission.

"What the Nkomati Accord Means for Africa." *The Black Scholar* 15, no. 6 (1984): 15–22. http://www.jstor.org/stable/41067114.

World Fact Book, "Congo, Democratic Republic of the" (9 March 2021). https://www.cia.gov/the-world-factbook/countries/congo-democratic-republic-of-the/.

Wright, K., and R. Black. "Poverty, Migration and Human Well-being: Towards a Post-crisis Research and Policy Agenda." *Journal of International Development* 23, no. 4 (2011): 548–54.

Xu, L., S. S. Saatchi, A. Shapiro, et al. "Spatial Distribution of Carbon Stored in Forests of the Democratic Republic of Congo." *Scientific Reports* 7, no. 15030 (8 November 2017). https://www.nature.com/articles/s41598-017-15050-z.pdf.

Yankoski, M., and D. Yankoski. *Zealous Love: A Practical Guide to Social Justice*. Grand Rapids: Zondervan, 2009.

Zeufack, Albert G., Cesar Calderon, Gerard Kambou, Megumi Kubota, Catalina Cantu Canales, and Vijdan Korman. "Africa's Pulse 22." (October 2020) Washington, DC: World Bank. https://openknowledge.worldbank.org/bitstream/handle/10986/34587/9781464816482.pdf.

Milton Keynes UK
Ingram Content Group UK Ltd.
UKHW011301110923
428462UK00022B/698